THE EUROPEAN JUDICIARY

This open access book provides a compelling re-examination of the European Union judiciary, encompassing the European Court of Human Rights, the Court of Justice of the European Union and constitutional courts, as explored by prominent scholars from the Spanish academic community.

Organised into three substantive parts, the book explores the essential interplay between these judicial bodies, emphasising how their distinct roles, challenges and evolutions are deeply interconnected. Together, these institutions form a cohesive yet occasionally tension-filled 'community of judges' that collaborates, interacts, and sometimes diverges in shaping the legal landscape of Europe.

The first part examines the institutional framework and the foundational role of the European Court of Human Rights, focusing on its influence on European legal norms and human rights protections. The second part addresses the institutional challenges faced by the Court of Justice of the European Union, including its function as a cornerstone of EU law and its interactions with other courts. The final part investigates the role of constitutional courts within EU Member States, highlighting their responses to European integration and their dynamic relationships with supranational courts.

By exploring the interdependencies, mutual influences, and occasional tensions within this 'community of judges', the book reveals how these courts, in collaboration with European scholarship, collectively contribute to a broader 'community of law' that continues to shape the legal and political order of Europe.

Volume 133 in the Series Modern Studies in European Law

Modern Studies in European Law

Recent titles in this series:

The European Integrated Border Management: Frontex, Human Rights, and International Responsibility
Giulia Raimondo

Private Autonomy in EU Internal Market Law: Parameters of its Protection and Limitation
Rufat Babayev

Free Movement and Welfare Access in the European Union: Re-Balancing Conflicting Interests in Citizenship Jurisprudence
Victoria Hooton

EU Trade and Investment Treaty-Making Post-Lisbon: Moving Beyond Mixity
Gesa Kübek

The Normative Foundations for EU Criminal Justice: Powers, Limits and Justifications
Jacob Öberg

EU Neighbourhood Law: Wider Europe and the Extended EU's Legal Space
Alessandro Petti

The Dynamics of Powers in the European Union
Edited by Christina Eckes, Päivi Leino-Sandberg and Anna W Ghavanin

The European Convention on Human Rights and Private Law: Comparative Perspectives from South-Eastern Europe
Edited by Mateja Durovic and Cristina Poncibò

Judging Composite Decision-Making: The Transformation of European Administrative Law
Filipe Brito Bastos

EU Diplomacy in Multilateral Fora
Edited by Christine Kaddous and Frank Hoffmeister

The Market Citizenship Illusion: Free Movement Rights for Atypical Workers
Alice Welsh

Actors and Roles in EU Disability Law
Edited by Delia Ferri and Eva S Krolla

The Impact of War (in Ukraine) on the EU
Edited by Inge Govaere, Sacha Garben and Eleanor Spaventa

The European Judiciary: A Community of Law and a Community of Judges
Edited by Alejandro Saiz Arnaiz and Joan Solanes Mullor

For the complete list of titles in this series see www.bloomsbury.com/uk/series/modern-studies-in-european-law/

The European Judiciary

A Community of Law and a Community of Judges

Edited by
Alejandro Saiz Arnaiz
and
Joan Solanes Mullor

•HART•
OXFORD • LONDON • NEW YORK • NEW DELHI • SYDNEY

HART PUBLISHING

Bloomsbury Publishing Plc

Kemp House, Chawley Park, Cumnor Hill, Oxford, OX2 9PH, UK

1385 Broadway, New York, NY 10018, USA

Bloomsbury Publishing Ireland Limited, 29 Earlsfort Terrace, Dublin 2, D02 AY28, Ireland

HART PUBLISHING, the Hart/Stag logo, BLOOMSBURY and the Diana logo are trademarks of Bloomsbury Publishing Plc

First published in Great Britain 2025

A catalogue record for this book is available from the British Library.

A catalogue record for this book is available from the Library of Congress.

ISBN: HB: 978-1-50997-570-9
ePDF: 978-1-50997-572-3
ePub: 978-1-50997-571-6

Typeset by Compuscript Ltd, Shannon

For product safety related questions contact productsafety@bloomsbury.com

To find out more about our authors and books visit www.hartpublishing.co.uk. Here you will find extracts, author information, details of forthcoming events and the option to sign up for our newsletters.

ACKNOWLEDGEMENTS

This book would not have been possible without the insightful contributions of its esteemed authors: Luis López Guerra, Rafael Bustos Gisbert, Paz Andrés Sáenz de Santa María, Daniel Sarmiento, Juan Ignacio Ugartemendía Eceizabarrena, Sara Iglesias Sánchez, Javier Díez-Hochleitner, Pedro Cruz Villalón, Xabier Arzoz, Maribel González Pascual and Cristina Izquierdo Sans. Their expertise and diverse perspectives have enriched this exploration of the European judiciary and its role in shaping the European legal landscape. We also extend sincere thanks to Bradley Hayes for his dedicated attention to the English language revision.

The significant debt this volume owes to the Jean Monnet Chair Programme must also be acknowledged; without whose generous support this project would not have been possible. The Jean Monnet Chair of Alejandro Saiz Arnaiz *Community of Law and Community of Judges: The European Judiciary and the Future of the Union* at Pompeu Fabra University (Ref. number: 101047901) provided the vital forum and essential foundation for the research, collaboration and intellectual exchange that led to the work compiled in these pages. By fostering a deeper understanding of European integration and especially its legal dimensions, the Jean Monnet Programme plays a key role in generating scientific knowledge and informed debate on the crucial issues currently facing the EU.

Finally, the book has benefited from the support of the research project funded by the Ministry of Science and Innovation of the Spanish Government entitled *Populismo y poder judicial: los retos para el Estado constitucional de derecho* (PRESP07023-AEI-PID2022–136707NB-100, funded by MICIU/AEI/10.13039/501100011033). This project provided the resources necessary for delving deeply into the complex relationship between populism, the judiciary and the rule of law within the EU. This funding facilitated extensive research, fostered collaboration among the contributing authors, and supported the organisation of academic events and discussions that significantly enriched the ideas presented in this book.

Co-funded by
the European Union

Jean Monnet Chair 101047901

Proyecto PRESP07023 - AEI-PID2022-136707NB-I00/AEI/10.13039/501100011033 financiado por:

Ministerio de Ciencia, Innovación y Universidades

Cofinanciado por la Unión Europea

Agencia Estatal de Investigación

CONTENTS

LIST OF CONTRIBUTORS

Xabier Arzoz is Professor of Administrative and EU law at National University of Distance Education (UNED).

Rafael Bustos Gisbert is Professor of Constitutional Law at Complutense University of Madrid.

Pedro Cruz Villalón is Professor of Constitutional Law at Autonomous University of Madrid.

Javier Díez-Hochleitner is Professor of Public International Law and EU law at Autonomous University of Madrid.

Maribel González Pascual is Professor of Constitutional Law at Pompeu Fabra University.

Sara Iglesias Sánchez is Professor of EU law and Administrative law at Complutense University of Madrid.

Cristina Izquierdo Sans is Professor of Public International Law and EU law at Autonomous University of Madrid.

Luis López Guerra is Professor of Constitutional Law at Carlos III University of Madrid.

Paz Andrés Sáenz de Santamaría is Professor of Public International Law at Oviedo University.

Alejandro Saiz Arnaiz is Professor of Constitutional Law at Pompeu Fabra University of Barcelona.

Daniel Sarmiento is Professor of EU law at Complutense University of Madrid.

Joan Solanes Mullor is Professor of Constitutional Law at Pompeu Fabra University.

Juan Ignacio Ugartemendía Eceizabarrena is Professor of Constitutional law and EU law at the Basque Country University.

The European Judiciary: A Community of Judges as a Functional and Evolving Instrument of Constitutional Pluralism

ALEJANDRO SAIZ ARNAIZ AND JOAN SOLANES MULLOR

1. The European Judiciary: Interconnecting Constitutional Pluralism

The concept of constitutional pluralism is inextricably linked to the experience of the European Union (EU). Indeed, constitutional pluralism has found in the EU its most genuine and unique expression.[1] The coexistence and interaction of multiple legal systems and sources of authority, from the supranational to the national level, lies at the heart of MacCormick's pluralist theory.[2] This pluralistic framework challenges traditional notions of a monolithic constitutional order, recognising the reality of multiple overlapping legal systems, each with its own claims to authority.[3] In this complex interplay of legal systems, the judiciary plays a central role in ensuring coherence, resolving conflicts, and facilitating the dynamic evolution of the EU legal order.

Different sub-theories within constitutional pluralism have attempted to conceptualise the idea of pluralism within the EU legal order. One foundational theory is multilevel constitutionalism as elaborated by Pernice. This theory highlights vertical interaction between supranational and national levels of authority, in which the European judiciary acts as a vital intermediary to ensure harmonious interaction between the two levels.[4] Besselink's composite constitutionalism, on the other hand, calls for understanding the EU as a composite system where different legal orders contribute to the overall framework.[5] Here the role of the European judiciary is described as a 'constitutional architect', ensuring coherence and resolving conflicts between the constituent parts.

[1] N MacCormick, 'Beyond the Sovereign State' (1993) 56 *The Modern Law Review* 1, 10–11.
[2] N MacCormick, *Questioning Sovereignty: Law, State and Nation in the European Commonwealth* (Oxford, Oxford University Press, 2002) 142.
[3] N Krisch, *Beyond Constitutionalism: The Pluralist Structure of Postnational Law* (Oxford, Oxford University Press, 2010) 5–7.
[4] I Pernice, 'The Treaty of Lisbon: Multilevel Constitutionalism in Action' (2019) 15 *Columbia Journal of European Law* 349, 372–85.
[5] LFM Besselink, *A Composite European Constitution* (Groningen, Europa Law Publishing, 2007) 3–6.

Bustos's notion of network constitutionalism, for its part, emphasises the decentralised nature of authority within the EU, envisioning different legal systems as interconnected nodes.[6] The European judiciary facilitates communication and cooperation between these nodes, ensuring the smooth flow of information and legal principles. Finally, Maduro's contrapunctual constitutionalism underscores the dynamic interplay and potential tensions between legal systems.[7] The European judiciary is tasked with harmonising these 'counterpoints', ensuring productive coexistence and interaction.[8]

Constitutional pluralism offers a distinctive lens through which European integration can be analysed, a lens that emphasises the crucial role of law and courts in shaping this process. Legal scholars have played an active part in developing the concept and practice of constitutional pluralism in the European integration process.[9] Their research and analysis have helped to identify and articulate the multiple sources and levels of legal authority within the EU system. By exploring the interactions and tensions between these different legal orders, legal scholars have contributed to the creation of that 'community of law' where diverse norms and values coexist and interrelate. They have highlighted the importance of dialogue and mutual respect between different legal actors and institutions, fostering a sense of shared responsibility for upholding the core values of constitutional democracy in times of resurgent populism.[10] In short, the role of legal scholars, alongside courts and lawmakers, is vital in shaping the 'community of law', contributing to the interpretation, development and cohesion of the pluralistic legal system.

Undoubtedly, constitutional pluralism as a concept is framed and driven by the EU legal community, and, in this sense, its interplay with political science theories of institutional evolution is limited.[11] This legal focus is not, however, inherently or necessarily detrimental, as its contribution to an understanding of the EU's legal evolution is extremely valuable. Still, a more integrated approach, one drawing on both legal and political science perspectives, might offer a richer and more nuanced understanding of the EU integration process, encompassing both institutional dynamics and legal

[6] See R Bustos Gisbert, *La Constitución red: un estudio sobre supraestatalidad y constitución* (Oñati, Instituto Vasco de Administración Pública, 2005).

[7] See MP Maduro, 'Contrapunctual Law: Europe's Constitutional Pluralism in Action' in N Walker (ed), *Sovereignty in Transition* (Oxford, Hart Publishing, 2003) 501–37.

[8] See MP Maduro, 'Europe and the Constitution' in JHH Weiler and M Wind (eds), *European Constitutionalism Beyond the State* (Cambridge, Cambridge University Press, 2003) 74–102.

[9] H Schepel and R Wesseling, 'The Legal Community: Judges, Lawyers, Officials and Clerks in the Writing of Europe' (1997) 3 *European Law Journal* 165, 165–66.

[10] See L Lazarus, 'Constitutional Scholars as Constitutional Actors' (2020) 48 *Federal Law Review* 483, 484–87.

[11] Political science offers a variety of theoretical frameworks for understanding the development of the EU institutional process, providing insights that go beyond a purely legal perspective. Ranging from historical institutionalism to rational choice and sociological institutionalism, these frameworks offer diverse lenses through which to analyse the EU's evolution (See P Hall and R Taylor, 'Political Science and the Three New Institutionalisms' (1996) 44 *Political Studies* 936, 938–44). In relation to the EU, political science has offered insightful institutional theories, such as neofunctionalism, which emphasises spillover effects and supranational institution-building (see the seminal work of EB Haas, *The Uniting of Europe: political, Social and Economic Forces, 1950–1957* (Notre Dame, University of Notre Dame Press, 2004), and intergovernmentalism, which highlights the role of national governments and state power in driving integration (see A Moravcsik, *The Choice for Europe. Social Purpose & Sate Power from Messina to Maastricht* (Ithaca, Cornell University Press, 1998)).

frameworks. Essentially, constitutional pluralism establishes a notion of a community of law and a community of judges, with a shared legal language forming the foundation of the European integration project. This shared language not only facilitates communication and cooperation but also fosters a sense of community and shared purpose among legal actors across the EU.

Within this shared legal language, the European judiciary emerges as a dynamic force and vital tool for ensuring coherence within the pluralistic framework. The European judiciary links Pernice's multiple levels, interconnects Besselink's components, facilitates transmission between Bustos' nodes, and harmonises Maduro's counterpoints. It can be conceptualised as a linchpin binding together the multiple layers of the EU legal order. Consequently, the European judiciary is an engine of EU constitutional pluralism and cannot be understood without this interconnecting function, which embodies the collaborative spirit of the legal community and the judges. The European judiciary, with its interconnecting function, is thus indispensable to the functioning of EU constitutional pluralism, ensuring the ongoing evolution of the EU legal order.

Building on this understanding of a shared legal language, and drawing insights from both law and political science, the European judiciary can be defined in terms of its function rather than of its components. In other words, the function of interconnecting all the nodes of the pluralistic legal community of the EU is what defines the European judiciary. A functionalist approach, unlike an institutional approach that focuses on the specific composition and structure of courts, emphasises the role and purpose of the judiciary in the broader legal and political system.[12] Under this functionalist approach, the European judiciary connects all the parts and makes possible the overall functioning of a pluralistic legal order, rendering unnecessary a strict delimitation of the European judiciary as composed solely of the Court of Justice of the European Union (CJEU), national judges, or even the European Court of Human Rights (ECtHR). While individual courts within the European judiciary undoubtedly have distinct roles and functions, overall, regardless of the level, the common function they perform defines the European judiciary and explains their common interaction and the principles that guide that interaction. This functionalist perspective is centered on the common purpose and interconnectedness of the European judiciary, regardless of the specific court or level of authority.

The function of conjoining pluralistic claims and resolving conflicts in a pluralistic context thus defines the nature of the European judiciary and provides a common purpose or sense of unity for all components of the EU community of judges, whether they are located at the EU or national level. In this sense, we approach the idea, defended elsewhere, that the European judiciary functions as a single, cohesive system, a supranational judicial (and quasi federal) system with a shared purpose and set of principles.[13] However, the concept of a single judicial system may not fully capture the nuanced reality of the EU legal order, which stands out for the diversity of its constituent parts. Instead of striving for complete unity, the idea of a community of law and judges

[12] See M Shapiro, *Courts: A Comparative and Political Analysis* (Chicago, University of Chicago Press, 1981).

[13] See KJ Alter, *Establishing the Supremacy of European Law: The Making on an International Rule of Law in Europe* (Oxford, Oxford University Press, 2001); J Zglisnki, 'The new judicial federalism: the evolving relationship between EU and Member State courts' (2023) 2 *European Law Open* 345–71.

committed to coherence within diversity is more appealing and fits better with the reality and narrative of the complex and cacophonous process of EU integration. The legal community and the community of judges share a common purpose – ensuring coherence while maintaining diversity – and in doing so, they have dynamically developed, as if in a shared partnership, principles and mechanisms that discipline their relationship.

2. A Community in Motion: The European Judiciary's Dynamic Response to European Challenges

The European judiciary is far from a static entity; it is a dynamic and evolving force, constantly adapting to the historical context and the ever-changing challenges facing the EU. This adaptability is crucial for understanding the judiciary's response to new realities and demands arising throughout the European integration process. As has been noted, the strategic development and adaptation of legal frameworks, or 'legal engineering', has been a constant element in the European legal order.[14] The European judiciary has thus always needed to refine its relationships according to the needs and aspirations of the European integration process. Dynamism, evolution and innovation have been hallmarks of both the European integration process and the European judiciary. Law, and the relationships within the legal community and the components of the European judiciary, have undergone intensive transformation in response to the evolving needs of European integration. This adaptability has enabled the European judiciary to effectively fulfill its role in ensuring coherence and resolving conflicts within the EU's complex, multilayered legal system.

The dynamic function of the European judiciary and its evolving relationships are vividly illustrated by its response to three key challenges: (1) the recognition of fundamental rights in EU law; (2) the scope of EU powers and the control of its institutions; and (3) the response to the rule of law backsliding. These three challenges, each demanding a unique response from the European judiciary, highlight its remarkable adaptability to the evolving challenges facing European integration. Moreover, these examples demonstrate the crucial role played by the European judiciary in navigating crises within the EU to provide stability and uphold core values during periods of uncertainty. The EU, forged in crisis,[15] has often been able to rely on its judiciary to navigate turbulent times.

The incorporation of fundamental rights into the core of EU law is a dynamic story of evolution, one made remarkable by the fascinating interplay between the CJEU and national courts. The early focus of European integration was primarily on economic matters, so much so that the founding treaties remained silent on the protection of fundamental rights. The prevailing assumption was that fundamental rights would find sufficient protection at the national level and from the Council of Europe. Then, however, came the CJEU's assertion of the primacy of EU law, which raised concerns

[14] B De Witte, 'The European Union's COVID-19 Recovery Plan: The Legal Engineering of an Economic Policy Shift' (2021) 58 *Common Market Law Review* 635.

[15] J Monnet, *Mémoires* (Paris, Fayard, 1976) 494.

among national courts, particularly in Germany, about the potential conflict between EU law and national constitutional rights.[16] The German Federal Constitutional Court's decision in *Solange I*,[17] driven by concerns over potential clashes between supreme EU law and national constitutional fundamental rights, was elaborated in direct dialogue with the CJEU and its doctrine protecting fundamental rights as general principles of EU law.[18] A clear compromise was struck: the primacy of EU law would be acceptable only if it ensured the protection of fundamental rights. The CJEU, acknowledging the concerns of its national counterparts, affirmed its commitment to protecting fundamental rights.

Then came the Euro-crisis of 2008, which triggered a soul-searching debate over the powers of the European Central Bank (ECB). Here again we find a compelling example of the evolving role of the European judiciary in balancing EU and national powers. This debate brought to the forefront the role of the European judiciary, particularly the CJEU and the German Federal Constitutional Court, in delineating the boundaries between EU and national competences, and determining the appropriate level of scrutiny for EU institutions. The German Federal Constitutional Court, in *Gauweiler* and *Weiss*,[19] severely criticised a possible overreach by the ECB and the questionable level of scrutiny applied by the CJEU. While the tension between the two courts persists,[20] this dialogue has largely been conducted within the framework of the preliminary reference procedure by which national courts refer questions of EU law to the CJEU for interpretation and which itself is a telling indication of the degree of cooperation and deference operating within the EU judicial system.

Finally, the rise of populism in recent years has posed a formidable challenge to the EU legal order, one requiring a coordinated response from the European judiciary, including the ECtHR. The crisis came to a head when national judiciaries in Poland and Hungary sought support from European institutions after populist governments curtailed their independence by, for example, forcing judges into retirement, initiating disciplinary proceedings against critical judges, and changing the procedures for judicial appointment.[21] The CJEU responded by taking a strong stance in defence of EU values and principles, prompting some scholars to argue that the rule of law backsliding in Europe has triggered a new wave of constitutionalisation within the EU.[22]

[16] See, for a seminal text regarding the tension between primacy of EU law and the protection of fundamental rights at national constitutional systems, JHH Weiler, 'The Transformation of Europe' (1991) 100 *Yale Law Journal* 2403, 2417–19.

[17] *Solange I-Beschlub*, 29 May 1974, BVerfGE 37, 271 2BvL 52/71.

[18] *Internationale Handelsgesellschaft mbH v Einfuhr- und Vorratsstelle für Getreide und Futtermittel*, Case 11/70, EU:C:1970:114.

[19] Case C-62/14 *Peter Gauweiler and Others v Deutscher Bundestag*, EU:C:2015:400; Case C-493/17 *Weiss and Others*, EU:C:2018:1000.

[20] A Bobic and M Dawson, 'Making sense of the "incomprehensible": the PSPP Judgment of the German Federal Constitutional Court' (2020) 57 *Common Market Law Review* 1953, 1994.

[21] See L Pech and KL Scheppele, 'Illiberalism Within: Rule of Law Backsliding in the EU' (2017) 19 *Cambridge Yearbook of European Legal Studies* 3.

[22] N Scicluna and S Auer, 'Europe's constitutional unsettlement: testing the political limits of legal integration' (2023) 99 *International Affairs* 769.

The ECtHR, for its part, buttressed the principle of judicial independence by providing crucial protection for national judiciaries against undue political interference.[23] The collective response of national judiciaries, the CJEU and the ECtHR to the rule of law backsliding underscores the collaborative nature of the European judiciary and its commitment to safeguarding the integrity of the European integration process.

In conclusion, the adaptability of the European judiciary has been amply demonstrated through its responses to challenges such as imposing the assimilation of fundamental rights into EU law, the delineation of EU competences when the Eurozone's fate was uncertain and erecting a legal backstop against populist attempts to hamstring political opposition. A major reason for the resilience and effectiveness of the EU legal order, particularly during times of crisis, has been the European judiciary's responsiveness to the ever-changing needs of European integration. The collaborative spirit within the European judiciary, exemplified by the ongoing dialogue between the CJEU, national courts and the ECtHR, underscores its commitment to the integrity of the European project. As the EU continues to navigate uncertain waters, the flexibility and responsiveness of its judicial system will remain crucial for its unique legal order and core values.

3. The Glue that Binds the European Judiciary Together: Principles of Judicial Interaction

These two key defining principles of the European judiciary – its adhesive function within a pluralistic constitutional framework; and its evolving, dynamic character – permeate the legal doctrines that orient the relationships between all the components. These doctrines grew out of the need to balance the diversity of national legal traditions and the evolving nature of EU law. By providing the 'glue', these practices ensure cohesion within a framework of constitutional pluralism. To achieve the necessary cohesion, the interactions between different parts of the European judiciary must accommodate the diversity of its components while remaining sensitive to evolving legal circumstances.

One of the most crucial principles binding the CJEU to its national counterparts is the principle of primacy of EU law.[24] This principle, functionalist in nature, has as its objective harmony between national and EU law, effectively 'gluing' the two levels together. Primacy is essential for the resolution of conflicts within this complex legal system. The principle has evolved dynamically by virtue of contributions made from all

[23] PA Sáenz de Santamaría, 'Rule of Law and Judicial Independence in the Light of CJEU and ECtHR Case Law' in C Izquierdo Sans, C Martínez Capdevila and M Nogueira Guastavino (eds), *Fundamental Rights Challenges* (Cham, Springer, 2021) 167–87.

[24] At the time of writing, the principle remains a case law development of the CJEU (see, as the seminal case, Case 6/64, *Flaminio Costa v ENEL*, EU:C:1964:66). The Treaty establishing a Constitution for Europe of 2004 tried to codify the principle (Article I-6) but the Treaty of Lisbon of 2007 did not ultimately codify it. However, the Intergovernmental Conference in which the Treaty of Lisbon was elaborated included the following declaration: 'The Conference recalls that, in accordance with well settled case law of the Court of Justice of the European Union, the Treaties and the law adopted by the Union on the basis of the Treaties have primacy over the law of the Member States, under the conditions laid down by the said case law.'

corners of the European judiciary. While the CJEU has been the driving force, national courts have also played a significant role. For instance, the 'counter-limits' doctrine developed by national constitutional courts safeguards fundamental rights[25] and the 'ultra-vires' control by national courts prevents the EU from exceeding its treaty-mandated powers.[26] Even the CJEU's emphasis on a robust notion of primacy to ensure the effectiveness of EU law exemplifies this collaborative effort.[27] This ongoing dialogue between courts at all levels frames a wide scope of interaction and ensures the framework's legal cohesion within the EU.

More recently, debate surrounding the concept of 'constitutional national identity' has emerged as another key area of interaction between EU law and national law.[28] Similar to the principle of EU law primacy, understanding this concept requires a pluralistic framework that respects the diversity of Member States' traditions and values.[29] The entire European judiciary has contributed to shaping this principle. The CJEU particularly has grappled with the challenges posed by this clause, especially in the context of the recent rule of law crisis.[30] In response, the CJEU, along with the broader legal community, are developing a new understanding of EU law. This understanding involves 'constitutionalising' the EU's legal architecture and the 'EU constitutional identity',[31] a concept nascent in CJEU case law.[32] In the wake of the rule of law crisis, recognition of the need to reinforce the core values of European integration has grown. The diverse mechanisms employed to achieve this objective highlight the dynamic and evolving nature of the European judiciary.[33] This ongoing process demonstrates the EU's commitment to balancing national identity with the overarching goals of the Union.

Even outside times of crisis, the European judiciary has actively fostered coherence within its legal system. One example is the 'Bosphorus doctrine', which seeks to harmonise the relationship between the CJEU and the ECtHR, even though the EU

[25] M Cartabia, 'The Italian Constitutional Court and the Relationship Between the Italian legal system and the European Union' in AM Slaughter, A Stone Sweet and JHH Weiler, *The European Court and National Courts. Doctrine and Jurisprudence* (Oxford, Hart Publishing, 1998) 133–46, 138–39.

[26] P Craig, 'The ECJ and ultra vires: A conceptual analysis' (2011) 48 *Common Market Law Review* 395–437.

[27] See the aftermath of the *Melloni* case (Case C-399/11 *Stefano Melloni v Ministerio Fiscal*, EU:C:2013:107. See also A Torres Pérez, 'Melloni in Three Acts: From Dialogue to Monologue' (2014) 10 *European Constitutional Law Review* 308.

[28] See F Fabbrini and A Sajó, 'The dangers of constitutional identity' (2019) 25 *European Law Journal* 457; P Cruz Mantilla de los Ríos, *La identidad nacional de los Estados miembros en el Derecho de la Unión Europea* (Pamplona, Aranzadi, 2022).

[29] J Scholtes, 'Abusing Constitutional Identity' (2021) 22 *German Law Journal* 534, 540–42.

[30] G Halmai and J Scholtes, 'Illiberal Constitutionalism and the Abuse of Constitutional Identity' in R Hirschl and Y Roznai, *Deciphering the Genome of Constitutionalism. The Foundations and Future of Constitutional Identity* (Cambridge, Cambridge University Press, 2024) 272–85.

[31] P Faraguna, 'Constitutional Identity in the EU – A Shield or a Sword?' (2017) 18 *German Law Journal* 1618, 1622–25; Pablo Cruz Mantilla de los Ríos, 'Constitutional Identity of the European Union: a legal category under construction' (2022) 79 *Estudios de Deusto*; T Drinóczi and P Faraguna, 'The Constitutional Identity of the EU as a Counterbalance for Unconstitutional Constitutional Identities of the Member States' (2023) *European Yearbook of Constitutional Law 2022*, 57–87.

[32] See Case C-156/21 *Hungary v Parliament and Council of the European Union*, EU:C:2022:97, para 232; and Case C-157/21 *Republic of Poland v European Parliament and Council of the European Union*, EU:C:2022:98, para 264.

[33] About the interplay between political and judicial mechanisms deployed by the EU to fight the rule of law crisis, see M Bonnelli, 'The rule of law crisis and the constitutionalisation of the EU' in G Moreno González (ed), *El Estado de Derecho en el siglo XXI* (Valencia, Tirant lo Blanch, 2024) 257–92.

has yet to formally join the European Convention on Human Rights (ECHR).[34] This doctrine, developed by the European judiciary, exemplifies a proactive approach to legal challenges. While the relationship between EU law and the ECHR system remains ambiguous,[35] the CJEU has emphasised the importance of preserving the effectiveness of EU law even when under external review by the ECtHR.[36] This thorny issue is central in the ongoing negotiations over EU accession to the Convention. While a formal agreement may eventually address the issue, the CJEU and the ECtHR will doubtlessly base their relationship going forward on the needs of their respective legal systems. Looking ahead, it seems likely that the European judiciary will continue to refine the balance between ECtHR oversight of EU law and the CJEU mandate to ensure its effectiveness. This ongoing process highlights the dynamic nature of the European judiciary and its commitment to preserving coherence among all its components.

Theories of judicial deference also helped in securing consistency within the European judiciary, in this case regarding the relationship between the CJEU and the ECtHR with national courts, as exemplified by the preliminary reference procedure, a key mechanism for dialogue between the CJEU and national courts. This procedure enables the CJEU to provide guidance to national courts while granting them discretion to apply that guidance in their specific national context.[37] The ECtHR, lacking a similar mechanism,[38] developed its own judicial deference doctrine. The 'margin of appreciation' and the principle of subsidiarity allow the ECtHR to respect the discretion of national judiciaries while upholding standards derived from the Convention.[39] At the national level, doctrines such as the 'interpretation of conformity' or 'consistent interpretation' promote coherence by encouraging national courts to interpret their own laws in alignment with both EU law and the ECHR.[40] Ultimately, this combination of top-down and bottom-up approaches to judicial deference has, over time, fostered a high degree of coordination within the European legal community. Such coordination enables diverse legal systems to work together effectively, respecting both national diversity and the overarching principles of the European legal order.

The European judiciary stands as a testament to the intricate balance between unity and diversity within a complex legal system, and therefore plays a cohesive role within a pluralistic constitutional framework. Its ability to 'glue' together disparate national traditions while remaining adaptable to an ever-changing legal landscape is truly

[34] *Bosphorus Hava Yollari Turizm ve Ticaret Anomim Sirketu v Ireland*, judgment (Grand Chamber) 30 June 2005, Application no 45036/98.

[35] The negotiations for the accession of the EU to the Convention are still ongoing. See for a resume of the negotiations see https://www.coe.int/en/web/human-rights-intergovernmental-cooperation/accession-of-the-european-union-to-the-european-convention-on-human-rights.

[36] See CJEU Opinion 2/13 *Accession of the European Union to the ECHR*, EU:C:2014:2454.

[37] P Schroeder, 'Seizing opportunities: the determinants of the CJEU's deference to national courts' (2023) 31 *Journal of European Public Policy* 2986, 2986–89.

[38] At the time of writing, the advisory opinion based on Protocol no 16 to the Convention has been scarcely employed and, as such, its potential as a mechanism comparable to the preliminary reference proceeding in the EU remains uncertain.

[39] J Gerards, 'Pluralism, Deference and the Margin of Appreciation Doctrine' (2011) 17 *European Law Journal* 88, 102–15.

[40] G Betlem and A Nollkaemper, 'Giving effect to Public International Law and European Community Law before Domestic Courts. A Comparative Analysis of the Practice of Consistent Interpretation' (2003) 14 *Journal of International Law* 569, 588–89.

remarkable. This delicate dance is achieved through a combination of innovative legal doctrines, a commitment to dialogue and a nuanced approach to judicial deference. The ongoing interaction between the CJEU, the ECtHR and national courts fosters a collaborative environment where legal interpretation and application respect both the overarching principles of EU law and the unique characteristics of individual Member States. Ultimately, the EU legal order serves as a model for navigating the complexities of a multilayered legal system in a globalised world. Its success lies in its ability to foster unity without sacrificing diversity, to adapt to change without compromising fundamental principles, and to promote dialogue and cooperation within a framework of mutual respect. As the EU continues to evolve, its judiciary will undoubtedly play a crucial role in shaping a legal landscape that reflects both the shared values and the rich tapestry of its Member States.

4. An Overview of the Book to Map the Terrain

This volume explores the intricate workings of the European judiciary, a complex system characterised by constitutional pluralism and the interplay of three key components: the ECtHR; the CJEU, and national constitutional courts. Divided into three parts, it delves into the distinct roles of each component, their interaction with one another, and the challenges they face in navigating the overlapping legal orders of the EU and its Member States. From upholding fundamental human rights to ensuring the primacy of EU law, this book examines the effect of these judicial bodies on the European legal landscape and the elaboration of a shared legal culture.

This book offers a unique perspective on EU law by leading Spanish scholars from diverse legal fields, including constitutional law, administrative law and public international law. The authors' varied approaches illuminate the intricate connections between these legal orders, contributing to a vibrant 'community of law' within the EU's pluralistic framework. These Spanish legal scholars make a significant contribution to the understanding of the EU as a shared community of legal values and principles, reflecting the complex and interconnected nature of the European integration project.

Transcending traditional analyses of individual courts and doctrines, this work focuses on the dynamic interactions and dialogues between these three pillars of the European judiciary. It highlights the tensions and convergences that arise as they grapple with issues of sovereignty, integration and the protection of fundamental rights. Ultimately, this exploration reveals the emergence of a 'community of judges' and a 'community of law', demonstrating how collaboration and mutual learning contribute to the construction of a cohesive and effective European legal space.

Part I, 'The European Court of Human Rights: Protecting Human Rights in a Pluralistic Europe', examines the complexities of upholding human rights within a diverse European legal landscape. It analyses the ECtHR's efforts to reconcile its overarching principles with the specificities of individual legal systems, highlighting the dynamic interplay between different legal levels and the crucial role of lower courts in driving the adoption of human rights standards. This part also explores the challenges faced by the ECtHR in addressing human rights violations within the context of international armed conflicts, calling for comprehensive reforms to strengthen the ECHR system in times of war.

Part II, 'The Court of Justice of the European Union: Managing the Challenges of Primacy and Pluralism', shifts the focus to the relationship between national and EU law. It critically examines the challenges to the primacy of EU law, advocating for procedural mechanisms to foster consensus and address concerns arising from national perspectives. This part also analyses the obligation of national courts to interpret national law in conformity with EU law, highlighting their role in fostering coherence and upholding EU law primacy. In addition, it explores the implications of recent reforms to the EU judicial architecture, emphasising the evolving roles of the CJEU and the General Court in shaping the interpretation and application of EU law.

Finally, Part III, 'Constitutional Courts: Navigating Integration and Autonomy', delves into the evolving role of constitutional courts in the European legal order. It examines the impact of the Charter of Fundamental Rights of the European Union (CFR) on national constitutional review processes, highlighting the tension between upholding national constitutional supremacy and accommodating EU law. This part also analyses the growing role of constitutional courts in shaping a European criminal law framework grounded in fundamental rights, emphasising the shift towards active collaboration between constitutional courts and the CJEU. It concludes by examining the Spanish Constitutional Court's (SCC) approach to ensuring the effective application of EU law, underscoring its evolving role in navigating the complex relationship between national and EU law.

4.1. Part I. The European Court of Human Rights: Protecting Human Rights in a Pluralistic Europe

Chapter one of Part I by Luis López Guerra delves into the complexities of human rights protection within the European legal landscape. The chapter highlights the inherent tension between the ideal of a unified European system and the reality of diverse national legal orders. While the ECHR strives for supremacy, its practical application is constrained by the need to coordinate with existing national and supranational frameworks. Despite this inherent complexity, the author suggests an underlying 'will' towards a more integrated system driven by the shared goal of human rights protection. Ultimately, the text emphasises the dynamic interplay between different legal levels and the ongoing efforts to reconcile the ECHR's overarching principles with the specificities of individual legal systems.

In chapter two, Rafael Bustos Gisbert examines the complex relationship between the ECtHR's rulings and their implementation within national legal systems, with a specific focus on Spain. While apex courts sometimes resist incorporating new European standards that clash with national precedents, lower courts often directly apply these standards, creating 'bottom-up' pressure for legal change. This phenomenon, rooted in the 'contrapunctual law' framework proposed by Maduro, highlights the evolving role of lower courts in driving the adoption of human rights standards, even in the face of resistance from higher courts. This dynamic ultimately strengthens the principle of subsidiarity within the ECHR framework by fostering shared responsibility among all levels of the judiciary to uphold Convention mandates.

Finally, in chapter three, Paz Andrés Sáenz de Santamaría analyses the challenges faced by the ECtHR in addressing human rights violations within the context of international armed conflicts, particularly the recent ones in Georgia, Ukraine and Armenia/Azerbaijan. The author highlights the Court's struggle to handle the increased workload and complexity of these cases, as well as its limited capacity to provide timely resolution. The chapter emphasises the need for comprehensive reforms, which include increasing the Court's resources and putting greater focus on political solutions within the framework of the Council of Europe. Ultimately, the author calls for a collective response to address the root causes of these conflicts and strengthen the ECHR system, so it better protects human rights during times of war, while keeping in mind that lasting solutions require both legal and political action.

4.2. Part II. The Court of Justice of the European Union: Managing the Challenges of Primacy and Pluralism

Part II starts chapter four, in which Daniel Sarmiento focuses on the significant threat that questioning the primacy of EU law poses to the unity and effectiveness of the European project, particularly in the face of contemporary challenges. The author criticises the use of 'constitutional identity' arguments to undermine EU law, linking the notion to destructive nationalism. While acknowledging the persistence of such views, the author advocates for procedural mechanisms, such as a mixed chamber with representatives from both national courts and the CJEU, to address these concerns and foster consensus. This approach, the author suggests, will allow for the expression of dissenting opinions while ultimately reinforcing the legitimacy and necessity of EU law primacy for a cohesive and functional EU.

In chapter five, Juan Ignacio Ugartemendía Eceizabarrena dives into the complex relationship between national and EU law, focusing on the obligation of national courts, including constitutional courts, to interpret national law in conformity with EU law. This obligation, the author argues, serves not only as a tool to ensure the effectiveness of EU law, but also as a mechanism for controlling the 'Europeanness' of national law. The author highlights the far-reaching implications of this obligation, extending as far as the interpretation of national constitutions and fundamental rights provisions. While acknowledging the potential tension between national and EU legal orders, the author ultimately emphasises the role of this interpretative obligation in fostering coherence and upholding the primacy of EU law within the national legal landscape.

Chapter six by Sara Iglesias Sánchez analyses the proposed reform of the EU judicial architecture by which certain preliminary rulings would be transferred from the CJEU to the General Court. While acknowledging the potential for increased efficiency, the author emphasises the reform's broader implications for the identity and roles of both courts. The author argues that this shift signifies a 'deconstitutionalisation' of the preliminary ruling procedure, allowing the CJEU to focus on its constitutional role while consolidating the General Court's apex position in specific areas. The author also highlights the potential challenges of maintaining consistency in EU law interpretation across the two courts and underscores the reform's implicit commitment to a centralised system of interpretation, even with allowance for internal decentralisation. Ultimately, the reform is presented as a significant step in the evolution of the EU judicial system that will potentially have long-term consequences for the balance between national and EU courts in shaping the interpretation and application of EU law.

Part II ends with chapter seven by Javier Díez-Hochleitner that critically examines the CJEU's jurisdiction over the Common Foreign and Security Policy (CFSP), arguing that the CJEU should adopt a more expansive interpretation of its powers. The author contends that the CJEU's current approach, which relies on 'legerdemain' to assert jurisdiction over CFSP acts with administrative or financial implications, insufficiently guarantees effective judicial protection. Instead, the author proposes a clearer criterion – whether or not a CFSP act involves 'sovereign' foreign policy choices – to determine the boundaries of the CJEU's jurisdiction. This approach, the author argues, would better align with the right to effective judicial protection enshrined in the CFR and the ECHR, ensure greater accountability and prevent potential conflicts with fundamental rights guarantees.

4.3. Part III. Constitutional Courts: Navigating Integration and Autonomy

Chapter eight, authored by Pedro Cruz Villalón, explores the evolving role of the CJEU as a 'surrogate guardian' of the constitutions of EU Member States, highlighting the increasing interconnectedness between national and European legal orders. The author proposes a novel framework for understanding the 'EU Member State Constitution' (EUMSC) comprising three tiers: a Europeanised tier shaped by EU law; a self-determined tier encompassing residual national constitutional provisions; and a contested tier where national and EU law potentially clash. This framework illuminates the complex interplay between national and supranational legal authorities, with the CJEU and national courts acting as associated guardians of the EU Member State Constitutions, while national courts retain primary responsibility for the self-determined tier. The contested tier, however, remains a site of potential conflict, requiring ongoing negotiation between national and European guardians to ensure both the integrity of national constitutions and the primacy of EU law.

In chapter nine, Xabier Arzoz examines the impact of the CFR on national constitutional review processes, prompting a 'Europeanisation' of these systems. The author analyses the strategies employed by various European constitutional courts to align their review parameters with the Charter, highlighting the tension between upholding national constitutional supremacy and accommodating EU law. While some courts have boldly embraced the Charter, others, like Spain's, have sought less disruptive adjustments. The author argues that this adaptation, driven by the evolving nature of EU law, ultimately reshapes the role of national constitutional courts within the broader European legal landscape, forcing them to navigate a complex interplay between national sovereignty and supranational integration.

In chapter ten, Maribel González Pascual examines the growing role of constitutional courts in shaping a European criminal law framework grounded in fundamental rights. It highlights the shift from initial reluctance to active collaboration between constitutional courts and the CJEU, particularly in cases concerning the European Arrest Warrant (EAW). By engaging with the CJEU through preliminary rulings, constitutional courts have successfully advocated for stronger fundamental rights protections within the EAW framework, prompting the CJEU to refine its jurisprudence and enhance the protection of individual rights. This collaborative dialogue, the author suggests, signifies a promising trend towards a shared understanding of fundamental rights within the evolving landscape of European criminal law, although challenges remain, particularly with regard to substantive criminal law and the principle of legality.

Part III closes with chapter eleven, in which Cristina Izquierdo Sans analyses the SCC's approach to ensuring the effective application of EU law within the Spanish legal system. The author highlights the SCC's proactive role in safeguarding effective judicial protection, having even anticipated certain pronouncements of CJEU. The author commends the SCC's restrained approach to reviewing cases where national courts have applied EU law without seeking a preliminary ruling, emphasising the importance of respecting the role of ordinary judges as 'judges of the Union'. However, the author also calls for greater precision and care from the SCC when exercising its 'reinforced reasoning' canon of control, particularly to avoid encroaching on the CJEU's interpretative authority. Ultimately, the author underscores the SCC's evolving role in navigating the complex relationship between national and EU law, recognising its contribution to upholding EU law primacy while maintaining respect for the ordinary judicial process.

5. Acknowledgments

This book would not have been possible without the insightful contributions of its esteemed authors: Luis López Guerra, Rafael Bustos Gisbert, Paz Andrés Sáenz de Santamaría, Daniel Sarmiento, Juan Ignacio Ugartemendía Eceizabarrena, Sara Iglesias Sánchez, Javier Díez-Hochleitner, Pedro Cruz Villalón, Xabier Arzoz, Maribel González Pascual and Cristina Izquierdo Sans. Their expertise and diverse perspectives have enriched this exploration of the European judiciary and its role in shaping the European legal landscape. We also extend sincere thanks to Bradley Hayes for his dedicated attention to the English language revision.

The significant debt this volume owes to the Jean Monnet Chair Programme must also be acknowledged; without whose generous support this project would not have been possible. The Jean Monnet Chair of Alejandro Saiz Arnaiz *Community of Law and Community of Judges: The European Judiciary and the Future of the Union* at Pompeu Fabra University (Ref. number: 101047901) provided the vital forum and essential foundation for the research, collaboration and intellectual exchange that led to the work compiled in these pages. By fostering deeper understanding of European integration and especially its legal dimensions, the Jean Monnet Programme plays a key role in generating scientific knowledge and informed debate on the crucial issues currently facing the EU.

Finally, the book has benefited from the support of the research project funded by the Ministry of Science and Innovation of the Spanish Government entitled *Populismo y poder judicial: los retos para el Estado constitucional de derecho* (PRESP07023-AEI-PID2022-136707NB-100, funded by MICIU/AEI/10.13039/501100011033). This project provided the resources necessary for delving deeply into the complex relationship between populism, the judiciary and the rule of law within the EU. This funding facilitated extensive research, fostered collaboration among the contributing authors, and supported the organisation of academic events and discussions that significantly enriched the ideas presented in this book.

Bibliography

Alter, KJ, *Establishing the Supremacy of European Law: The Making of an International Rule of Law in Europe* (Oxford, Oxford University Press, 2001).

Besselink, LFM, *A Composite European Constitution* (Groningen, Europa Law Publishing, 2007).

Betlem, G and Nollkaemper, A, 'Giving effect to Public International Law and European Community Law before Domestic Courts. A Comparative Analysis of the Practice of Consistent Interpretation' (2003) 14 *Journal of International Law* 569.

Bobic, A and Dawson, M, 'Making sense of the "incomprehensible": the PSPP Judgment of the German Federal Constitutional Court' (2020) 57 *Common Market Law Review* 1953.

Bonnelli, M, 'The rule of law crisis and the constitutionalisation of the EU' in G Moreno González (ed), *El Estado de Derecho en el siglo XXI* (Valencia, Tirant lo Blanch, 2024) 257–92.

Bustos Gisbert, R, *La Constitución red: un estudio sobre supraestatalidad y constitución* (Oñati, Instituto Vasco de Administración Pública, 2005).

Cartabia, M, 'The Italian Constitutional Court and the Relationship Between the Italian Legal System and the European Union' in AM Slaughter, A Stone Sweet and Weiler, JHH, *The European Court and National Courts. Doctrine and Jurisprudence* (Oxford, Hart Publishing, 1998) 133–46.

Craig, P, 'The ECJ and ultra vires: A conceptual analysis' (2011) 48 *Common Market Law Review* 395.

Cruz Mantilla de los Ríos, P, 'Constitutional Identity of the European Union: a legal category under construction' (2022) 79 *Estudios de Deusto* 153.

—— *La identidad nacional de los Estados miembros en el Derecho de la Unión Europea* (Pamplona, Aranzadi, 2022).

De Witte, B, 'The European Union's COVID-19 Recovery Plan: The Legal Engineering of an Economic Policy Shift' (2021) 58 *Common Market Law Review* 635.

Drinóczi, T and Faraguna, P, 'The Constitutional Identity of the EU as a Counterbalance for Unconstitutional Constitutional Identities of the Member States' in *European Yearbook of Constitutional Law 2022* (2023) 57–87.

Fabbrini, F and Sajó, A, 'The dangers of constitutional identity' (2019) 25 *European Law Journal* 457.

Faraguna, P, 'Constitutional Identity in the EU – A Shield or a Sword?' (2017) 18 *German Law Journal* 1617.

Gerards, J, 'Pluralism, Deference and the Margin of Appreciation Doctrine' (2011) 17 *European Law Journal* 88.

Haas, EB, *The Uniting of Europe: Political, Social and Economic Forces, 1950–1957* (Notre Dame, University of Notre Dame Press, 2004).

Hall, P and Taylor, R, 'Political Science and the Three New Institutionalisms' (1996) 44 *Political Studies* 936.

Halmai, G and Scholtes, J, 'Illiberal Constitutionalism and the Abuse of Constitutional Identity' in Hirschl, R and Roznai, Y, *Deciphering the Genome of Constitutionalism. The Foundations and Future of Constitutional Identity* (Cambridge, Cambridge University Press, 2024) 272–85.

Krisch, N, *Beyond Constitutionalism: The Pluralist Structure of Postnational Law* (Oxford, Oxford University Press, 2010).

Lazarus, L, 'Constitutional Scholars as Constitutional Actors' (2020) 48 *Federal Law Review* 483–96.

MacCormick, N, 'Beyond the Sovereign State' (1993) 56 *The Modern Law Review* 1.

—— *Questioning Sovereignty: Law, State and Nation in the European Commonwealth* (Oxford, Oxford University Press, 2002).

Maduro, MP, 'Contrapunctual Law: Europe's Constitutional Pluralism in Action' in N Walker (ed), *Sovereignty in Transition* (Oxford, Hart Publishing, 2003) 501–37.

—— 'Europe and the Constitution' in Weiler, JHH and Wind, M (eds), *European Constitutionalism Beyond the State* (Cambridge, Cambridge University Press, 2003) 74–102.

Monnet, J, *Mémoires* (Paris, Fayard, 1976).

Moravcsik, A, *The Choice for Europe. Social Purpose & Sate Power from Messina to Maastricht* (Ithaca, Cornell University Press, 1998).

Pech, L and Scheppele, KL, 'Illiberalism Within: Rule of Law Backsliding in the EU' (2017) 19 *Cambridge Yearbook of European Legal Studies* 3.

Pernice, I, 'The Treaty of Lisbon: Multilevel Constitutionalism in Action' (2019) 15 *Columbia Journal of European Law* 349.

Sáenz de Santamaría, PA, 'Rule of Law and Judicial Independence in the Light of CJEU and ECtHR Case Law' in Izquierdo Sans, C, Martínez Capdevila, C and Nogueira Guastavino, M (eds), *Fundamental Rights Challenges* (Cham, Springer, 2021) 167–87.

Schepel, H and Wesseling, R, 'The Legal Community: Judges, Lawyers, Officials and Clerks in the Writing of Europe' (1997) 3 *European Law Journal* 165.

Scholtes, J, 'Abusing Constitutional Identity' (2021) 22 *German Law Journal* 534.

Schroeder, P, 'Seizing opportunities: the determinants of the CJEU's deference to national courts' (2023) 31 *Journal of European Public Policy* 2986.

Scicluna, N and Auer, S, 'Europe's constitutional unsettlement: testing the political limits of legal integration' (2023) 99 *International Affairs* 769.

Shapiro, M, *Courts: A Comparative and Political Analysis* (Chicago, University of Chicago Press, 1981).

Torres Pérez, A, 'Melloni in Three Acts: From Dialogue to Monologue' (2014) 10 *European Constitutional Law Review* 308.

Weiler, JHH, 'The Transformation of Europe' (1991) 100 *Yale Law Journal* 2403.

Zglisnki, J, 'The new judicial federalism: the evolving relationship between EU and Member State courts' (2023) 2 *European Law Open* 345.

PART I

The European Court of Human Rights: Protecting Human Rights in a Pluralistic Europe

1

Formal and Informal Integration in the European System of Human Rights Protection

LUIS LÓPEZ GUERRA

1. Introduction

To start with, some nuance of the title of this chapter is needed, for it remains (as yet) impossible to speak of a single 'European system for human rights protection', given the superposition of several legal orders, whether national, international or supranational (which do not always coincide). Rather, it would be more accurate to speak of the 'multilevel scheme' of human rights protection to convey that the system into which these legal orders are integrated is not completely coherent. Yet it is also true that, in practice, what has been called 'multilevel European constitutionalism' has frequently been touted as a way towards integrated coordination for the protection of human rights (at least in its basic principles) in Europe.

With respect to the level of protection represented by the European Convention on Human Rights (ECHR), the questions that its coordination with other, national or supranational instruments poses are similar to those posed in general concerning the intersectional relationship of international law with the national legal orders. In this aspect, chronology is important, as the international norms (including the ECHR) were superimposed upon preexisting national norms that remain subject to their own principles, which implies the need for coordination between levels – coordination that often requires experimentation and refinement in evolving circumstances that together make adaptation, in form as well as in practice, also needed. This coordination is not only necessary to preserve coherence between both types of norms, but also to sustain the relationships between the organs responsible for applying human rights law (mostly judicial organs) at different levels.

Looking at the ECHR and its relationship to normative authorities at other levels, national or supranational, no formal homogeneity is apparent. It cannot be seen in the effect of its mandates, its relationships to the different Member States or its impact on the legal order of the European Union (EU). As will be shown, the effects of its mandates are affected by very different regulations. It is thus logical that no common dogmatic or doctrinal approach in this matter can be found (except in the form of proposals or suggestions for future action). Still, again, in practice, the different legal levels have been learning to coexist, which might be explained (among other causes) if not by the existence of a European system of human rights per se, at least by an intellectual 'will' for such a system present within the process of European integration.

As an initial point of departure, from the ECHR's perspective (that is, the Strasbourg Court's perspective vis-à-vis the ECHR), the primacy of conventional law over national law has been consistently reaffirmed by the institutions monitoring conventional compliance. Their repeated proclamation of primacy derives not only from the general principles of international law such as *pacta sunt servanda*. With respect to the ECHR, the Convention not only explicitly declares in Article 1 that Member States are bound by its mandates, representing the first time in history that the States' responsibility vis-à-vis their own citizens' rights has been recognised by an international charter, but also assigns the European Court of Human Rights (ECtHR) institutional jurisdiction over all matters concerning the interpretation and application of the Convention (Article 32.1 ECHR). The Convention also established the contracting States' commitment 'to abide by the final judgment of the Court in any case to which they are parties' (Article 46.1 ECHR). The result (even without any express *Costa/Enel*-type pronouncement on the part of the ECtHR) is the general assumption by the institutions that the ECHR must be applied with preeminence over any internal norm.

This reading of Convention primacy, however, is not universally accepted by national authorities all of the time. The general attitude of national authorities, particularly concerning the rank of their constitutional law, is often precisely the opposite. Despite the increasingly frequent proclamations inserted into constitutional texts boldly affirming the vocation toward European integration and human rights protection, the principle of national constitutional supremacy clearly remains operative. It is present, for instance, in the requirement that treaties containing clauses that contradict constitutional mandates must be preceded by constitutional amendment for ratification, or in the repeated 'warnings' found in the case law of constitutional courts concerning the permanent conditioning of the application of international or supranational conventional norms to their compatibility with basic constitutional principles. Although the ECHR is mentioned explicitly in some constitutional texts (as in Article II.7 of the Constitution of Bosnia Herzegovina) or indirectly (as in Article 10.2 of the Spanish Constitution), its binding force derives from the constitutional recognition, not from any recognition of some 'natural' hierarchical superiority. A similar consideration, *mutatis mutandis*, may also extend to the references to the ECHR in the Treaty of the European Union (Article 6 TEU) or the Charter of Fundamental Rights of the European Union (Preamble and Article 52.1 CFR).

Yet the lack of a universally accepted conceptual framework for the relation of conventional and internal norms and decisions (as evidenced on occasion by contradictory declarations by international convention-based and national high courts) has not impeded the progressive evolution of the ECHR system. Indeed, the institutions involved (mainly the courts at the national and Conventional levels) have increasingly sought convergence between the different levels of legal norms through practical means. Furthermore, the relationship between conventional and internal law is not explicitly regulated in many of the Member States, making an understanding of 'practical concordance' between internal and conventional norms only possible through a realistic approach that looks closely at the positions previously adopted by internal authorities and, more significantly, the courts themselves.

2. Integration Formulae

One expression (or rather result) of the absence of an authentic European system of human rights protection is the variety of formulae by which the different legal orders, by means of their constitutional courts, have integrated Conventional mandates in their internal law in specific types of cases of potential contradiction between Conventional mandates and national legal norms. The positions of constitutional courts on the ramifications of these contradictions and the ways to solve them vary considerably.

3. Conventional Supralegality and Diffuse Control: The French Approach[1]

The French formula for questions involving the conventionality control of internal legal norms separates this type of control from the control of constitutionality, a separation which is based on the progressive development of the domestic case law. Conventionality control in this case law is in principle eminently formal and derives from Article 55 of the Constitution of the French Republic: 'The agreements or treaties duly ratified and approved shall prevail, after their publication, over Parliament statutes, subject to their application by the other party.' Following the interpretation of this article in the case law of French courts, when an internal (judiciary or administrative) authority has to rule on conflicts or collisions between an internal norm and a mandate imposed by international treaty, the court must take its starting point as the formal prevalence established in Article 55, independently of the substantive mandates in the rest of the Constitution.[2] One result of that formal approach is the competence of ordinary judicial or administrative courts to decide conflicts between internal and international norms.

The origin of this system, which concedes to ordinary courts the control of conventionality of internal norms with respect to the ECHR, may be found in the *Conseil Constitutionnel*'s interpretation of the cited Article 55 of the French Constitution in its famous decision on 15 January 1975 in the case *Interruption volontaire de grossese*. The *Conseil* considered that the ECHR did not form part of the *bloc de constitutionnalité*,

[1] N Maestracci, 'L'ouverture implicite aux sources exterieures. Le cas de la France' in L Bourgorgue-Larsen (ed), *Les défis de l'interprétation et de l'application des droits de l'homme* (Paris, Pedone, 2017), 159–68. See C Lageot, 'France' in J Garard and J Fleuren (eds), *Implementation of the European Convention on Human Rights and of the Judgments of the ECtHR in national case law. A Comparative Analysis* (Cambridge/Antwerpen, Intersentia, 2014) 217–60; C Grewe, 'The ECHR in French Law: Status, Implementation and Debates' in K Ziegler (ed), *The U.K and European Human Rights. A strained relationship?* (Oxford, Hart, 2015) 341–77.

[2] After the 2008 constitutional reform, the Courts may request (via the *Cour de Cassation* or the *Conseil d'État*) a consult of constitutionality from the *Conseil Constitutionnel*. For an example of the complex relationship between the question of unconstitutionality and the control of conventionality (referred to EI law), see the judgment of the CJEU in the well-known case C-188/10 *Aziz Melki*, 22 June 2010.

and therefore should not be taken as a point of reference in the examination of the constitutionality of an internal norm. As a result, the eventual contradiction between a domestic norm and the ECHR was not deemed a matter for the constitutionality control, but rather only a matter of conflict between infra-constitutional norms, which should not be adjudicated by the *Conseil Constitutionnel* (competent only for the control of constitutionality), but rather by the judicial or administrative courts charged with applying the law in question. The consequence of this decision was that the ordinary courts, and not the *Conseil Constitutionnel*, became responsible for controlling the conventionality of internal norms with respect not only to EU law, but also with respect to the mandates of the ECHR, as interpreted by the ECtHR. In other words, these ordinary courts should be the authorities that decide, in case of conflict, whether to apply domestic law or conventional mandates, taking into account the primacy of conventional law established by Article 55 of the Constitution. Following the position staked out by the *Conseil Constitutionnel*, the appeals court (*Cour de Cassation*) recognised the primacy of conventional over internal law both with respect to EU law (*Societé des cafés Jacques Vabre*, 24 May 1975, a civil case) and with respect to the ECHR (*Respino* judgment, 3 June 1975, a criminal case). For its part, the *Conseil d'État* took more time before accepting the primacy of conventional law over domestic legal norms and applying conventionality control, which it finally did in *Niccolo* (20 October 1989).

4. Convention Supralegality and Concentrated Constitutionality Control: The Italian Case

The Italian experience represents a different path to attaining practical concordance between internal and conventional norms.[3] In this case, the constitutional case law concerning the relationship between the ECHR and internal legal norms resulted in a formula that, although based on general principles similar to those applied by the French *Conseil Constitutionnel*, has very different consequences concerning the type of courts that must rule on the compatibility of the two types of norms. In the Italian system, ordinary judges have no authority to decide cases of conflict or contradiction between internal and conventional (ECHR) law, nor to make pronouncements on the constitutionality or unconstitutionality (and eventual nullity) of an internal norm allegedly in conflict with the Convention.

The Italian formula is not expressly established by any internal norm; rather it arose from the case law of the *Corte Costituzionale*, specifically the court's judgments 348 and 249, both handed down in 2007, which interpreted Article 117(1) of the Italian Constitution following its reform in 2001. The reformed article establishes that 'Legislative power is performed by the State and the Regions, respecting the Constitution as well as the bounds derived from the European Community law and from international

[3] See the analysis of O Pollicino in 'The European Court of Human Rights and the Italian Constitutional Court: No "Groovy Kind of Love"' in Ziegler (n 1) 361–77, and T Groppi, 'La jurisprudence de la Cour européenne des droits de l'homme dans les décisions de la Cour constitutionnelle italienne: une recherche empirique' in Bourgorgue-Larsen (n 1) 323–64.

obligations.' The Italian Constitutional Court considered that the ECHR did not have direct effect on the Italian legal order 'in such a way that they would give power to the competent national judges not to apply the national mandates incompatible with them.'

According to the reasoning of the *Corte Costituzionale*, Article 117(1) of the Italian Constitution confers a superior level to the ECHR over subsequent internal norms, and consequently, the introduction in the internal legal order of any infra-constitutional norm contrary to the ECHR would incur a violation of the reformed constitutional article. As the duty to defend the Constitution against infra-constitutional norms is assigned to the Constitutional Court, only this Court, and no other, possesses the competence to (through the procedure for determining unconstitutionality) take up the question of the presence and consequences of a conflict between internal and conventional norms, derived from the ECHR.

One implication of this case law is that, should an ordinary court perceive a contradiction between the ECHR and internal norms in a specific case before it, it should send the question of unconstitutionality to the *Corte Costituzionale*, asking it to determine the compatibility of the internal norm with Article 117(1) of the Italian Constitution. In other words, the two norms are compared twice, initially by the ordinary judge, and then by the Constitutional Court, in light of Article 117(1) of the Italian Constitution and the ECtHR's interpretation.[4] Should a conflict be found, it must be decided according to the primacy system established by the cited Article 117(1). Final, definitive control is reserved for the Constitutional Court, while the role of ordinary courts is confined to formulating the initial question of unconstitutionality about the possible contradiction between internal and ECHR law.

5. From Concentrated to Diffuse Control? The Spanish Case

In the Spanish legal order, as in the Italian case, conventionality control of internal norms appears intimately related to the constitutionality control of norms that Spain's Constitutional Court is to perform. In practice, the case law of the Constitutional Court with respect to the conventionality control, in cases of conflict between internal and ECHR law, followed, until its STC 140/2018 judgment of 20 December 2018, a reasoning based on a mandate in Article 10.2 of the Spanish Constitution: 'The norms concerning fundamental rights, and freedoms recognized by the Constitution shall be interpreted according to the Universal Declaration of Human Rights and the treaties and international agreements on these matters ratified by Spain.' As the Constitutional Court understands this article, constitutional fundamental rights must be interpreted according to the ECHR, and, furthermore, according to the interpretation of the Convention by the case law of the ECtHR.[5]

[4] The *Corte Costituzionale*, in judgment 49/2015, established as a reference point the *consolidated* case law of the ECtHR. See G Ragone, 'Nota a Corte cost. 49/2015. Giurisprudencia CEDU e ordinamento interno: nuove istruzioni per l'uso da parte della Corte costituzionale italiana' *DPCE online 2015* 2,www.dpceonline.it/index.php/dpceonline/article/view/172.

[5] See L López Guerra, 'Constitución y protección internacional de derechos humanos. El proceso de internalización del Convenio Europeo de Derechos Humanos' in B Pendás (ed), *España Constitucional (1978–2018) Trayectorias y perspectivas. Vol I* (Madrid, CEPC, 2018) 771–87.

In practice, this article has guided the Spanish courts when they encounter a potential contradiction between internal law and the ECHR. A reason for this approach is that the list of fundamental rights contained in the Spanish Constitution includes, almost without exception, the rights recognised in the Convention and its Protocols. Thus, any internal norm contrary to the ECHR (as interpreted by the Strasbourg Court) should also be considered contrary to the Spanish Constitution. Therefore, the control of conventionality would coincide with a (substantive) control of constitutionality.

In the Spanish system, the Constitutional Court has exclusive jurisdiction over the constitutional control of statutes. Consequently, if an ordinary court in any proceeding considers a statute contrary to any conventional mandate, as interpreted by the ECtHR, and as a result (following Article 10.2 of the Constitution) unconstitutional, it should, before pronouncing any position on the case, submit a question of unconstitutionality before the Constitutional Court. The Constitutional Court will then decide the compatibility between internal and conventional norms. In other words, the Constitutional Court does not decide the question because of conflict with the Convention (or to the case law of the Strasbourg Court), but because of any violation of fundamental rights recognised in the Constitution. Although the fundamental rights coincide, basing any ruling on the constitutionality of a statute on the Constitution, not the Convention, is consequential.

It means that the judgment of the Constitutional Court does not derive from the hierarchical superiority of the ECHR (as an international treaty) over internal law, but from the (possible) contradiction between the internal norm in question and the constitutional mandates potentially affected. Moreover, the Constitutional Court has maintained in its own case law that the Strasbourg case law has 'a singular interpretative value' since STC 50/1989 of 21 February 1989. When examining the compatibility of a statute with a constitutional right equivalent to any one recognised by the Convention, the argument goes, the Strasbourg case law is a determinant factor to establish the content and extent of that right.

Another factor worthy of consideration is that, paralleling developments in Latin America, discussion has begun in Spain concerning the possible introduction of what might be denoted as diffuse conventionality control. The Constitution exclusively assigns to the Constitutional Court the power to control the constitutionality of statutes, so ordinary courts are excluded from this task. However, according to Article 96 of the Spanish Constitution, international treaties have greater force than parliamentary statutes. Therefore, if a statute contradicts obligations contracted by international treaty, the treaty obligations preempt. According to prevailing academic opinion and the Constitutional Court's own case law, in such cases the parliamentary statute need not be considered unconstitutional, but rather, simply, it must not be applied.

An alternative solution is the proposal to apply Article 96.1 of the Spanish Constitution[6] when a judge considers a parliamentary statute contrary to the ECHR, as interpreted by the ECtHR. In such cases, the ordinary court will not need to submit a question of unconstitutionality to the Constitutional Court, proceeding immediately to

[6] 'Validly concluded treaties, once officially published in Spain, shall form part of the internal legal order. Their provisions may only be repealed, amended or suspended in the manner provided in the treaties themselves or in accordance with the general rules of international law.'

ignore the internal norm, applying instead the ECHR. According to this interpretation, the Constitutional Court would retain its function of concentrated control of constitutionality, while ordinary courts would practice diffuse control.

This proposal enjoyed a surprising reception by the Constitutional Court in the above-mentioned judgment 140/2018. In it, expressly citing the doctrine of the Inter-American Court of Human Rights in *Almonacid Arellano*, the Spanish Court maintained that

> The existing legal-constitutional framework makes the conventionality control, in the Spanish system, to be only a criterion to select the applicable law, what must be made, case by case, by the courts of ordinary jurisdiction. As previous case law has established consistently, determining what is the norm to be applied on each concrete case is a matter of legality which must not be solved by the Constitutional Court, *but, in principle, by the ordinary courts, in the exercise of the jurisdictional function conferred on them, with an exclusive character, by Article 117.3 of the Spanish Constitution* (par. 6). (author's emphasis).

It remains to be seen whether the Spanish Constitutional Court maintains this line (sustained up to now in solely one judgment) going forward. Sustaining this case law would signify a change towards the 'French' model that separates conventionality control from substantive control of constitutionality.

6. Discrepancies between Constitutional Courts and the European Court of Human Rights

The lack, to this day, of a fully integrated system of human rights protection is not only keenly felt in matters of integrating the mandates of the ECHR system into the internal national legal orders, but also, on occasion, where discrepancies arise between the ECtHR and national constitutional courts over interpretation of the meaning and binding force of the Strasbourg case law.

One such discrepancy (since solved but still relevant) resulted from the Italian Constitutional Court judgment 49 of 26 March 2015, which addressed the binding force of the ECtHR judgments. The Italian Court analysed the degree to which ordinary courts, applying Italian law, were bound by the ECtHR doctrine for the interpretation of ECHR mandates and when Italian judges should apply the mandate in concrete cases. The Italian *Corte Costituzionale* considered that the binding force of the ECtHR case law should carefully nuance its judgments in consideration of the circumstances of each case, including, and examining, which authority or branch of the ECtHR had issued the relevant judgments for its interpretation. According to the Italian Court,

> It is not always immediately clear whether a certain interpretation of the provisions of the ECHR has become sufficiently consolidated at Strasbourg, especially in cases involving rulings intended to resolve cases that turn on highly specific facts, which have moreover been adopted with reference to the impact of the ECHR on legal systems different from that of Italy. In spite of this, there are without doubt signs that are capable of directing the national courts during their examination: the creativity of the principle asserted compared to the traditional approach of European case-law; the potential for points of distinction or even contrast from other rulings of the Strasbourg Court; the existence of dissenting opinions, especially if fueled

> by robust arguments; the fact that the decision made originates from an ordinary division and has not been endorsed by the Grand Chamber; the fact that, in the case before it, the European court has not been able to assess the particular characteristics of the national legal system, and has extended to it criteria for assessment devised with reference to other member states which, in terms of those characteristics, by contrast prove to be little suited to Italy.
>
> When all or some of these signs are apparent, as established in a judgment which cannot disregard the specific features of each individual case, *there is no reason to require the ordinary courts to use the interpretation chosen by the Strasbourg Court in order to resolve a particular dispute, unless it relates to a 'pilot judgment' in a strict sense*' (author's emphasis).

The ECtHR explicitly rejected this type of affirmation. In *Giem S.L.* of 28 June 2018, the Grand Chamber, after quoting the position of the Italian Court, declared that all of its judgments had equal legal value. Its binding force and interpretative authority, hence, did not depend on the configuration that the Court issuing them used (paragraph 252). This solved one aspect of the question. But other aspects remain ambiguous. One good example of the tension that remains between the Strasbourg Court and national constitutional courts, not to mention the lack of consolidated procedures to solve the tension might be one involving a country presently outside the Convention system yet indicative of a situation requiring an ad hoc formula to keep the system operative, might be found in *Anchugov and Gladkov v Russia*, handed down on 4 July 2013, and its effects.

In this case, it bears repeating, besides the concrete circumstances of the judgment, the question concerned the consequences of the rulings of the Strasbourg Court on the freedom of action of the Member States. The Russian response referred to a judgment in the line of *Hirst*, on prisoners' voting rights. The confrontation began after the *Hirst* doctrine was applied to a blanket prohibition in Russia on the right to vote of any person convicted and was imprisoned, a prohibition that violates, according to the ECtHR's judgment in *Anchugov*, Article 3 of Protocol no 1. The case was peculiar in that the deprivation of the vote was not established by a parliamentary norm, but by Article 32 of the Russian Constitution itself.

The complex legislative process then witnessed the 'backlash' of the Russian legal order against the ECtHR's judgment. After the ECtHR judgment in *Anchugov*, a group of deputies in the Russian Duma asked the Russian Constitutional Court to declare unconstitutional the law incorporating the Russian Federation to the Conventional system, as the Strasbourg Court ruling applying the Convention challenged an explicit mandate of the Constitution. The Constitutional Court dismissed that claim while pointing out that the Russian Parliament could enact legislation to avoid the execution of Strasbourg judgments contrary to the Constitution.

Unsurprisingly, given the foul mood caused by the Strasbourg ruling, a few months later the Government presented a law that the Russian Parliament approved empowering the Government to request the Constitutional Court to declare that the execution of a concrete Strasbourg ruling would be in contradiction with constitutional mandates and, as such, would be unenforceable. And that was precisely what the Russian Government did, filing a demand at the Constitutional Court immediately after the approval of the law with respect to the execution of *Anchugov*, complaining that the *Hirst* doctrine's application in this case was directly opposed to Article 32 of the Russian Constitution.

In a 2016 judgment, the Russian Constitutional Court ruled that the judgment in *Anchugov* was effectively unenforceable, contrary to the mandates of the Russian Constitution.

At first sight, that situation could seem as a direct challenge to the ECHR and, as such, making the Russian Federation's membership in the system incompatible. As a matter of fact, however, with the well-known care that courts methodologically put into judicial dialogue, the Russian Constitutional Court proposed a middle ground solution to avoid future confrontation.

To start with, it must be remembered that, from the applicants' point of view, the execution of the *Anchugov* judgment presented no problems: the Strasbourg Court had not required the state to economically compensate the applicants, and furthermore, the two men had been released and consequently recovered their right to vote. The pressing question was how to comply with the general effects resulting from the Strasbourg Court ruling, looking for general measures the Russian Federation could adopt to avoid future violations of the right to vote.

This would seem daunting. The Russian Constitutional Court explicitly mandated through Article 32 of the Constitution no right to vote to convicted prisoners, a general ban that could not be lifted by a parliamentary law. Even a partial solution seemed unavailable, as all convicted prisoners, according to the wording of the Constitution were to be deprived of that right, no matter the severity of the penalty. The Constitutional Court, however, attentive to the reformulation of the *Hirst* doctrine by the Strasbourg Court in *Scoppola*, found a way to avoid future clashes between the Convention and its constitutional mandates in this area. According to *Scoppola*, the deprivation of the right to vote would be compliant with the Convention if imposed not as an indiscriminate, blanket ban, but as the outcome of a measure proportional to the imposed penalty. The Constitutional Court considered that the Russian law that the Douma could change was the one setting penalties. It could be changed to impose lighter penalties (no imprisonment) for minor crimes, while imprisonment (and loss of the voting rights) would be reserved for serious crimes. In this way, the Federation would comply with both the mandate of proportionality in *Scoppola* and the constitutional mandate of Article 32. The strategy worked in that a direct confrontation between the Russian Constitutional Court and the Strasbourg Court was avoided; in September 2019, the Committee of Ministers of the Council of Europe declared the *Anchugov* judgment as executed and closed the case. However, the ad hoc solution left unresolved the contradiction between a constitutional mandate and the case law of the ECtHR.

Even resorting to an ad hoc solution, a third case seems more difficult. In this case, the unfinished character of the 'system' also stands out: the conflict between the Strasbourg Court and the Polish Constitutional Court deriving from the ECtHR judgment in *Xero Flor v Poland* of 7 May 2021. In *Xero Flor*, the Strasbourg Court stated that Poland had violated the right to due process enshrined in Article 6 ECHR; the issue being a judgment issued by the Polish Constitutional Court joined by a judge whose appointment, according to the ECtHR standards established, inter alia, by *Gudmundur Andri Astradsson*, had failed to meet the criteria for judicial independence and impartiality. The Polish court responded in its judgment K6/21 of 24 November 2021, in which it declared that the Strasbourg Court's interpretation of Article 6 ECHR was unconstitutional, inasmuch as it applied the term 'court' to the Constitutional Court and gave the ECtHR the power to review the legality of the election of judges to that court. An implication of the Polish court's reasoning would be that it has jurisdiction to decide which judgments of the Strasbourg Court are binding and which are not, on grounds of ultra vires. To justify its position, the Constitutional Court affirmed that the interpretation of Article 6 ECHR handed down by the Strasbourg Court was not foreseeable when Poland ratified the Convention.[7]

7. Informal and Formal Coordination

As can easily be deduced from the examples above, the coexistence of very different principles concerning, on the one hand, the constitutional regimes of the states (which form part of their constitutional identity) and, on the other hand, the basic tenets of an international Convention claiming primacy in the protection of human rights sometimes leads to conflicts and differences. Such conflicts make necessary (if the will to maintain an effective level of protection of human rights is genuine) continuous coordination and integration, subject to unceasing evolution, which, hopefully, will eventually transform the 'scheme' into an authentic European 'system' of human rights protection. The national and international mechanisms for oversight currently differ significantly, as do their procedures. In a first step, we can identify a series of informal practices or techniques that the higher judicial bodies, including the ECtHR, the Court of Justice of the European Union (CJEU) and the national constitutional courts have developed. We can also identify several formalised techniques meant to incorporate into international instruments mechanisms for coordination among the different European bodies of human rights protection.

7.1. Informal Coordination

An initial example of informal coordination are the fora for discussion and dialogue between members of the judicial bodies in charge of the application of the Convention, that is, the judges on apex national courts plus those on the international courts in Strasbourg and Luxembourg. These fora may be permanent organisations or of a more occasional format; sometimes they involve judges from many countries and sometimes are bilateral arrangements. One example of an institutionalised forum is the Conference of Constitutional Courts,[8] which includes among its 40 members the ECtHR and the CJEU. Another is the Superior Courts Network, organised by the ECtHR, which includes 103 high courts (supreme and constitutional) from forty-four countries.[9]

[7] See E Lettowska, 'The honest (though embarrassing) coming out of the Polish Constitutional Tribunal', *Verfassungsblog* 29 November 2021, verfassungsblog.de/the honest-though embarrassing-coming-out-of-the-polish-constitutional-tribunal.

[8] See A Von Bogdandy, C Grabenwarter and PM Huber, 'Justicia Constitucional en el espacio jurídico europeo' in A Von Bogdandy and JM Pérez de Nanclares (eds), *La justicia constitucional en el espacio jurídico europeo* (Valencia, Tirant Lo Blanch, 2022) 1548.

[9] Useful information about these questions can be found on the ECtHR webpage.

Besides these multinational fora, other relevant examples are periodic bilateral meetings of the Strasbourg Court with other courts, such as the CJEU (usually annually) or the German Federal Constitutional Court. Understandably, these meetings do not yield binding decisions or mandates, but they are useful, as shown in practice, as space for clarification of common interest matters for all affected jurisdictional levels.

A second way by which national legal orders and conventional mandates informally and progressively coordinate is through the frequently cited 'dialogue between courts'. This expression has been employed with very different connotations, ranging from the mere quotation by one court of another court's decision to reciprocal interaction and influence among several courts that is made manifest in their case law. In this last sense, 'dialogue between courts' may genuinely contribute to the elaboration of an authentic European 'system' of fundamental rights protection. This level of dialogue between courts could serve as an instrument of joint action and establish common patterns of conventional rights application to overcome discrepancies stemming from practices inherent to each national legal order. Of course, that would often require making changes to the interpretation of international, statutory, and constitutional norms by the national courts (and, in some cases, by the Strasbourg Court as well).

Several examples of this type of reciprocal interaction are well known. In Spain, keen attention has been devoted to alterations of the national case law made in response to Strasbourg case law. The Supreme and Constitutional Courts' case law concerning wiretapping, for instance, has evolved as a consequence of the *Valenzuela Contreras* judgment, evolution which the Strasbourg Court acknowledged in its inadmissibility decision in *Coban*. With respect to Germany, one example are the changes in the case law made by the Constitutional Court concerning the right to one's personal image and the privacy of public figures following the ECtHR judgment in *Von Hannover I* (2004), changes which were also acknowledged and reinforced by the ECtHR in its 2012 judgment in *Von Hannover II*. Lastly, with respect to the CJEU, an example of such dialogue between courts is the change of the Luxembourg Court's case law on the inviolability of the domicile of legal persons after the ECtHR's judgment in *Niemetz*.

It is worth pointing out that 'dialogue between courts' has, on a few occasions, also resulted in changes to the case law of the Strasbourg Court. For instance, in its Grand Chamber judgment in *Al Khawaja and Tahery*, the Court revoked the Chamber's previous judgment after considering the British Supreme Court's judgment in *The Crown v Horncastle*. More recently, the nuances on Strasbourg court's *ne bis in idem* doctrine introduced in its *A and B v Norway* judgment are worth mentioning. These modifications reflected the reasoning of the Luxembourg Court in *Akerberg Fransson*. Also worth noting is the adoption by the CJEU, continuing the dialogue, of the reasoning, in its subsequent *Luca Menci* judgment articulated by the ECtHR in, among other cases, *A and B*.[10]

Regarding informal coordination of the ECtHR with the EU and the CJEU in the area of human rights protection, one very useful formula has emerged that could be defined as '*iuris tantum* presumption of conventionality' which applies to the compliance

[10] See L López Guerra, 'La Carta de Derechos Fundamentales de la Unión Europea y la Jurisprudencia del Tribunal Europeo de Derecho Humanos', in L López Guerra (ed), *Protección multinivel de los derechos humanos. Sistemas europeo e interamericano* (Lima, Palestra, 2021) 304–25.

of Union actions with certain requisites. This presumption was first advanced by the Strasbourg Court in its *Bosphorus v Ireland* judgment of 30 June 2005.

In that case, the question before the Strasbourg Court was the violation of a conventional right by a Member State of both the Convention and of the EU for executing a mandate of EU law although the Member State did not have any margin of appreciation in that execution. Put another way, the Member State had only one path at its disposal to execute the mandate, but that path (according to the applicant) led to a violation of a conventional right. The concerned Member State was obliged to protect that right, but at the same time, as a Member of the EU had to comply with EU law. In such cases, the Strasbourg Court must forcibly, when judging the Member State's action, also make a pronouncement on the Union mandate behind the state action in question. ECtHR pronouncements on Union mandates therefore seem inevitable, even though the Union is not party to the Convention.

In *Bosphorus*, the European Council decided, applying instructions from the United Nations, that an airplane belonging to a Serbian company and operated by a Turkish airline was to be grounded, which the Irish Government effectuated. The Turkish airline, after the Luxembourg Court established the legality of the airship's grounding, appealed to the Strasbourg Court, claiming that the Irish Government violated its conventional rights. Because the Irish Government's action directly derived from a Union order, however, any judgment on that action would amount to a pronouncement on a Union mandate.

In its *Bosphorus* judgment, the Strasbourg Court pointed out that the EU, through its substantive and material norms, as well as by virtue of its procedural organisation, offered equivalent guarantee of fundamental rights to the protection afforded by the Convention and that, for that reason, the action of Union Member States enjoyed what it called a presumption of conventionality.[11] By this principle, acts condoned by the Luxembourg Court should be considered in agreement with the ECHR, and, consequently, the Strasbourg Court did not consider a new examination of the case necessary. The presumption, in any case, was not *iuris et de iure*, but only *iuris tantum*. If the ECtHR, in another instance, considered that the Union accorded insufficient protection to a conventional right, it would take up claims brought against state actions executing EU law. This *Bosphorus* doctrine, as it is now known, has been consistently applied by the ECtHR since 2005, and has prevented the Court from making indirect pronouncements on acts of the Union, which remains an entity that is not party to the Convention.

The entry into force of the Lisbon Treaty and the binding force that the CFR then attained have reinforced, for the time being (until an eventual accession of the Union to the Convention is concluded), the application of the *Bosphorus* doctrine. Its main principles have been somewhat codified in *Michaud v France* (6 December 2012), when the ECtHR examined the possibility of applying the doctrine to the case at hand and reasserted the binding nature of the Convention even when Member States carrying out obligations that derive from other international arrangements to which some of their sovereignty has been relegated. The ECtHR considered that the performance of such obligations may be presumed compatible with the Convention when the international

[11] L Garlicki, 'Cooperation of Courts: The Role of Supranational Jurisdictions in Europe' (2008) 6 *International Journal of Constitutional Law* 50, 527.

organisation substantively and procedurally ensures an equivalent level of protection of the right in question as the European Convention, and the mechanisms for that protection (particularly those of the CJEU) have been activated. The presumption of conventionality is only to be rejected when some lack of protection of the right is allegedly manifest.

The ECtHR also pointed out two other relevant factors. Firstly, the presumption will not be applied if the state enjoys a margin of discretion in the execution of its obligations (for instance, when transposing a directive). Secondly, the *Bosphorus* doctrine cannot be applied if, in the Court's opinion, the existing guarantees in the international organisation presented in the case are manifestly insufficient for the protection of the fundamental right at stake. Wherever the relationship between the Convention and the EU is not formally consolidated, in any case, the *Bosphorus* doctrine seems to be an adequate technique for at least provisional coordination and integration between the European Convention and the Union.

7.2. Formal Integration

Besides these informal fora that facilitate the coordination and evolutive integration towards (it is hoped) a consolidated European system of protection of human rights and that came about on the initiative of jurisdictional bodies themselves, several formal arrangements have also been proposed. A couple have even been put into effect by means of international instruments with binding force. One of these arrangements that involves the EU is still under development and a second, which involves the interpretative high Courts of the Member States of the Convention, concerning its interpretation, is already in practice.

In respect to the first formal arrangement, with the aim being the creation of an authentic European system of human rights protection, Article 6.2 TEU establishes that 'The Union shall accede to the European Convention for the Protection of Human Rights and Fundamental Freedoms. This accession shall not modify the competences of the Union defined in the Treaties.'[12] This mandate's parallel in the ECHR is Article 59.2, which only goes as far as saying that 'The European Union may accede to the Convention.' The accession of the EU to the Convention would solve many present difficulties. As an example of these difficulties, the present overlap of two competent jurisdictions on human rights, namely the ECtHR as the authoritative interpreter of the Convention and the CJEU as interpreter of the CFR, makes divergent case law more probable, with ensuing complications for consistent interpretation on the part of the Member States of the two organisations.

The EU's accession to the ECHR through Article 6 TEU and Article 59.2 ECHR, would certainly contribute considerably to the EU institutions' capacity to promote and

[12] For an explanation of the elaboration of Art 6.2 TEU, see S Leutheuser-Schnarrenberger, 'Der Beitritt der EU zur EMRK: Eine schier unendliche Geschichte' in C Hohmann-Dennhart, P Masuch and M Villiger (eds), *Grundrechte und Solidarität. Festchrift für Renate JAEGER* (Kehl, Engel Verlag, 2010) 135–46; for the particularities of the accession process see D Engel, *Der Beitritt der Europäische Union zur EMRK* (Tübingen, Mohr Siebeck, 2015).

defend human rights, the rule of law and democracy. Indeed, accession would not only reconfirm the EU's commitment to the values enshrined in the Convention (values that already form part of the basic principles of the EU) and the rights it proclaims (rights also included in EU law via the Charter), but would also acknowledge external control of the actions of EU institutions relative to those rights. The 27 Member States of the Union are already members of the Convention and are therefore subject to the control of the ECtHR. EU accession to the Convention would extend this control to actions of the Union institutions regarding human rights. So far, as shown above, the absence of such external control has given rise to difficulties when complaints against the Union have been brought before the Strasbourg Court because of action by EU institutions that is allegedly contrary to the rights recognised in the Convention, or because of alleged violations of the ECHR by Member States in mandatory execution of EU law.

In view of the provision of Article 6 TEU, the European Council gave the European Commission a mandate on 4 June 2010 to commence accession negotiations with specific terms of reference. On the Council of Europe's side, the Committee of Ministers mandated the Steering Committee for Human Rights to conduct the necessary negotiations with the EU and prepare an agreement for the EU's accession to the ECHR.

The Working Group created by the Steering Committee met with representatives of the EU and drew up a draft agreement. Because it was a draft international treaty binding on the EU, in accordance with Article 218 of the Treaty on the Functioning of the EU (TFEU) it would be scrutinised by the CJEU for compatibility with EU law. In due course, the European Commission requested the CJEU's opinion from the CJEU in July 2013. In its Opinion 2/2013, the CJEU held that the draft agreement on EU accession to the ECHR was incompatible with EU law and therefore accession under the terms of the draft agreement was disallowed.[13] Negotiations have continued, however, and, at present, the prospects of reopening the access procedures seem to be increasing.

A second formal arrangement for coordination between jurisdictional bodies occurred with the entry into force in 2018 of Protocol no 16 to the Convention, which provides an additional formula to facilitate the work of the Court. This Protocol introduces a new procedure by which high courts of Member States may ask the Court to weigh in on the proper interpretation and application of conventional mandates in cases they are deciding. The particularities of this new procedure are distinct from other types of consulting opinions at an international level. For instance, Article 47 ECHR establishes a procedure by which the Committee of Ministers of the Council of Europe may ask the Court for its opinion but (unlike the procedure established by Protocol no 16) the request does not come from a judicial body, and it cannot refer to questions connected to Conventional rights. For another comparison, in the Inter-American Human Rights System, Article 64 of the Inter-American Convention opens the possibility of requests about the proper interpretation of Conventional rights from the Inter-American Court by the Member States or the Organization of American States, but in this case the request cannot be made by the Member States' courts.

[13] For an exposition of the objections of the CJEU and possible solutions, see L López Guerra, *Strengthening cooperation with the Council of Europe* (Policy Department for Citizens' Rights and Constitutional Affairs, Directorate General for Internal Policies, European Parliament, 2021), wwweuroparl.europa.eu/supporting-analyses.

Creating the consulting opinion procedure of Convention Protocol no 16 was inspired by the mechanism for preliminary questions established by Article 267 TFEU, but the characteristics of the consulting opinion procedure of Protocol no 16 differ considerably from the preliminary consulting opinions that the CJEU issues. The procedure before the ECtHR is regulated in a Protocol that is separate from the Convention text; only the courts of the Member States that voluntarily ratify the Protocol will have recourse to this procedure, whereas the preliminary question to the CJEU is an essential element of the functioning of the Union and is to be applied in all Member States. The request for an opinion from the Strasbourg Court will only be open to the high courts specified by each state, not to any court whatsoever. Furthermore, while a request for a consulting opinion is always optional, Article 267 TFEU makes it obligatory in certain circumstances. Finally, at least in theory, the Strasbourg Court's reply to the consulting opinion will not be binding.

Several reasons justify adopting such a procedure through Protocol no 16. The basic reason has to do with the will to make it possible for the judicial bodies of the Member States, taking into account the ECtHR's opinion, to adopt general interpretive patterns for the Convention and national law, not only in solving concrete cases, but also in initiating or promoting reforms of norms that clash with the Convention, thus reducing the amount of space for violations of the conventional rights and the need to seek the protection of the Strasbourg Court. The procedure would therefore reduce the number and range of Convention violations in the future and would, furthermore, improve the communication between national and European courts. It is for this reason that the Protocol has been called the 'Dialogue Protocol'. Once a Member State ratifies the Protocol, we would expect fewer 'systemic' violations of the Convention. The high national courts that handle violations of human rights allegedly derived from 'systemic' deficiencies in the national legal order (for instance, whenever its legal norms are in tension with the Convention), would ask for an opinion of the Strasbourg Court before adopting its own general jurisprudential line in order to clarify the content of the Convention. In this way, taking the opinion of the Court into account before establishing highly consequential doctrine would both avoid 'systemic' violations of the Convention and reduce the Strasbourg Court's caseload.

One might ask how such expectations are playing out in reality. Granted, because of the (slow) pace with which these types of innovations are implemented, it is still too soon to draw a conclusion. Yet the initial results do not seem very encouraging. On one side, only a small number of Member States have ratified Protocol no 16, and among the countries that have not are the United Kingdom, Germany, Italy, Spain and Poland. Moreover, not many opinions have been requested. Some reflection on the role the Court plays in encouraging requests might be useful to reassess the procedure's purpose and effectiveness.

Bibliography

Engel, D, *Der Beitritt der Europäische Union zur EMRK* (Tübingen, Mohr Siebeck, 2015).

Garlicki, L, 'Cooperation of Courts: The Role of Supranational Jurisdictions in Europe' (2008) 6 *International Journal of Constitutional Law* 509.

Grewe, C, 'The ECHR in French Law: Status, Implementation and Debates' in K Ziegler (ed), *The U.K and European Human Rights. A strained relationship?* (Oxford, Hart, 2015) 341–77.

Groppi, T, 'La jurisprudence de la Cour européenne des droits de l'homme dans les décisions de la Cour constitutionnelle italienne: une recherche empirique' in Bourgorgue-Larsen, L, *Les défis de l'interprétation et de l'application des droits de l'homme* (Paris, Pedone, 2017) 323–64.

Lageot, C, 'France' in Garard, J and Fleuren, J (eds), *Implementation of the European Convention on Human Rights and of the Judgments of the ECtHR in national case law. A Comparative Analysis* (Cambridge/Antwerpen, Intersentia, 2014) 217–60.

Lettowska, E, 'The honest (though embarrassing) coming out of the Polish Constitutional Tribunal', *Verfassungsblog* 29 November 2021, verfassungsblog.de/the honest-though embarrassing-coming-out-of-the-polish-constitutional-tribunal/.

Leutheuser-Schnarrenberger, S, 'Der Beitritt der EU zur EMRK: Eine schier unendliche Geschichte' in Hohmann-Dennhart, C, Masuch, P and Villiger, M (eds), *Grundrechte und Solidarität. Festchrift für Renate JAEGER* (Kehl, Engel Verlag, 2010).

López Guerra, L, 'Constitución y protección internacional de derechos humanos. El proceso de internalización del Convenio Europeo de Derechos Humanos' in Pendás, B (ed), *España Constitucional (1978–2018) Trayectorias y perspectivas. Vol I* (Madrid, CEPC, 2018) 771–87.

—— 'La Carta de Derechos Fundamentales de la Unión Europea y la Jurisprudencia del Tribunal Europeo de Derecho Humanos' in López Guerra, L (ed), *Protección multinivel de los derechos humanos. Sistemas europeo e interamericano* (Lima, Palestra, 2021) 304–25.

—— *Strengthening cooperation with the Council of Europe* (Policy Department for Citizens' Rights and Constitutional Affairs, Directorate General for Internal Policies, European Parliament, 2021), wwweuroparl.europa.eu/supporting-analyses.

Maestracci, N, 'L'ouverture implicite aux sources exterieures. Le cas de la France' in Bourgorgue-Larsen, L (ed), *Les défis de l'interprétation et de l'application des droits de l'homme* (Paris, Pedone, 2017) 159–68.

Pollicino, O, 'The European Court of Human Rights and the Italian Constitutional Court: No "Groovy Kind of Love"' in K Ziegler (ed), *The U.K and European Human Rights. A strained relationship?* (Oxford, Hart, 2015).

Ragone, G, 'Nota a Corte cost. 49/2015. Giurisprudencia CEDU e ordinamento interno: nuove istruzioni per l'uso da parte della Corte costituzionale italiana' *DPCE online 2015* 2, www.dpceonline.it/index.php/dpceonline/article/view/172.

Von Bogdandy, A, Grabenwarter, C and Huber, PM, 'Justicia Constitucional en el espacio jurídico europeo' in Von Bogdandy, A and Pérez de Nanclares, JM (eds), *La justicia constitucional en el espacio jurídico europeo* (Valencia, Tirant Lo Blanch, 2022) 15–48.

2

Contrapunctual Dialogue with the European Court of Human Rights?

RAFAEL BUSTOS GISBERT

1. Introduction. Contrapunctual Law in the European Conventional System: Some Methodological Issues

In a seminal essay, Miguel Maduro[1] coined the expression 'contrapunctual law' to describe the legitimacy of EU law based on logic distinct from the conventional justifications for its creation and subsequent constitutionalisation. By his own account, Maduro sought to 'reconstruct this process by contrasting the top-down character of that traditional rhetoric with the bottom-up legitimacy that it presupposed and, in fact, modulated the European legal order'.[2] One of the main theses he sustained in the essay focuses on the need to abandon the view that the Court of Justice of the European Union (CJEU) is the sole actor in the construction and constitutionalisation of European Union (EU) law. Instead, this process involved 'a larger group of actors that can be described as forming an European legal community', meaning 'the success of his creation of a European legal order was only possible because the (EU) Court looked for and found the cooperation of national legal actors'.[3] This explains the choice of a musical metaphor in the term 'contrapunctual law', for:

> [C]ounterpointing is the musical method of harmonising different melodies that are not in a hierarchical relationship *inter se* .... In law we have to learn how to manage the non-hierarchical relationship between different legal orders and institutions and to discover how to gain from the diversity and choices thereby offered us without generating conflicts that ultimately will destroy those legal orders and the values they sustain.[4]

In this chapter I will borrow some of the theses put forward by Maduro and assess whether they can be extended beyond the scope of EU law. Specifically, I want to

[1] M Maduro, 'Contrapunctual Law: Europe's Constitutional Pluralism in Action' in N Walker (ed), *Sovereignty in Transition* (Oxford, Hart Publishing, 2003) 501–37.
[2] ibid 502.
[3] ibid 512.
[4] ibid 523–24.

determine whether, behind the application of the European Convention on Human Rights (ECHR) at the national level, some 'contrapunctual law' responding to bottom-up logic as described by the former Advocate General can be found.

The main thesis I wish to advance in this chapter could be summarised as follows. The traditional approach to the application of the Convention and the case law of the European Court of Human Rights (ECtHR) at the national level is based on top-down logic. In this approach, both the Convention and the case law of the ECtHR first pass to the apex national courts (the constitutional court where it exists and supreme courts where it does not). The higher courts are the first to review and ensure the consistency of national human rights law with European standards by providing, when necessary, complementary interpretation of the human rights standards in question. These high court interpretations are then spread downward throughout the various levels of the judiciary. This 'mediator' function facilitates simultaneous respect for European human rights standards and equal application of national law by domestic courts. In this model, higher courts may sometimes exercise a degree of 'veto power' over the application of the Convention as interpreted by the ECtHR. This construction also implies that, if the ECtHR case law does not pass through national apex courts, it will not reach the lower instances of adjudication. In this chapter I will argue that there are situations in which this 'traditional' approach does not adequately explain all the processes of application of the Convention, which can be, in certain circumstances, better explained by bottom-up logic by which the application of European standards is first carried out by the lower courts and only climbs back up to the higher courts by way of appeal. If my argument is valid, such a process may significantly influence the concrete application of the ECtHR case law.

My thesis confronts an important methodological question. Conclusively determining whether ordinary courts directly apply, without the mediation of higher courts, the case law of the ECtHR would require examining each direct application of that case law in thousands of cases, a Herculean task in any context and one that certainly exceeds the capacity of a chapter limited to 8,000 words. Thus, in this chapter, I focus on two sagas that unfolded in Spanish courts that encountered problems in adapting the national legal system to new standards established by the ECtHR concerning the freedom of expression. While adopting a case study methodology narrows the weight of the conclusions, it still offers interesting insight.

2. First Case Study: Freedom of Speech and Privacy in the Harassment of Public Figures

In the ECtHR's well-known *Von Hannover (1) v Germany* judgment of 24 June 2004, the ECtHR first held that taking photographs of public figures in public spaces without the applicant's knowledge and in the context of daily harassment by photographers could amount to a violation of the applicant's right to privacy. Furthermore, the Court underscored the capacity of new communication technologies (in 2004) to systematically take photographs and disseminate them to the public, increasing the risks to the right to privacy of public figures. Because of this capacity, national courts were not to rely solely on the criterion of spatial isolation to conclude that such photographs do not violate the right of public figures. On the contrary, courts were also to consider other criteria definitively established eight years later in *Axel Springer v Germany and von Hannover (2) v Germany* (7 February 2012), following reluctance by the German Constitutional Court to apply the standards set by the ECtHR.[5]

Our interest in this case does not lie in the underlying substantive issue (the scope of privacy as a limit to freedom of information and the criteria for assessing the conflict between the two rights), but in the treatment of this case law in Spain. *Von Hannover (1)* immediately raised an important point as taking images of public persons in public places was deemed a legitimate exercise of freedom of information in the Constitutional Court's case law. Furthermore, Article 8.2.a of Organic Law 1/82, 5 May, established (and still does), with reference to personal images, that the right to one's own image shall not prevent: 'Its capture, reproduction or publication by any means in the case of persons holding a public office or exercising a profession of public renown or projection and the image is captured during a public act or *in places open to the public*' (italics added). Not surprisingly, the case law of both the Constitutional Court and the ordinary courts was consistent in finding no breach of the right to privacy in the capture and dissemination of images taken in public places when the persons concerned held a public office or were popular to the public for other reasons (generally those exercising professions with significant public projection or notoriety).[6] Put another way, the ECtHR judgment in the *Von Hannover (1)* case itself qualified as a triggering decision insofar as it changed the *status quo* of the understanding of the limits on imparting information that had been elaborated in Spain for over 20 years.

Considering the relevance of the conflict on a rather sensitive issue (the scope of public figures' freedom of information), it seems striking that the Constitutional Court did not make any reference to *Von Hannover (1)* until 2012[7] in a case on the use of hidden cameras in investigative journalistic reporting.[8] This case presented a slightly different situation which, as was subsequently clarified by the ECtHR, it was not exactly the same criteria to be followed.[9] It would not be until the end of 2013[10] that the Constitutional Court started to disapply its case law and align its reading of Article 8.2.a of Organic Law 1/82 with the new standards laid down in Strasbourg. Moreover, even in these cases, the shifts in the Constitutional Court's case law were triggered by the prior application of the ECtHR standards by ordinary courts when adjudicating the conflict between privacy and freedom of speech under Organic Law 1/1982.

[5] M González Pascual. *El Tribunal Constitucional Alemán en la Construcción del espacio europeo de los derechos* (Madrid, Thomson-Civitas, 2010).

[6] A violation of the right to privacy was only found for the taking of images of public figures in public places when other incriminating facts were present, such as when a friend and a relative leaked private photos (STC 139/2001 and STC 83/2002)) or when a video recorded the death of a bullfighter in the bullring dispensary (STC 231/1988).

[7] STC 12/2012, 30 January 2012, ECLI:ES:TC:2012:12.

[8] For a commentary on this judgment, see I Villaverde Menéndez, A propósito de la reciente jurisprudencia del Tribunal Constitucional sobre el empleo de cámaras ocultas (2012) 10 *Derecon* 21.

[9] See ECtHR, *Haldimann and Others v Switzerland*, 24 February 2015.

[10] See judgments 76/2013, 21 October; 190/2013, 18 November; 7/2014, 7 January, 19/2014, 10 February; and 18/2015, 16 February.

Indeed, the quickness with which the ordinary courts, unlike the Constitutional Court, adopted the *Von Hannover* standards is remarkable. The first time *Von Hannover (1)* is quoted by ordinary courts (also in a case concerning hidden cameras) is the judgment of Barcelona First Instance Court no 21 of 2 December 2004, less than six months after the ECtHR issued its judgment. Yet it is another case, the *Alvarez Cascos* saga, that led to the implementation of *Von Hannover* standards in Spain.

This saga concerns the capture of the image of the vice-president of the Spanish Government during holidays he spent with his family (he had recently divorced). These images, taken in public places thanks to the use of telephoto zoom lenses, were broadcast on four different television programmes, prompting four different legal proceedings for moral damages based on Organic Law 1/82. Four different first instance courts in Madrid decided the cases between April and December 2005. In each judgment, the *Von Hannover* standards were considered by the judges in charge of the procedures, although the final decisions of the cases varied. In one case, the application was dismissed, and in the other three cases the damage awards differed significantly. The three cases in which the television programmes were condemned to pay damages were appealed to the second instance court (Audiencia Provincial de Madrid), but they were allocated to three different panels within the court. In two cases they upheld the decisions of the first instance courts but changed the amount of damages awarded to the applicant. In the third case, the second instance court quashed the first instance decision, maintaining no violation of the right to privacy had occurred. These three judgments were appealed before the Supreme Court through a cassation procedure. At this level the Supreme Court sought to unify the doctrine on the topic, finding no violation of the right to privacy. In the Supreme Court opinion, because the case concerned a public person who held an extremely important office (vice-president of the Government), information concerning his holidays was of public interest. For that reason, an exception expressly stated in *Von Hannover (1)* was applicable. Yet this uniformity reached at the *cassational* level, did not extend to the constitutional level. Indeed, Alvarez Cascos appealed to the Constitutional Court demanding a consistent response. The inconsistency alleged deserves attention.

The lack of uniformity in the Constitutional Court decision derives from the specific characteristics of the *amparo* instrument for appeal in Spain. This type of appeal is specifically designed to give the Constitutional Court responsibility to protect certain rights. Since 2005, however, appellants must demonstrate the 'special constitutional relevance' of their case before its merits will be considered. In the prolonged trajectory of the cases under study it should be disconcerting (and may possibly be unacceptable) that only one of the cases was considered 'especially relevant' from a constitutional point of view when, as we have pointed out, all three cases involved the same factual situation (the same images, the only difference being the television programme on which they were broadcast). Even more importantly, all referred to the same, essential constitutional question; that is, the scope of the limits on the right to information about persons holding political offices. Be that as it may, the final solution of the case took into consideration the standards laid down in

Von Hannover (1)[11] and began adapting the Constitutional Court's previous case law in the judgments issued in 2014.

Table 2.1 Overview of the cases

First Instance Court Madrid no 3817 March 2005 Dismissal	First Instance Court Madrid no 9 28 April 2005 Favourable (Damages awarded: €200,000)	First Instance Court Madrid no 12 9 December 2004 Favourable (Damages awarded: €120,000)	First Instance Court Madrid no 52 27 April 2005 Favourable (Damages awarded: €600)
No appeal	Second Instance Court: Audiencia Provincial Madrid, Section: 8ª 8 September 2006 Partially Favourable (Damages awarded: €18,000)	Second Instance Court: Audiencia Provincial Madrid, Section: 19ª 7 March 2009 Favourable to appellants (No damages awarded)	Second Instance Court: Audiencia Provincial Madrid, Section: 8ª 8 September 2006 Partially Favourable (Damages awarded: €18,000)
	Supreme Court, Judgment: 452/2011, 28 June Cassation estimated (No damages awarded)	Supreme Court Judgment: 611/2009, 7 October Cassation dismissed (No damages awarded)	Supreme Court, Judgment: 719/2009, 16 November Cassation estimated (No damages awarded)
	Constitutional Court: inadmissibility of the application for *amparo*. Lack of especial constitutional relevance	Constitutional Court: inadmissibility of the application for *amparo*. Lack of especial constitutional relevance	Constitutional Court, Judgment 176/2013, 21 October Nullity of the Supreme Court Judgment
		ECtHR Communicated case 36866/10, 26 May 2015. Withdrawal of Appellants declared 15 March 2016	Supreme Court, Judgment 1812/2014, 30 April. Declares the first instance judgment to be final (Damages awarded: €600)

From the point of view of the application of *Von Hannover (1)*, some observations from this case study jump out.

First, the first court to apply the case law the ECtHR established in *Von Hannover v Germany* on the limits to public persons' right to privacy was not the Constitutional Court, or even the Supreme Court. In fact, it took five years for the Supreme Court and

[11] Even though, as we have argued elsewhere, incorrectly. See R Bustos Gisbert, 'Vida privada y derecho a la información. Desarrollos jurisprudenciales 2013–2014: la extraña y tardía recepción de Carolina en España' (2016) 36 *Revista Española de Derecho Constitucional* 369.

eight for the Constitutional Court to take note of this jurisprudence. Ordinary courts were the first to apply the new rules, which they did quite promptly, less than a year had elapsed between the issuance of the ruling and its adoption at national level.

Secondly, the higher courts only took the new case law into account when it reached them from appeals (through cassation to the Supreme Court and through *amparo* to the Constitutional Court) brought against judicial decisions in which the reasons given in the *Von Hannover* case had been previously and explicitly considered by the courts of first instance. In other words, the higher courts did not address the consequences of the ECtHR rules for the Spanish legal system until the new *Von Hannover* rules reached them through appeal because they were taken up in the judgments of first instance. The higher courts thus did not themselves (*ex officio*) introduce the ECtHR rules, only taking up the task when compelled by their prior consideration in the first instance.

A third observation that jumps out is the heterogenous 'national judicial dialogue' that *Von Hannover (1)* triggered over the scope and effects of the new rules in the interpretation of Article 8.2.a of Organic Law 1/82. The dialogue began with different solutions reached in the first and second instance of the proceedings. A unified response was not reached until the 'cassational' level. Yet even this solution would be overturned by the Constitutional Court, whose approach has hitherto been applied consistently by all the courts.

3. Second Case Study: Freedom of Speech and Offences Directed against National Symbols and Figureheads

3.1. The Triggering Case: *Otegi Mondragon*

This second case study focuses on the problems that (at least some) Spanish courts have encountered when attempting to keep the national legal order in line with ECtHR case law on the admissibility of limits to freedom of speech based on the protection of dignity of important national symbols (flags) or persons (heads of state).

The case law in this respect was clearly laid down by the ECtHR in *Colombani and others v France* of 25 June 2002, in which journalists were condemned for insulting a foreign head of state. The Court criticised the national law that shielded the honour of a foreign head of state 'beyond general law … solely on account of their function or status irrespective of whether the criticism is warranted', which 'amounts to conferring on foreign heads of State a special privilege that cannot be reconciled with modern practice and political conceptions' (paragraph 68). In other words, a specific and privileged protection of the rights of the head of state of a foreign state is not admissible under the Convention. The argument is even stronger when applicable to the national head of state as affirmed in *Artun et Güverner v Turkey*, 26 June 2007 at paragraph 31.[12]

[12] 'A cet égard, la Court estime que ce qui a été énoncé dans l'arrêt *Colombani et autres c. France*, au sujet des chefs d'Etats étrangers, vaut à plus forte raison s'agissant de l'intérêt d'un Etat de protéger la réputation de son propre chef d'Etat: pareil intérêt ne saurait justifier de conférer à ce dernier un privilège ou une protection spéciale vis-à-vis du droit d'informer et d'exprimer des opinions à son sujet. Penser autrement ne saurait se concilier avec la pratique et les conceptions politiques d'aujourd'hui.'

Contrast the clear jurisprudence of the ECtHR with Article 490.3 of the Spanish Criminal Code (still):

> Anyone who falsely accuses or insults the King or any of his ascendants or descendants, the Queen consort or the consort of the Queen, the Regent or any member of the Regency, or the Crown Prince, in the exercise of his or her duties or on account of or in connection with them, shall be liable to a term of imprisonment of between six months and two years if the false accusation or insult is of a serious nature, and otherwise to a day-fine payable for between six and twelve months.

The disparity between the two positions made interpretative conflict unavoidable. The conflict first arose because of public statements made by a well-known leader of radical Basque independence accusing the head of the Spanish state of protecting torturers. The High Court of Justice of the Basque Country handed down the first instance assessment of these statements in a judgment of 18 March 2005 considering that Mr Otegui's statements did not amount to a crime because they were linked to political debate of maximal public interest. This decision was quashed, however, by the Supreme Court in its judgment of 31 October 2005, which sentenced Mr. Otegui to a one-year prison term in pursuance of Article 490.3 of the Criminal Code. The Constitutional Court declined to hear the appeal for *amparo* filed by the appellant in the surprising Auto 213/2006, of 3 July 2006; it did not find the offence or the sentence of sufficient special constitutional relevance for the Constitutional Court to give it further consideration.

The ECtHR, as was to be expected, would eventually show its discord, which occurred in *Otegi Mondragón v Spain* of 15 March 2011.[13] Paragraph 55 of the judgment is crystal clear:

> [I]n convicting the applicant, the domestic courts relied on Article 490 § 3 of the Criminal Code, which affords the Head of State a greater degree of protection than other persons (protected by the ordinary law on insults) or institutions (such as the government and Parliament) with regard to the disclosure of information or opinions concerning them, and which lays down heavier penalties for insulting statements (see paragraphs 27–29 above). In that connection, the Court has already stated that providing increased protection by means of a special law on insults will not, as a rule, be in keeping with the spirit of the Convention.

After citing *Colombani* and *Artun et Güverner* (among other judgments), the ECtHR affirms the full applicability of its previous jurisprudence to a monarchy such as the Spanish one in paragraph 56:

> The Court considers that, despite the differences compared with a republican system like that of Turkey, the principles established in its own case-law in that regard are also valid in relation to a monarchy like Spain, where the King occupies a unique institutional position, as pointed out by the Government.

In short: the ECtHR underscored the non-compatibility with the Convention of a differentiated and more severe criminal offence to protect the honour and dignity of the king.

[13] On this judgment see M Sánchez de Diego Fernández de la Riva, 'Las injurias al Rey a la luz de la Jurisprudencia del TEDH' (2011) 24 *Revisa General de Derecho* Europeo and E Gómez Corona, 'El prestigio de las instituciones como límite a la libertad de expresión de los ciudadanos. El caso Otegi Mondragón c. España' (2011) 151 *Revista General de Derecho Administrativo.*

3.2. A Controversial Dialogue between the Constitutional Court and the ECtHR: *Stern Taulats*

One would expect the Spanish Constitutional Court to react by bringing Article 490.3 of the Criminal Code into line with the ECtHR ruling by repealing or, more likely, revising the statute's content, but it did not. In its Judgment 177/2015, 13 March 2015, ECLI:ES:TC:2015:177, the Court faced an appeal for amparo in which the applicants, expressly invoking the case of *Otegi Mondragón v Spain*, regarded the application of the same Article 490.3 of the Criminal Code as a violation of their freedom. The application of the statute resulted in a criminal conviction for publicly burning a photograph of the King and Queen of Spain during a secessionist demonstration. The Constitutional Court upheld the conviction but modified its previous stance on the issue. In its new approach, the grounds for conviction under Article 490.3 was not the protection of the King's honour, but the defence of public order. The Court held that the burning of the photograph was a variant of hate speech that should not be protected under freedom of expression. This new approach must be emphasised because the conviction of the appellants by both ordinary courts (the Central Court and the Criminal Section of the Audiencia Nacional) were grounded on the offence to the King's honour. The change in the Constitutional Court's reasons behind its judgment belies consciousness of the inconsistency of the first-instance reasoning with ECtHR standards. Indeed, no fewer than four dissenting opinions were penned by the minority of the Constitutional Court pointing out the inconsistency.

As many expected,[14] the appellants won their case before the ECtHR in the judgment *Stern Taulats et Roura Capellera v Spain*, 13 March 2018.[15] In its judgment the Court found that no incitement to violence could be inferred from the elements used to stage the event nor from the context in which it took place. In addition, imposing a criminal penalty for an offence committed in the context of political debate was considered disproportionate and unnecessary in a democratic society. As to the issue at the heart of this disagreement between the ECtHR and the Spanish court – the existence of a differentiated criminal standard to protect the head of state's honour, the ECtHR recalled in para 35:

> *En matière d'offense envers un chef d'État, la Cour a déjà déclaré qu'une protection accrue par une loi spéciale en matière d'offense n'est, en principe, pas conforme à l'esprit de la Convention (Colombani et autres c. France, no 51279/99, §§ 66–69, CEDH 2002-V, Pakdemirli c. Turquie, no 35839/97, §§ 51–52, 22 février 2005, Artun et Güvener c. Turquie, no 75510/01, § 31,*

[14] It seems highly significant that two of the commentators on this judgment considered it a 'chronicle of a condemnation foretold'. See M Presno Linera, 'Crónica de una condena anunciada. El asunto Stern Taulats y Roura Capellera c España sobre la quema de las fotos del Rey' (2018) 42 *Teoría y Realidad Constitucional* and J Bilbao Ubillos, 'La STEDH de 13 de marzo de 2018 en el asunto Stern Taulats y Roura Capellera contra España. La crónica de una condena anunciada' (2018) 28 *Revista General de Derecho Constitucional*.

[15] The literature on this judgment is vast. A useful approach to the diverging opinions can be consulted in the Academic Survey on freedom of speech put together by a well-known constitutional law journal in consultation with seven prominent freedom of speech experts (M Carrillo López, L Corredoira Alfonso, A Rodríguez Vergara, R Sánchez Ferriz, JJ Solozábal Echavarría, J Urías Martínez, I Villaverde Menéndez). These experts were specifically asked about the effect of *Stern Taulats* on the constitutional framing of freedom of speech in Spain. See *Teoría y Realidad Constitucional* (2019) 44, pp 15–73.

> *26 juin 2007, et Otegi Mondragon c Espagne, no 2034/07, §§ 55–56, CEDH 2011). En effet, l'intérêt d'un Etat de protéger la réputation de son propre chef d'Etat ne peut justifier de conférer à ce dernier un privilège ou une protection spéciale vis-à-vis du droit d'informer et d'exprimer des opinions à son sujet (Otegi Mondragon précité § 55)*

As to the concrete circumstances of the case, the Court held in at paragraph 36 that no personal offence was present:

> *Tous ces éléments permettent de conclure qu'il ne s'agissait pas d'une attaque personnelle dirigée contre le Roi d'Espagne, ayant pour but de mépriser et de vilipender la personne de ce dernier, mais d'une critique envers ce que le Roi représente, en tant que chef et symbole de l'appareil étatique et des forces qui, selon les requérants, avaient occupé la Catalogne – ce qui relève du domaine de la critique ou dissidence politique et correspond à l'expression d'un rejet de la monarchie en tant qu'institution.*

As for the Constitutional Court's qualification of the applicants' conduct as incitement to hatred, it is dismissed by the ECtHR in paragraph 40. Although the Court does not analyse the issue any further, its criticism of the national court's assessment of the criteria for incitement to hatred established in European case law is clear. These criteria can be summarised as the need to assess the context of the expression considered as incitement to hatred on the basis of the content of the speech, the intention of the author and the likelihood of harm. Following this approach, the likelihood of causing harm depends on the actual political and social context at the time of the speech and the impact of the message, which requires considering: the publicity, authorship, and audience; the importance and credible nature of the potential harm. These criteria were not evaluated by the Constitutional Court, which only relied on the potential (not actual) effect of the speech on public order.

Last but not least, the Court underscored its well-known case law on the prima facie disproportionality of imposing criminal penalties in the exercise of freedom of speech in public interest debates in paragraph 42:

> *[U]ne peine d'emprisonnement imposée par une infraction commise dans un cadre de débat politique, en ce qu'elle représente la plus forte réprobation juridique d'un comportement, constitue une ingérence dans la liberté d'expression qui n'était pas proportionnée au but légitime poursuivi ni nécessaire dans une société démocratique.*

3.3. More Resistance from the Constitutional Court: *Puta Bandeira*

The *Stern Taulats* case has been cited by the Constitutional Court in six judgments,[16] in all but one of which, STC 190/2020, the references were inconsequential. In those cases, the references to *Stern Taulats* were clearly indirectly related to the decisions' reasoning.

[16] STC 56/2020, 15 June 2020, ECLI:ES:TC:2020:56; STC 190/2020,15 December 2020, ECLI:ES:TC:2020:190; STC 91/2021, 22 April 2021, ECLI:ES:TC:2021:91; STC 106/2021, 11 May 2021, ECLI:ES:TC:2021:106; STC 121/2021, 2 June 2021, ECLI:ES:TC:2021:121; and STC 58/2022, 7 April 2022, ECLI:ES:TC:2022:58.

For that reason, we can focus on the outlier, STC 190/2020, 15 December 2020 (*Puta Bandeira*).[17] The appellant, Fragoso Dacosta, was convicted for insulting the Spanish flag as it was being hoisted in a military facility during a demonstration due to a labour conflict. In this case, it was not the honour of the King as protected by Article 490.3 of the Criminal Code at stake, but rather the honour of Spanish symbols as protected by Article 543 of the Criminal Code: 'Offence or insults conveyed publicly, by means of utterances, writing or actions, against Spain, its Autonomous Communities or the symbols or emblems thereof shall be punished by a day-fine payable for between seven and twelve months.'

Even though the honour protected differed (the flag instead of the King) the arguments set forth in *Stern Taulats* were fully applicable to the case. Yet instead of applying them, the Constitutional Court focused its efforts on undermining them.

First, it is worth emphasising the lack of any reference to hate speech or incitement to violence by the two judicial decisions by ordinary courts previous to the *amparo* appeal. The first instance judgments focused on the insults to the flag without any reference to hate speech or incitement to violence. It is also important to note the public prosecutor's backing of the appeal at the constitutional level. The arguments set forth by the parties to the *amparo* proceedings were therefore united in favour of an estimative judgment and the declaration of a violation of freedom of speech. Even so, the Constitutional Court declared the application unfounded and that no violation of the right could be found.

Reviewing the Constitutional Court's references to its own judgment 177/2015 is highly instructive. The Spanish court uses 13 such references to qualify its position without acknowledging that the ECtHR completely rejected that position in *Stern Taulats*. The scarce (two) references to *Stern Taulats* were only made to insist on the importance of the concurrence of elements that may justify a limitation of freedom of speech based on incitement to violence.[18] In this sense, the key question for the Court would be evaluating the risk to the public order as protected by law. The case analysis thus parallels the one it issued in 2015 that was considered unsatisfactory by the ECtHR. To distinguish the flag case from the photograph burning case, the Constitutional Court emphasised the difference between the object of the offensive behaviour. In the case at hand, it was not a public figure being attacked, but a national symbol. Public figures must tolerate attacks on their private life (including honour), but attacks on symbols, the Spanish court argued, touch all citizens. Finally, the Court attempted to justify the proportionality of the penalty imposed with the argument that it was *only* a fine and did not involve imprisonment.

Five judges issued dissenting opinions deploring the lack of respect for its arguments by the ECtHR in *Stern Taulats* even though those arguments were discussed during the Spanish court's deliberations. The dissenting opinions thus reveal the express will of the majority of the Court not to follow the ECtHR on this point.

[17] For a deeper analysis of the antecedents and the content of this judgment see J Bilbao Ubillos, 'La protección penal de los símbolos nacionales. El delito de ultraje a la bandera' (2022) 126 *Revista Española de Derecho Constitucional* 13 and I Álvarez Rodríguez, 'Libertad de expresión y ultraje a la bandera de España. Comentario a la STC 190/2020, de 15 de octubre' (2021) 24 *Foro. Revista de Ciencias Jurídicas y Sociales* 343.

[18] A 'fleeting double allusion' would be considered in the dissenting opinion of Judge Ollero at para 4.

As was easily expected, Fragoso took his case to the ECtHR and the ECtHR again found the Constitutional Court in violation of Article 10 of the Convention in *Fragoso Dacosta v Spain*, 8 June 2023.[19] In it, the Court acknowledged that insults to a person may lead to different conclusions than insults to national symbols. In paragraph 27 it expressly acknowledged that, 'in principle, the national authorities are better placed than the international judge to assess the significance and impact of offensive words, in particular where they are directed at a national symbol'. It also notes, however, that 'the principle of subsidiarity imposes a shared responsibility between the States Parties and the Court, and that national authorities and courts must interpret and apply the domestic law in a manner that gives full effect to the Convention'. In the next paragraph, however, the ECtHR found that despite the reference by the Constitutional Court to a 'feeling of intolerance' projected by the applicant, 'it did not examine whether there were sufficient grounds to find that his statements amounted to hate speech, such as the existence of a tense political or social background or the capacity of the statements to lead to harmful consequences'. Accordingly, the Court declared the violation of Article 10 insofar as no hate speech could be found in insulting the flag during a peaceful demonstration. In this case, the ECtHR thus criticises the Constitutional Court's determination of hate speech without due regard for the criteria necessary to justify limits on freedom of speech.

The Constitutional Court's attempt to 'rescue' the provisions of the Criminal Code related to the defence of Spanish symbols (both the King and the flag) by framing them as crimes of incitement to hatred proved unsuccessful. Incitement to hatred has its own criteria that must be met in each case and cannot be easily extended to crimes related to the protection of collective honour through symbols.

3.4. Apparent Compliance

A very similar approach can be found in the case law of the Spanish Supreme Court. A search in the Spanish Jurisprudence Database found citations of *Stern Taulats* in 72 court decisions. In these rulings, the Spanish Supreme Court references the case in different ways.

First, *Stern Taulats* is cited by both the Civil Chamber and the Criminal Chamber of the Court. The Civil Chamber deals with damages arising from the violation of the right to privacy, while the Criminal Section assesses cases involving defamation of persons and symbols that constitutes a criminal offence.

The Civil Chamber first cited *Stern Taulats* in 2013 to emphasise the stricter interpretation of limits on freedom of expression in cases where a matter of public interest is at stake. *Stern Taulats* appears only as one of the various ECtHR decisions on the subject, in other words, merely one judgment in a longer list starting, typically, with the seminal case *Handyside v United Kingdom*.

[19] About this case see, I Alvarez Rodríguez, 'Ultraje a la bandera y convenio europeo de derechos humanos. Comentario a la STEDH Fragoso Dacosta contra España' (2023) 88 *REDE: Revista Española de Derecho Europeo* 145 and C Quesada Alcalá, 'Los ultrajes a la bandera y el clamor general del Consejo de Europa: análisis comparativo de la STEDH Fragoso Dacosta c España' (2023) 61 *Revista General de Derecho Europeo*.

For its part, the Criminal Chamber of the Supreme Court, while associating the judgment with the need for stricter scrutiny of any limit to freedom of expression in cases where a matter of public interest is at stake in the same sense as the Civil Chamber, emphasises that criminal sanction is only acceptable when the speech in question goes beyond protected speech because it qualifies as hate speech.

The Supreme Court therefore changed its position regarding injuries to symbols codified in Articles 490.3 (for the King) and 543 (for other symbols such as the flag) of the Criminal Code. This shift, however, is the same as the Constitutional Court's in its judgment 177/2015 that the ECtHR rejected as not in accordance with European standards both in *Stern Taulats* and *Fragoso Dacosta* if the assessment of hate speech was not made at the national level following the specific jurisprudence on the subject laid down by the ECtHR.

The Supreme Court took positive steps in declaring the prevalence of freedom of expression in cases brought after a far-right pseudo-union filed abusive criminal complaints alleging politicians and even ministers had insulted the crown or national symbols. In these decisions, the Supreme Court found no hate speech of any kind.

However, the Court upheld criminal convictions in cases where, together with insults to symbols, profanations were made, mostly in the context of secessionist or radical movements, that could be considered threats to the King and therefore, in the Supreme Court's opinion, qualified as hate speech.

The Supreme Court's reception of *Stern Taulats* is far from satisfactory. The judgment did cite it, and formally complied with it. Yet in truth, when deciding whether the statement made against the symbols amounted to hate speech, the Supreme Court did not follow the standards laid out by the ECtHR. In fact, the Supreme Court, following the approach of the Constitutional Court in its judgment 177/2015, considers incitement to hatred to exist whenever a statement may somehow potentially disturb public order, without taking up the stringent criteria of incitement to hatred established by the ECtHR. In any such cases, the Supreme Court considers any insult to the Crown (or to the symbols) as incitement to hatred insofar as the insult is likely to provoke some public disorder. Furthermore, the Court has always (except in cases of abusive complaints) considered the disruptive effect of the insult likely irrespective of the perpetrator, the form, the context and the probability of provoking violence. In short, the Supreme Court formally applies the *Stern Taulats* ruling, but in practice fails to comply with the substantive criteria the ruling established.

This assertion has been confirmed recently in a Supreme Court judgment of 19 October 2023. In it, the Supreme Court ruled on an appeal against a conviction under Article 490 of the Criminal Code for statements made by the appellant against the former King. However absurd they were, the statement could in no way be regarded as incitement to hatred because they alleged the former King was involved in the kidnapping, rape, torture and murder of three young women 30 years previously; terrible crimes that shocked the Spanish public at the time. The plaintiff argued that Article 490 granting greater protection to the honour of the King and his family than to other citizens was unconstitutional, an argument the Court rejected. First, the Court placed the question of law within the scope of a conflict with the right to honour of the King Emeritus: 'The facts declared proven have an unequivocal meaning of offence to the honour and dignity of the aggrieved person, in this case, Mr. …., King Emeritus' (paragraph 2.3). In a second step, the Court held that Article 490 of the Criminal Code does not raise any human rights issues insofar as:

> The legislator is free to reorder axiologically the values at stake in the face of attacks that go beyond the undermining of the personal honour and dignity of the addressee. When the offences transcend the personal level and undermine the institutional integrity which, in each case, is embodied by the offended party, the creation of a specific type of offence covering the disvalue of the injurious or defamatory conduct is fully justified (paragraph 4.4.1)

The essence of the *Stern Taulats* judgment (the inconsistency of a privileged criminal offence to protect the honour of the head of state with the Convention) is thus completely excluded in the case despite the fact that the appellant invoked the 177/2015 judgment of the Constitutional Court. Unsurprisingly, *Stern Taulats* is not mentioned anywhere in the judgment.

3.5. Actual Compliance

This bleak picture contrasts sharply with the implementation of the criteria set out in *Stern Taulats* by some Spanish courts of first instance. A first example related to Article 490.3 of the Criminal Code (Insults to the King) can be found in the decision of the Investigation Judge of the Audiencia Nacional, dated 6 May 2019, regarding the burning of photographs of the King during a demonstration precisely organised to celebrate the *Stern Taulats* judgment. The magistrate decided against criminal conviction because, as stated in the *Stern Taulats* judgment that the judge cited explicitly, the burning could not be considered hate speech.

However, even more interesting (and to a certain extent more striking in view of the Supreme Court's approach) might be the application of the criteria established in *Stern Taulats* by some courts of first instance charged with determining criminal liability for infringing Article 543 of the Criminal Code. The competent courts of first instance for this type of criminal charge are the *Audiencia Provinciales* (provincial courts), an apparent trivial detail with consequential difference with respect to Article 490.3, whose jurisdiction is centralised in the Audiencia Nacional. The Provincial Court of Barcelona in particular has established case law that fully meets the criteria set forth in *Stern Taulats* and has repeatedly ruled that insults to Spanish symbols or institutions do not merit a criminal conviction under Article 543 to the extent that they do not involve incitement to hatred.[20] In its decision of 12 December 2018, the Provincial Court of Barcelona fully recognised the significance of *Stern Taulats* and its impact on the constitutional interpretation of freedom of expression. In fact, it refers to *Stern Taulats* as a judgment that 'corrects the criterion of judgment 177/2015 of the Constitutional Court'. The Audiencia thus declares in its ruling (in direct contrast to what the Constitutional Court would consider two years later) that burning the flag is not 'a collective insult of hatred', but a political questioning directed at the State through its symbols.

[20] See Decision 7 June 2018 (even before the *Taultats* judgment became final), Decision 12 December 2018 or Decision 6 May 2019.

This line of reasoning that requires hate speech must be proven after assessing the criteria established by the ECtHR in order to declare a criminal conviction for insulting Spanish institutions or symbols is found not only in Barcelona, but also in courts in other Spanish provinces. It should be noted that some of these rulings came after the Constitutional Court's ruling 190/2020. Put another way, while the Constitutional Court declared Article 543 of the Criminal Code as justifying a conviction for insulting a symbol, some provincial courts have ruled to the contrary, relying on the criteria established in *Stern Taulats*.[21]

In short, some courts of first instance are applying the ECtHR criteria more faithfully than either the Constitutional Court or the Supreme Court. Moreover, they are fully aware that, in doing so, they are departing from national case law and, instead, directly applying European precedents. The cases cited above have not been appealed before the Supreme Court and are therefore now *res iudicata*. Future appeals in similar cases will give both the Supreme Court and the Constitutional Court the opportunity to review their case law, although I am not holding my breath for them to veer substantially from their previous jurisprudence.

4. Contrapunctual Law at Work: Some Tentative Conclusions

Some provocative conclusions can be drawn from the cases as they have been presented. They should be considered only 'tentative' conclusions because they are drawn from only two case studies. To be considered generalisable, the conclusions would have to draw on a longer, more thorough study that is not feasible in this chapter.

First, the apex courts (Constitutional and Supreme) are able to oppose or simply ignore the application of European case law in the interpretation of national rights when those courts do not agree with the conclusions of the ECtHR or when the ECtHR rulings are completely divergent from previous national rulings. This is a well-known phenomenon that often leads to judicial back-and-forth between national high courts and European courts, dialogue that did indeed take place in the cases reviewed. The dialogue proved fruitful in the *Von Hannover* case, even if the constitutional approach differs slightly from the approach adopted by the ECtHR. It is also worth underscoring that the Constitutional Court took almost 10 years to begin aligning itself with the ECtHR case law. In contrast, the judicial dialogue over differentiated standards of protection for the right to honour of the head of state or of national symbols has been fruitless. The Spanish high courts have repeatedly tried to justify and maintain their understanding of the legal issues. After they were rebuked (in the *Stern Taulats* and *Fragoso Dacosta*) they returned to the interpretation of the rules of the Criminal Code from before the Strasbourg Court began to find them in violation of Article 10.

The attempts of the higher courts to block the application of newly established European standards contrast starkly with the traditional assumption that ECtHR case law is transmitted to national jurisdictions following top-down logic (first to apex

[21] See, eg Judgment Audiencia Provincial of San Sebastián, 13 May 2022, Decision Audiencia Provincial of Cáceres, 27 December 2021, Judgment Audiencia Provincial of Málaga, 13 September 2021.

courts and then on to lower courts). In one of the cases studied, the apex court simply ignored the new rules for nearly a decade; in the other, the two courts resisted by applying the rules by either following ratiocination in direct tension with that envisaged by the ECtHR or by simply acting as if the Strasbourg judgments did not exist.

Second, the paralysis or opposition of the higher courts in applying the new European standards that are inconsistent with national law has been counterbalanced by the direct application of these new standards by lower courts on a case-by-case basis, even before the higher courts ever cited the new ECtHR judgments. This direct effect of the new European standards has served two different purposes: (i) as a warning that a new approach to rights must be adopted (*Von Hannover*); and (ii) as a direct challenge to the case law adopted by the apex national courts before and after the ECtHR judgments (*Stern Taulats*). The assimilation of the ECtHR rulings by lower courts contradicts claims that higher courts have de facto 'veto power' over ECtHR findings. The lower courts often explore paths that circumvent a national jurisprudence when the apex courts ignore rulings by the ECtHR. Thus, contrapunctual law (in the sense theorised by Maduro for EU law) may be making its way into the realm of the ECHR, which would represent a new way in which European standards may be applied under bottom-up logic of jurisprudence and compensate for, if not overcome, the resistance of higher courts to developments in the interpretation of human rights.

In any case, and this would be the third and last conclusion, European judges of first and second instance are increasingly aware of and attentive to ECtHR case law, and not only the higher courts that are sufficiently staffed to keep abreast of it. New tools for disseminating its case law and intensive training programmes for legal professionals (not only judges, but also prosecutors and lawyers) in the European Convention system may have started to bear first fruits in the form of direct application of treaty rights immediately by the courts of first instance without the intermediation of the higher courts, or even against them. A new legal community in the sense outlined by Maduro can now be seen within the scope of the ECHR, which lies outside the realm of EU law.

This scenario is consistent with the operation of the principle of subsidiarity and, in particular, with one of its most remarkable derivatives: the principle of shared responsibility that implies the involvement of all domestic authorities (courts in particular) in ensuring compliance with ECHR rights. Ordinary courts seem to be assuming their role as European courts and developing the Convention system in an unexpected twist on the principle of shared responsibility that might help to fulfil the Convention's mandates as interpreted by the ECtHR. In short: the case studies show the usefulness of contrapunctual law is not only for EU Law, but for the ECHR as well.

Bibliography

Álvarez Rodríguez, I, 'Libertad de expresión y ultraje a la bandera de España. Comentario a la STC 190/2020, de 15 de octubre' (2021) 24 *Foro Revista de Ciencias Jurídicas y Sociales*343.

—— 'Ultraje a la bandera y convenio europeo de derechos humanos. Comentario a la STEDH Fragoso Dacosta contra España' (2023) 88 *REDE: Revista Española de Derecho Europeo* 145.

Bilbao Ubillos, J, 'La protección penal de los símbolos nacionales. El delito de ultraje a la bandera' (2022) 126 *Revista Española de Derecho Constitucional* 13.

—— 'La STEDH de 13 de marzo de 2018 en el asunto Stern Taulats y Roura Capellera contra España. La crónica de una condena anunciada' (2018) 28 *Revista General de Derecho Constitucional.*

Bustos Gisbert, R, 'Vida privada y derecho a la información. Desarrollos jurisprudenciales 2013–2014: la extraña y tardía recepción de Carolina en España' (2016) 36 *Revista Española de Derecho Constitucional.*

Carrillo López, L et al, 'Academic Survey on Freedom of Speech' (2019) 44 *Teoría y Realidad Constitucional.*

Gómez Corona, E, 'El prestigio de las instituciones como límite a la libertad de expresión de los ciudadanos. El caso Otegi Mondragón c. España' (2011) 151 *Revista General de Derecho Administrativo.*

González Pascual, M, *El Tribunal Constitucional Alemán en la Construcción del espacio europeo de los derechos* (Madrid, Thomson-Civitas, 2010).

Maduro, M, 'Contrapunctual Law: Europe's Constitutional Pluralism in Action' in N Walker (ed), *Sovereignty in Transition* (Oxford, Hart Publishing, 2003) 501–37.

Presno Linera, M, 'Crónica de una condena anunciada. El asunto Stern Taulats y Roura Capellera c España sobre la quema de las fotos del Rey' (2018) 42 *Teoría y Realidad Constitucional.*

Quesada Alcalá, C, 'Los ultrajes a la bandera y el clamor general del Consejo de Europa: análisis comparativo de la STEDH Fragoso Dacosta c España' (2023) 61 *Revista General de Derecho Europeo.*

Sánchez de Diego Fernández de la Riva, M, 'Las injurias al Rey a la luz de la Jurisprudencia del TEDH' (2011) 24 *Revisa General de Derecho* Europeo.

Villaverde Menéndez, I, 'A propósito de la reciente jurisprudencia del Tribunal Constitucional sobre el empleo de cámaras ocultas' (2012) 10 *Derecon* 21.

3

The European Court of Human Rights in Inter-State Applications Relating to International Armed Conflicts: Prospects and Difficulties

PAZ ANDRÉS SÁENZ DE SANTAMARÍA

1. Introduction

The number of inter-state applications filed in connection with international armed conflicts in Eastern Europe has significantly increased since 2007, opening up a new field of jurisprudence for the European Court of Human Rights (the Court, ECtHR).[1] Of the 14 cases based on Article 33 of the Convention for the Protection of Human Rights and Fundamental Freedoms (ECHR) currently pending,[2] 12 relate to international armed conflict, some during the war phase, others during subsequent situations of occupation and some with respect to specific incidents where violent force was used.[3] Of these 12 cases, so far only a judgment on the merits has been reached in the case *Georgia v Russia (II)*.[4]

One result of the increasing tendency to seek recourse from international tribunals in the context of warring factions has been the enshrining of the concept of vicarious protection of human rights as a form of 'judicialisation of foreign policy, using the courts as one more element of the persistent political and armed conflict between states, rather than [as] a tool in the service of genuine dispute settlement'.[5] Accordingly, K Dzehtsiarou and VP Tzevelekos have asserted that:

[1] See www.echr.coe.int/inter-state-applications.

[2] There are currently 14 inter-state cases pending (covering in total 18 applications) before the Court (see ECtHR, Press Unit, Q & A on Inter-State Cases, January 2024, 3–5).

[3] The only cases that do not relate to armed conflict are *Liechtenstein v the Czech Republic*, application no 35738/20, and *Ireland v the United Kingdom (III)*, application no 1859/24.

[4] Judgment (Grand Chamber) 21 January 2021, Application no 38263/08. This judgment was followed by another on 28 April 2023 on the issue of just satisfaction.

[5] EW Petit de Gabriel, 'Georgia, Rusia, la CIJ y el TEDH. Límites jurisdiccionales, complementariedad y protección vicaria de los derechos humanos' in S Torrecuadrada García-Lozano and C Espósito (eds), *Los desafíos de la Corte Internacional de Justicia frente a los Derechos Humanos* (Las Rozas, Madrid, Wolters Kluwer Legal & Regulatory España, 2022) 224. See an analysis of the causes of the judicialisation of political conflicts in S Steininger and N Deitelhoff, 'Against the Masters of War: The Overlooked Functions of Conflict Litigation by International Courts' (2021) 84, *Law and Contemporary Problems* 95.

> The absence in international law of other effective avenues and means for states to solve such international disputes creates a gap that states request the ECHR mechanism to fill. In other words, states invite the ECtHR to stretch the ECHR ambit to peace and security.[6]

The recently joined case *Ukraine and the Netherlands v Russia*,[7] which bundles complaints against the Russian military operations in Ukraine since 24 February 2022 and the conflict in eastern Ukraine involving pro-Russian separatists since 2014, including those related to the downing of Malaysia Airlines flight MH17, exemplifies how these disputes transcend the specific application: before the ECtHR, 26 states have applied for intervention under Article 36.2 ECHR, a particularly significant figure considering that overall applications for intervention now comprise 11 per cent of the total,[8] and that single cases have never before bundled such a high number of demands for intervention.[9]

This trend opens up new perspectives and at the same time poses fresh difficulties because, while it gives the Court the opportunity to ensure respect for human rights, at the same time it obliges it to rule on issues related to a context of use of force in which norms from other sectors of the international order are also applicable.[10] This was not the situation when the ECHR was drafted. It adds a new typology of inter-state claims that not only responds to the logic of the guarantee of European public order and the protection of the rights of individuals, but also configure a dispute settlement mechanism, a situation which brings in political motivations and factors.[11]

[6] K Dzehtsiarou and V P Tzevelekos, 'The Aggression Against Ukraine and the Effectiveness of Inter-state Cases in Case of War' (2022) 3, *European Convention on Human Rights Law Review* 165, 169.

[7] Applications nos 8019/16, 43800/14, 28525/20 and 11055/22. This case includes in total 31 third-party interveners (see Press Release Update on the third-party intervention requests granted in the inter-State case *Ukraine and the Netherlands v. Russia*, ECtHR 082 (2023), 17 March 2023).

[8] A figure calculated by K Dzehtsiarou, 'Conversations with friends: "friends of the Court" interventions of the state parties to the European Convention on Human Rights' (2023) 43, *Legal Studies* 381, 388.

[9] The significant increase in the number of applications for intervention explains why, on 20 March 2023, the ECtHR amended the Rules Court regarding third-party intervention and published a Practice Direction on the modalities of Third-Party Intervention; see Press Release, European Court clarifies third-party intervention: amendments to Rules of Court and new guidelines, ECtHR 084 (2023), 20 March 2023. See also J Batura, 'The Objective Friends of the Court – New Insights into the Role of Third Parties before the European Court of Human Rights', *EJIL: Talk!*, 19 April 2023, www.ejiltalk.org/the-objective-friends-of-the-court-new-insights-into-the-role-of-third-parties-before-the-european-court-of-human-rights. On the value of third-party interventions, see J Batura and I Risini, 'Of Parties, Third Parties, and Treaty Interpretation: Ukraine v. Russia (X) before the European Court of Human Rights', *EJIL: Talk!*, 26 September 2022, www.ejiltalk.org/of-parties-third-parties-and-treaty-interpretation-ukraine-v-russia-x-before-the-european-court-of-human-rights.

[10] K Dzehtsiarou and VP Tzevelekos point to a number of challenges for the Convention system caused by inter-State applications in the event of war, including the difficulties caused by a combination of the limited resources at its disposal, the large increase in workload that may be detrimental to individual applications and the risks to the reputation of the Court and the effectiveness of its decisions, which may end up being merely symbolic (n 6, 169–73).

[11] D Janer Torrens, *Conflictos Territoriales y Convenio Europeo de Derechos Humanos* (Pamplona, Aranzadi, 2023) 126. As A Mondré notes, 'An Inter-State application can be viewed as another piece in the diplomatic toolbox', adding that 'An application to an international court is also publically putting blame on the opposing state as an alleged perpetrator of human rights violations' ('Studying the Increase in Inter-State Applications' in *Inter-State Cases under the European Convention on Human Rights. Experiences and Current Challenges, Proceedings of the Conference organised under the aegis of the German Presidency of the Committee of Ministers (Berlin, 12–13 April 2021)* (Council of Europe, March 2022) 47, 48–9, rm.coe.int/interstate-cases-under-the-echr/1680a5e82c).

In this way, particularities generally present in inter-state claims are amplified, since it is clear that, as Judge Keller pointed out in her concurring opinion in *Georgia v Rusia (II)*, 'the judicial function entrusted to the Court by the Convention cannot be discharged in precisely the same fashion in inter-State cases (under Article 33) as in cases originating in individual applications (under Article 34)'.[12] This is why the specific problems posed by this growing practice and its impact on the effectiveness of the Convention system has already been taken up by the Council of Europe. A Declaration was adopted during the High-Level Conference meeting in Copenhagen on 12 and 13 April 2018, to which the Committee of Ministers was invited and in consultation with the Court. The purpose was to explore options to handle more effectively cases related to inter-state disputes, as well as individual applications arising out of situations of inter-state conflict, options that would not thereby limit the jurisdiction of the Court and took into consideration the specific features of these categories of cases.[13] This task was entrusted by the Committee of Ministers to the Steering Committee for Human Rights (CDDH),[14] which submitted its report in December 2022.[15]

In its Declaration on the effective processing and resolution of cases relating to inter-state disputes, adopted on 5 April 2023, the Committee of Ministers invited the Court to continue to reflect on its working methods and allocate appropriate human resources to ensure the effective and speedy examination and resolution of applications stemming from inter-state disputes which often involve large-scale human rights violations. The Committee also committed itself to reviewing the political tools at its disposal in relation to inter-state disputes.[16]

Meanwhile, in Appendix IV of the Reikjavík Declaration issued after the 4th Summit of Heads of State and Government of the Council of Europe (16–17 May 2023), it is recognised that 'that the Court's current resources are insufficient and unsustainable to adequately deal with the influx of new and pending applications, including interstate applications arising from conflicts, many of which concern complex legal, political and societal issues'.[17]

[12] Judgment (Grand Chamber) 21 January 2021, Concurring opinion, para 9.

[13] Para 54(c) (rm.coe.int/copenhagen-declaration/16807b915c). The Declaration also referred to the individual applications arising out of situations of inter-State conflicts, which currently constitute a significant percentage of the total number of pending individual applications (see data provided at ECtHR, Press Unit, Q & A on Inter-State Cases, December 2023; see also CDDH, DH-SYSC-IV, *Statistical Report on conflict-related applications*, DH-SYSC-IV(2022)05REV, 25 October 2022, rm.coe.int/dh-sysc-iv-statistical-report-on-conflict-related-applications-05rev/1680a90dc2).

[14] CM(2021) 131-addfinal. The CDDH was instructed by the Committee of Ministers to present by 31 December 2022 a report on the effective processing and resolution of cases related to inter-state disputes, including possible proposals; the task was entrusted to the Drafting Group on Effective Processing and Resolution of Cases Relating to Inter-State Disputes (DH-SYSC-IV), under the authority of the Committee of Experts on the System of the European Convention on Human Rights (DH-SYSC).

[15] CDDH *Report on the effective processing and resolution of cases relating to inter-State disputes*, CDDH(2022)R97 Addendum 3, 16 December 2022, rm.coe.int/steering-committee-for-human-rights-cddh-cddh-report-on-the-effective-/1680a96acb.

[16] Decl (05/04/2023), paras 1, 4 and 7, search.coe.int/cm/Pages/result_details.aspx?ObjectId=0900001680aad39a.

[17] Also, the heads of state and government 'Support the Court's efforts to ensure that, through the expeditious processing of individual and interstate applications, particularly those arising from conflicts, States are held accountable for their actions'.

These types of inter-state claims raise important substantive and procedural issues.[18] As the former President of the ECtHR has pointed out:

> The processing of inter-State cases raises exceptional challenges for the Court, and indeed the States parties, in particular when they concern armed conflicts. Complicated legal issues of admissibility, jurisdiction, and the Convention's relationship to International Humanitarian Law must often be addressed. The factual situations also pose challenges, as does the relationship between the inter-State case itself and the hundreds if not thousands of related cases.[19]

This chapter will focus on the specific aspects that give rise to inter-state claims related to international armed conflicts, confined exclusively to matters that arise during hostilities. It deals with questions of jurisdiction, the interplay between the ECHR and the international humanitarian law (IHL), the interim measures adopted and the concurrence of claims before the ECtHR and the International Court of Justice (ICJ).

2. The Controversial Issue of Jurisdiction

Much criticism has been levelled at the methodology adopted by the Court in its 21 January 2021 judgment of the *Georgia v Rusia (II)* case which distinguished between the active hostility phase and subsequent events related to the conflict,[20] concluding that, in the course of military operations during an international armed conflict, one cannot generally speak of 'effective control' over an area because 'the very reality of armed confrontation and fighting between enemy military forces seeking to establish control over an area in a context of chaos means that there is no control over an area'.[21]

Judge Pinto de Alburquerque asserted that 'the Court will face a gargantuan task to restore the damage to its credibility caused by this judgment'.[22] Judge Chanturia, for his part, advanced some interesting judicial policy considerations in which he asked 'who else, if not the Court, should carry out supervision of human-rights protection during armed conflicts occurring on the European continent',[23] noting that 'The Court has not only a legal but also a moral obligation to stay active and exercise its duty of European supervision in the event of armed conflicts occurring within the legal space of the Convention'[24] and that 'the majority's ruling as regards the question of extraterritorial

[18] For an overview of these issues, see G Ulfstein and I Risini, 'Inter-State Applications under the European Convention on Human Rights: Strengths and Challenges', *EJIL: Talk!*, 24 January 2020, www.ejiltalk.org/inter-state-applications-under-the-european-convention-on-human-rights-strengths-and-challenges; I Risini, *The Inter-State Application under the European Convention on Human Rights: Between Collective Enforcement of Human Rights and International Dispute Settlement* (Leiden/Boston, Brill Nijhoff, 2018); P Leach, 'On Inter-State Litigation and Armed Conflict Cases in Strasbourg' (2021) 2, *European Convention on Human Rights Law Review* 27.

[19] R Spano, Speech delivered at the Conference on *Inter-State cases under the European Convention on Human Rights. Experiences and Current Challenges* (n 11) 15.

[20] Para 83.

[21] Para 126.

[22] Partly dissenting opinion Judge Pinto de Alburquerque, para 30.

[23] Partly dissenting opinion Judge Chanturia, para 53.

[24] Partly dissenting opinion Judge Chanturia, para 54.

jurisdiction during the active phase of hostilities has given birth to such a vacuum, and this runs counter to the spirit of the Convention'.[25]

In the doctrine, along with moderate assessments according to which 'The Court is visibly not at ease with its role to adjudicate human rights violations in an armed conflict between two States',[26] it has also been argued that 'the Court's reasoning on the key points of jurisdiction and the applicability of the European Convention in armed conflict is exemplary only in its arbitrariness. It is a retrograde step … The Court … sees such cases dealing with armed conflict as an existential danger, which it wants to avoid dealing with as much as it is possible to do so'.[27] It has even been suggested that 'the Court may have inadvertently decided that the Convention will not apply to World War Three, if such a horrible armed conflict generates cross-border hostilities in the territory of the contracting states',[28] going so far as to qualify it as an 'aberration'.[29]

A specific argument used in the judgment has also been criticised for its interpretation of the practice of the High Contracting Parties to refrain from derogation under Article 15 of the Convention in situations where they have engaged in an international armed conflict outside their own territory as meaning that the High Contracting Parties consider that in such situations, they do not exercise jurisdiction within the meaning of Article 1 of the Convention.[30] The weakness of this justification seems clear. As Judge Pinto de Albuquerque pointed out, 'The absence of an Article 15 derogation has obviously nothing to do with jurisdiction … The Court cannot give away its own *Kompetenz-Kompetenz* under Article 1 of the Convention just because the Contracting Parties have simply ignored Article 15.'[31]

In its 30 November 2022 decision on admissibility in the joined cases on Eastern Ukraine and flight MH17,[32] the Grand Chamber recalled the *Georgia v Russia (II)*

[25] Partly dissenting opinion Judge Chanturia, para 55. Instead, according to Judge Keller, the contrary conclusion of some of her colleagues is ultimately founded on an overly expansive vision of the Court as an adjudicator of the totality of armed conflict (Concurring opinion, para 4).

[26] I Risini, 'Georgia v. Russia (II) Before the European Court of Human Rights' *Verfassungsblog*, 28 January 2021, verfassungsblog.de/human-rights-in-the-line-of-fire. In a similar vein, F Tan and M Zwanenburg consider that 'The Court appears to have been moved by motives of legal policy relating to the practical difficulties it must face in deciding cases relating to armed conflict and in doing so denies many victims of war recourse to the Convention and the Court' ('One step forward, two steps back? Georgia v. Russia (II), European Court of Human Rights, Appl No 38263/08') (2021) 22, *Melbourne Journal of International Law* 136, 154.

[27] M Milanovic, 'Georgia v. Russia No. 2: The European Court's Resurrection of Bankovic in the Contexts of Chaos', *EJIL: Talk!*, 25 January 2021, www.ejiltalk.org/georgia-v-russia-no-2-the-european-courts-resurrection-of-bankovic-in-the-contexts-of-chaos. In the opinion of K Dzehtsiarou, 'A court designed to be a bulwark against totalitarianism and war is here deciding not to deal with human rights violations because they are too complex and demanding' ('Georgia v. Russia (II)' (2021) 115, *American Journal of International Law* 288, 293).

[28] M Longobardo and S Wallace, 'The 2021 ECtHR Decision in *Georgia v Russia (II)* and the Application of Human Rights Law to Extraterritorial Hostilities' (2022) 55, *Israel Law Review* 145, 147.

[29] Longobardo and Wallace (n 28) 177. According to J Gavron and P Leach, 'the consequences of this finding are seriously deleterious to the international system of human rights protections and will inevitably lead to unconscionable results' ('Damage control after Georgia v. Russia (II) – Holding States Responsible for Human Rights Violations during Armed Conflict', *StrasbourgObservers*, 8 February 2021, strasbourgobservers.com/2021/02/08/damage-control-after-georgia-v-russia-ii-holding-states-responsible-for-human-rights-violations-during-armed-conflict).

[30] Para 139.

[31] Partly dissenting opinion, para 28.

[32] Grand Chamber Decision 30 November 2022, Applications nos 8019/16, 43800/14 and 28525/20.

judgment regarding the active phase of hostilities during the five days of armed conflict.[33] However, it also pointed out that since the judgment

> found jurisdiction to exist in respect of the detention and treatment of civilians and prisoners of war even during the 'five-day war' … there can be no doubt that a State may have extraterritorial jurisdiction in respect of complaints concerning events which occurred while active hostilities were taking place. The *Georgia v Russia (II)* judgment cannot, therefore, be seen as authority for excluding entirely from a State's Article 1 jurisdiction a specific temporal phase of an international armed conflict.[34]

This assertion can easily be understood as opening the door for further clarification.[35] It remains to be seen how this excursus will develop and what future interpretations the Court may find in relation to the exception to its jurisdiction established in *Georgia v Russia (II)*.[36] Whatever happens, the criticism described above is undoubtedly well founded, yet account must also be taken of another dimension that the Court noted in the judgment: the factual difficulties in establishing the facts. Accordingly, the Court pointed out:

> However, having regard in particular to the large number of alleged victims and contested incidents, the magnitude of the evidence produced, the difficulty in establishing the relevant circumstances … the Court considers that it is not in a position to develop its case-law beyond the understanding of the notion of 'jurisdiction' as established to date.[37]

Such obstacles may lead one to believe that the current ECHR and its Protocols leave the ECtHR ill-equipped to deal with international armed conflicts, as some authors have argued.[38] In this sense, the CDDH, in its December 2022 report, pointed out that

[33] ibid paras 557–58, 576 and 698.

[34] ibid para 558.

[35] M Milanovic, 'The European Court's Admissibility Decision in Ukraine and the Netherlands v Russia: The Good, the Bad and the Ugly – Part I', *EJIL: Talk!*, 26 January 2023, www.ejiltalk.org/the-european-courts-admissibility-decision-in-ukraine-and-the-netherlands-v-russia-the-good-the-bad-and-the-ugly-part-i.

[36] See a restrictive interpretation of the expression 'military operations during an active phase of hostilities' and its impact on jurisdiction in F Romani and G Gaggioli, *Third-Party Intervention on Behalf of the Geneva Academy of International Humanitarian Law and Human Rights. Ukraine and the Netherlands v. Russia (nos. 8019/16, 43800/14, 28525/20 & 11055/22)* 3–5, geneva-academy.ch/joomlatools-files/docman-files/Third%20party%20intervention%20ECtHR%20Geneva%20Academy.pdf; see also, H Duffy, 'Georgia v. Russia: Jurisdiction, Chaos and Conflict at the European Court of Human Rights', *Justsecurity*, 2 February 2021, www.justsecurity.org/74465/georgia-v-russia-jurisdiction-chaos-and-conflict-at-the-european-court-of-human-rights. For their part, M Milanovic and S Shah argue, in the *Amicus Curiae Brief* submitted on behalf of the Human Rights Law Centre of the University of Nottingham in *Ukraine and the Netherlands v Russia (nos 8019/16, 43800/14, 28525/20, 11055/22)*, that 'while it is reasonable to exclude the application of the spatial conception of jurisdiction to immediate areas in which intense fighting on the ground is taking place, and for such time as it is taking place, many areas proximate to the fighting will nonetheless clearly be within the control of one of the parties. There is no bar to applying the Convention fully in such areas. Put differently, a "context of chaos" cannot justify failing to apply the Convention to a town or village under the control of one of the parties to the conflict in which civilians or prisoners of war are unlawfully killed or mistreated', www.nottingham.ac.uk/hrlc/documents/news-holding/amicus-brief-mh17-final.pdf, 2.

[37] Para 141.

[38] As K Dzehtsiarou and VP Tzevelekos point out, 'Such inter-state cases, especially in the context of military confrontation, require the Court to examine and assess an enormous amount of evidence, witnesses, and claims concerning a major number of victims' (n 6) 169. Two different positions on the desirability of the Court dealing with fact-finding are found in P Leach, 'Enhancing Fact-finding in Inter-State Cases: A Critical Challenge for the European Court of Human Rights', *Völkerrechtsblog*, 29 April 2021, voelkerrechtsblog.org/enhancing-fact-finding-in-inter-state-cases and T Marauhn, 'Less is More: Limited Fact-Finding to Avoid

Inter-State cases raise exceptional difficulties for the Court regarding the establishment and assessment of evidence, in particular when they concern armed conflicts involving thousands of people and taking place over a significant period of time across a vast geographical area.[39]

3. The Interplay between the ECHR and IHL

In its judgment in the *Georgia v Russia (II)* case, the Court attempted to compensate for its declared lack of jurisdiction during the active phase of hostilities by palliatively pointing out that this does not permit the states involved to act outside any legal framework because they remain obliged to comply with the very detailed rules of IHL.[40] It also held that Russia had an obligation to carry out an effective investigation of the crimes allegedly committed during the active phase of the hostilities 'in accordance with the relevant rules of international humanitarian law',[41] and therefore found a violation of Article 2's procedural aspect.[42]

As for the assessment of the respondent's conduct in the post-hostilities phase, the Court relied on ICJ case law[43] and its own 2014 judgment in *Hassan v the United Kingdom*[44] to rule that 'the Convention must be interpreted in harmony with other rules of international law of which it forms part … This applies no less to international humanitarian law'.[45] Notwithstanding, the Court also warned that, in the specific case, it would examine the interrelation between the two legal regimes with regard to every aspect of the case and Convention Article allegedly breached in order to verify 'whether there is a conflict between the provisions of the Convention and the rules of international humanitarian law'.[46] In the corresponding analyses, the Court found no conflict of interpretation.[47]

In its 30 November 2022 decision on admissibility in *Ukraine and the Netherlands v Russia*, the Court reiterated this general approach to IHL,[48] adding that, 'Since no conflict arose in respect of any of the complaints, the Court determined them by reference to Convention principles only'.[49] In the case at hand, it left to the merits stage the specific question of determining how Article 2 ought to be interpreted with respect to

Overburdening the European Court of Human Rights in inter-State Cases', *Völkerrechtsblog*, 29 April 2021, voelkerrechtsblog.org/less-is-more. See also M Keller, 'The Challenge of Fact-Finding (Establishment of Facts) in Inter-State Cases' *Inter-State Cases under the European Convention on Human Rights. Experiences and Current Challenges* (n 11) 63–74 and. P Leach, 'Enhancing fact-finding – a critical role for the European Court of Human Rights' (ibid 75–8).

[39] n 15, para 42.

[40] Judgment (Grand Chamber) 21 January 2021, para 143.

[41] ibid para 331.

[42] ibid para 337.

[43] Advisory opinion of 8 July 1996 on *Legality of the Threat or Use of Nuclear Weapons*; advisory opinion of 9 July 2004 on *Legal Consequences of the Construction of a Wall in the Occupied Palestinian Territory*; judgment of 19 December 2005 in *Armed Activities on the Territory of the Congo (Democratic Republic of Congo-Uganda).*

[44] Judgment (Grand Chamber) 16 September 2014, Application no 29750/09.

[45] ibid para 94.

[46] ibid para 95.

[47] See ibid paras 199, 235, 267, 291 and 325.

[48] Grand Chamber Decision 30 November 2022, paras 718–19.

[49] ibid para 719.

the allegations of unintentional killing of civilians in the context of armed conflict, which relate to IHL,[50] delaying a conclusion by introducing an interesting waiting period.

Although some debate whether or not the ECtHR has fully recognised the relevance of IHL,[51] it is clear that 'the debate on the relationship between IHL and human rights law has mutated from a discussion of their coexistence to the determination of the standard applicable in the particular case, depending on the tribunal, the jurisdictional basis and the applicable law'.[52]

4. A New Dimension of Interim Measures

Inter-state applications in international armed conflicts also characteristically involve requests for interim measures. This new dimension in the practice of adopting interim measures was introduced by the ECtHR[53] in *Georgia v Russia (II)*, when, on 12 August 2008 – after hostilities had broken out – the President of the Court, acting as President of Chamber, at the request of Georgia, decided to apply Article 39 of the Rules, calling on both parties to respect their conventional commitments, in particular those relating to Convention Articles 2 and 3.[54] The call was reiterated in *Ukraine v Russia (Crimea)*,[55] and then in *Armenia v Azerbaijan*,[56] *Armenia v Türkiye*[57] and

[50] ibid para 720. As M Milanovic has pointed out, the Court 'very openly acknowledges that there is a potential norm conflict between some rules in the Convention and some rules of IHL, in particular as to the justifiability of deprivation of life' ('The European Court's Admissibility Decision in Ukraine and the Netherlands v Russia: The Good, the Bad and the Ugly – Part II', *EJIL: Talk!*, 26 January 2023, www.ejiltalk.org/the-european-courts-admissibility-decision-in-ukraine-and-the-netherlands-v-russia-the-good-the-bad-and-the-ugly-part-ii).

[51] In *Third-Party Intervention on Behalf of the Geneva Academy of International Humanitarian Law and Human Rights. Ukraine and the Netherlands v Russia (nos 8019/16, 43800/14, 28525/20 & 11055/22)*, it is argued that 'In this analysis, harmonization appears as a second-order eventuality: IHL enters the picture and has a bearing on the interpretation of ECHR only when there is a conflict of norms – otherwise, it does not affect how human rights rules are construed and applied' (n 36) 16.

[52] Petit de Gabriel (n 5) 217. An analysis of the relationship between the ECHR and IHL can be found in S. Meier, 'Reconciling the Irreconcilable? – The Extraterritorial Application of the ECCHR and its Interaction With IHL' (2019) 9, *Goettingen Journal of International Law* 395; also in H Duffy, *Trials and Tribulations: Co-Applicability of IHL and Human Rights in an Age of Adjudication*, Grotius Centre Working Paper Series No 2020/086-HRL, 29 January 2020, Leiden University Grotius Centre Working Paper Series No 2020/086-HRL, 29 January 2020, ssrn.com/abstract=3528156.

[53] N Vaiter-Romain has referred to the 'new potential' of Art 39 of the Rules of Court in the case of inter-state applications: 'La Cour Européenne des Droits de l'Homme, juge du "provisoire": effet de miroir ou réalité?' (2012) 89, *Revue trimestrielle des droits de l'homme* 71, 87–9.

[54] Press Release 581, 12 August 2020.

[55] Application no 20958/14. At the request of Ukraine, the President of the Third Section decided to apply the aforementioned Art 39 of the Rules of Procedure on 13 March 2014, calling on both parties to refrain from any measures, in particular those of military nature, which could lead to violations of the rights of the civilian population protected by the Convention, specifically those relating to Arts 2 and 3 of the Convention (Press Release ECtHR 073 (2014), 13 March 2014). The interim measure was lifted by the Decision on admissibility (Grand Chamber) of 16 December 2020.

[56] Application no 42521/20. Armenia requested interim measures which were decided on 29 September 2020 by a chamber of seven judges, with similar content to the Crimea case (Press Release ECtHR 265 (2020), 30 September 2020).

[57] Application no 43517/20. The Court responded by reapplying Art. 39 and calling on all states directly or indirectly involved in the conflict, including Turkey, to refrain from any act that would contribute to the

Azerbaijan v Armenia.[58] Lastly, Ukraine requested interim measures in *Ukraine v Russia (X)* that were adopted by the President of the Court.[59]

The generality of the measures is evident in all the cases, most strikingly in the Armenia case, which the Court even addressed to 'all States directly or indirectly involved in the conflict'. The measures are also abstract in nature, as they consist of requests to abstain from any action that would entail the violation of the rights protected by the ECHR. Hence, they are qualified as 'declaratory measures'.[60]

This attitude moves the ECtHR beyond its traditional scope of application of interim measures. These have usually been granted in individual lawsuits related to violations of the right to life, the prohibition of torture and inhuman or degrading treatment, exceptionally of the right to respect for private and family life, or for the purpose of ensuring the proper conduct of the proceedings,[61] and always and only when specific content could be linked to the circumstances of the case.

Although the novel issuance of abstract interim measures responds to the requirements of the war environment in which human rights violations occur, doubts over the relevance and effectiveness of such measures and even the appropriateness of the Court's involvement have been raised. In this regard, two opposing positions have clearly emerged. On one side are those that highlight the ineffectiveness of such interim measures and the consequences that this ineffectiveness may have on the reputation of the Court. On the other is the position that, by adopting provisional measures in wartime scenarios, the ECtHR fulfills its obligations as an international court and contributes to international peace and security, a precondition for the enjoyment of human rights.[62]

violation of the rights guaranteed to civilians under the Convention, and to respect their obligations under the Convention (Press Release ECtHR 276 (2020), 6 October 2020 and 314 (2020), 5 November 2020). In a statement on 4 November, the Court clarified that it was also referring to those captured during the conflict (Press Release 377 (2020), 16 December 2020). The measures on Turkey were lifted on 1 December (Press Release 349 (2020), 2 December 2020).

[58] Application no 47319/20. Azerbaijan also requested interim measures; the Court responded by recalling the measures already adopted (Press Release ECtHR 310 (2020), 27 October 2020). More recently, Armenia again requested interim measures to ensure compliance with the November 2020 Trilateral Agreement ending hostilities, in relation to the Lachin Corridor (*Armenia v. Azerbaijan (no 4)*, application no 15389/22); on 21 December 2022 the Court decided on measures instructing Azerbaijan to ensure the safe passage of sick and other persons in need (Press Release ECtHR 401 (2022), 21 December 2022).

[59] Application no 11055/22. On 1 March 2022, the President of the Tribunal appealed to the Russian Government to refrain from launching military attacks against civilians and civilian objects, including specially protected civilian habitations, relief vehicles and other civilian objects such as schools and hospitals, and to ensure the safety of health facilities, medical personnel and relief vehicles in the territory attacked or besieged by Russian soldiers (Press Release ECtHR 068 (2022), 1 March 2022 and 073 (2022), 4 March 2022). On 1 and 4 April, the Court recalled the measures already adopted and clarified them extensively (Press Release ECtHR 116 (2022), 1 April 2022).

[60] Risini (n 18) 203–04. As P Leach points out, 'Interim measures directions in conflict situations serve a potentially useful declaratory and symbolic purpose' (n 18) 74.

[61] A Saccucci, 'Interim Measures at the European Court of Human Rights: Current Practice and Future Challenges' in FM Palombino, R Virzo and G Zarra (eds), *Provisional Measures Issued by International Courts and Tribunals* (The Hague, TMC Asser Press, Springer, 2021) 215, 218–19. See an overview on the interim measures at the ECtHR in L Burgorgue-Larsen, 'Interims measures in the European system of Human Rights' (2009) 2, *Inter-American and European Human Rights Journal* 99; Y Haeck, C Burbano Herrera and L Zwaak, 'Strasbourg's Interim Measures Under Fire: Does the Rising Number of State Incompliances with Interim Measures Pose a Threat to the European Court of Human Rights?' (2011) 11, *European Yearbook on Human Rights* 375; S Watthée, *Les mesures provisoires devant la Cour européenne des droits de l'homme. La protection préventive des droits conventionnels en puissance?* (Brussels, Anthemis, 2014); Vaiter-Romain (n 53) 71–102.

[62] For a clear exposition of both positions, see K Dzehtsiarou and VP Tzevelekos, 'Interim Measures: Are Some Opportunities Worth Missing?' (2021) 2, *European Convention on Human Rights Law Review* 1.

Thus, while the former argue that issuing provisional measures of this kind and in these circumstances represents an opportunity that the Court should pass over, the latter point out that it would be far worse to remain silent when asked for assistance by a state party in a situation of developing hostilities and loss of life. In any event, it is interesting to note that the issue is not unique to the ECtHR, for it also arises with respect to the ICJ, particularly in the most recent cases.[63]

On the other hand, in *Georgia v Russia (II)*, the ECtHR has paradoxically declared, after having issued provisional measures, that it lacked jurisdiction during the active phase of the conflict. Longobardo and Wallace have pointed out that this weakens the position of the Court because, 'If, as stated in *Georgia v Russia (II)*, the Convention is inapplicable to the active phase of hostilities, why should states heed and implement interim measures purporting to safeguard Convention rights in situations of active hostilities?'[64]

To assess this new type of provisional measure, the shortcomings of the current method for adopting decisions on provisional measures based exclusively on Rule 39 of the Rules of the Court and developed through a judicial practice must be considered in need of improvement. Indeed, these decisions on interim measures are not attributed to a specific body,[65] are not reasoned or published by the Court, only being communicated

Within the abundant literature on the subject, see Y Haeck, and C Burbano Herrera, 'The Use of Interim Measures Issued by the European Court of Human Rights in Times of War or Internal Conflict' in A Buyse (ed), *Margins of Conflict. The ECHR and Transitions to and from Armed Conflict* (Antwerp, Intersentia, 2010) 77; K Dzehtsiarou, 'Can the European Court of Human Rights prevent war? Interim measures in inter-states cases' (2016), *Public Law* 254; VP Tzevelekos, 'Catch 22: The Interim Measures of the European Court of Human Rights in the Conflict between Armenia and Azerbaijan', *StrasbourgObservers*, 9 October 2020, strasbourgobservers.com/2020/10/09/catch-22-the-interim-measures-of-the-european-court-of-human-rights-in-the-conflict-between-armenia-and-azerbaijan; ibid 'On the Value of Interim Measures by the ECtHR on Inter-State Disputes', *StrasbourgObservers*, 3 February 2021, strasbourgobservers.com/2021/02/03/on-the-value-of-interim-measures-by-the-ecthr-on-inter-sate-disputes; I Risini, 'Interim Measures by the European Court of HumanRights in re Ukraine v Russia no. 10', *Verfassungsblog*, 3 March 2022, verfassungsblog.de/strasbourg-has-no-chance-and-uses-it; A Van Baelen, 'Interim measures by the European Court of HumanRights in the Ukrainian conflict: United against the Russian aggression', *StrasbourgObservers*, 22 March 2022, strasbourgobservers.com/2022/03/22/interim-measures-by-the-european-court-of-human-rights-in-the-ukrainian-conflict-united-against-the-russian-aggression.

[63] As M Alexianu points out, 'Even where compliance is very unlikely, the Court may want to continue issuing provisional measures orders for other reasons: to signal its commitment to and help consolidate the law, to outcast violators of international rules, or to enable other institutions to enforce those rules. But recent experience counsels the Court not to expect compliance in most cases, especially where the costs to the parties outweigh the benefits' ('Provisional, but Not (Always) Pointless: Compliance with ICJ Provisional Measures', *EJIL: Talk!*, 3 November 2023, www.ejiltalk.org/provisional-but-not-always-pointless-compliance-with-icj-provisional-measures.

[64] Longobardo and Wallace (n 28) 162. In the joint partly dissenting opinion accompanying the 2021 judgment on the *Georgia v Russia (II)* case, Judges Yudkivska, Wojtyczek and Chanturia pointed out: 'It is, however, striking, that having now fully rejected the jurisdiction under the Convention of any State in respect of the active phase of the hostilities, in September, October and November 2020 the Court still granted Rule 39 requests in three inter-State cases on hostilities in Nagorno-Karabakh: *Armenia v. Azerbaijan* (no.42521/20), *Armenia v. Turkey* (no. 43517/20) and *Azerbaijan v. Armenia* (no. 47319/20). Without any intention to comment on those cases as such, we note that by applying Rule 39 the Court admitted the existence of at least prima facie jurisdiction of the States involved during the active military phase – in clear contradiction to the conclusion reached by the majority in the present case' (para 12).

[65] Rule 39(1) states that 'the Chamber or, where appropriate, its President may … indicate to the parties any interim measure'.

by a notice from the Register of the Court and are only occasionally the subject of press releases.[66] This standard, which is much less stringent than that of other international tribunals,[67] has already drawn criticism in relation to individual claims,[68] but the shortcomings are more acute in the case of inter-state claims, particularly in cases of international armed conflict. Here again, comparison with the ICJ is timely because, before the ICJ, once the request for provisional measures has been filed by a party, public hearings take place and the decision is adopted by an Order that may be accompanied by opinions and statements by judges. However, it is also true that this more formalised procedure presents its own disadvantages, in particular the added delay that it takes for the issuance of provisional measures.[69]

Setting aside these factors, because the regulation and practice of provisional measures has already given rise both to criticism and proposals for improvement, the new dimension opened up by inter-state armed conflicts makes the task of establishing an adequate regulation of this tool even more necessary and urgent. In light of the shortfalls noted above, the Plenary Court has recently taken several decisions regarding interim measures and proposed amendments to Rule 39. Among other changes, the Court has decided to disclose the identity of the judges who render the decisions on interim measure requests while maintaining the practice of providing reasons for Rule 39 decisions on an ad hoc basis and issuing press statements where the circumstances of the cases so require. Formal judicial decisions are now also to be sent to the parties.[70]

5. The Parallelism between Proceedings before the ECtHR and the ICJ

Another feature of recent practice in this type of international conflict is simultaneous recourse to various tribunals and settlement mechanisms.[71] Conforming to this

[66] On the shortcomings of transparency in the adoption of interim measures by the ECtHR, see H Keller and C Marti, 'Interim Relief Compared: Use of Interim Measures by the UN Human Rights Committee and the European Court of Human Rights' (2013) 73, *Heidelberg Journal of International Law* 325, 338–39; see also G Gentile and D Sartori, 'Interim Measures as "Weapons of Democracy" in the European Legal Space' (2023), *European Human Rights Law Review* 26–7.

[67] The regulation and practice in the Inter-American Human Rights System stands out in this regard; see C Burbano-Herrera and Y Haeck, 'Provisional Measures: Inter-American Court of Human Rights (IACtHR)' in H Ruiz-Fabri (ed), *Max Planck Encyclopedia of International Procedural Law* (Oxford, Oxford University Press, 2019); C Burbano-Herrera, 'The Inter-American Court of Human Rights and Its Role in Preventing Violations of Human Rights through Provisional Measures' in Y Haeck et al (eds), *The Inter-American Court of Human Rights: Theory and Practice, Present and Future* (Cambridge, Intersentia, 2015) 353–73.

[68] See Saccucci (n 61) 247–49; Vaiter-Romain (n 53) 98–9.

[69] For a comparative analysis, see P Tzeng, 'Interim Measures in Inter-State Proceedings: Comparing the ECtHR and the ICJ', *Völkerrechtsblog*, 26 April 2021, voelkerrechtsblog.org/interim-measures-in-inter-state-proceedings; ibid, 'Interim Measures in Inter-State Proceedings', *Inter-State Cases under the European Convention on Human Rights. Experiences and Current Challenge* (n 11) 54–5.

[70] Press Release 308 (2023), 13 November 2023.

[71] See, eg, F Viljoen, 'Inter-state communications under the African human rights system', *Inter-State Cases under the European Convention on Human Rights. Experiences and Current Challenges* (n 11) 29–30 and D Keane, 'A Unique Jurisdiction: Inter-State Communications under Article 11 of the International Convention on the Elimination of Racial Discrimination' (ibid 39–43).

trend, Georgia/Russia,[72] Armenia/Azerbaijan,[73] Azerbaijan/Armenia[74] and Ukraine/Russia[75] cases have also reached the ICJ via settlement clauses of other human rights conventions.[76] In this regard,

> the increase of State to State litigation of claims based on human rights treaties is generally a good development for the effective protection of human rights. However, multi-forum litigation may burden the parties as well as the courts and lead to parallel proceedings, inconsistencies and contradiction.[77]

The overlap of ICJ and ECtHR jurisdiction also extends to the claimants' request for provisional measures. The ICJ has granted them in every case,[78] always insisting that 'both Parties shall refrain from any action which might aggravate or extend the dispute before the Court or make it more difficult to resolve', which is also in line with the approach followed by the ECtHR. The claims before the ICJ have raised doubts similar to those already noted in relation to the ECtHR questioning the true intention of the claims and the justification for jurisdiction. Hence, in the case concerning *Application of the International Convention on the Elimination of All Forms of Racial Discrimination (Georgia v Russian Federation)* it has been argued that recourse to the ICJ was used politically to draw the attention of the international community, as racial discrimination was at most a marginal aspect of a dispute involving the use of force, so much so that some have spoken of abuse of process.[79] The provisional measures were decided by

[72] Case concerning *Application of the International Convention on the Elimination of All Forms of Racial Discrimination (Georgia v Russian Federation)*, proceedings instituted on 12 August 2008.

[73] Case concerning *Application of the International Convention on the Elimination of All Forms of Racial Discrimination (Armenia v Azerbaijan)*, proceedings instituted on 16 September 2021.

[74] Case concerning *Application of the International Convention on the Elimination of All Forms of Racial Discrimination (Azerbaijan v Armenia)*, proceedings instituted on 23 September 2021.

[75] Case concerning *Application of the International Convention for the Suppression of the Financing of Terrorism and of the International Convention on the Elimination of All Forms of Racial Discrimination (Ukraine v Russian Federation)*, proceedings instituted on 16 January 2017; Case concerning *Allegations of Genocide under the Convention on the Prevention and Punishment of the Crime of Genocide (Ukraine v Russian Federation: 32 States intervening)*, proceedings instituted on 26 February 2022. This second case concerns the war in Ukraine after the Russian aggression in February 2022 and shares with the case brought before the ECtHR the particularity of the large number of intervening states.

[76] International Convention on the Elimination of All Forms of Racial Discrimination, 1965 and Convention on the Prevention and Punishment of the Crime of Genocide, 1948.

[77] Ulfstein and Risini (n 18). Chablais, chairperson of the Council of Europe Drafting Group on effective processing and resolution of cases relating to inter-state disputes, has also warned about the potential risks of double use or contradictory decisions that may occur (*Inter-State Cases under the European Convention on Human Rights. Experiences and Current Challenges* (n 11) 59.

[78] *Application of the International Convention on the Elimination of all Forms of Racial Discrimination (Georgia v Russian Federation), Provisional Measures, Order of 15 October 2008*, ICJ Reports 2008, 353; *Application of the International Convention on the Elimination of All Forms of Racial Discrimination (Armenia v Azerbaijan), Provisional Measures, Order of 7 December 2021*, ICJ Reports 2021, 361; *Application of the International Convention on the Elimination of All Forms of Racial Discrimination (Azerbaijan v Armenia), Provisional Measures, Order of 7 December 2021*, ICJ Reports 2021, 405; *Application of the International Convention for the Suppression of the Financing of Terrorism and of the International Convention on the Elimination of All Forms of Racial Discrimination (Ukraine v Russian Federation), Provisional Measures, Order of 19 April 2017*, ICJ Reports 2017, 104; *Allegations of Genocide under the Convention on the Prevention and Punishment of the Crime of Genocide (Ukraine v Russian Federation), Provisional Measures, Order of 16 March 2022*, ICJ Reports 2022, 211.

[79] P Okowa, 'The International Court of Justice and the Georgia/Russia Dispute' (2011) 11, *Human Rights Law Review* 739, 756.

the narrowest of margins, eight votes to seven, and the minority judges issued a joint dissenting opinion in which, among other observations, they noted that the acts imputed to Russia did not constitute acts of racial discrimination in the sense of Article 1 of the International Convention on the Elimination of all Forms of Racial Discrimination.[80] Furthermore, in the case concerning *Application of the International Convention on the Elimination of All Forms of Racial Discrimination (Armenia v Azerbaijan)*, Judge Yusuf pointed out in his dissenting opinion that:

> The Court has thrown wide open the gates of the Convention on the Elimination of Racial Discrimination … to all kinds of claims that have nothing to do with its provisions or with its object and purpose … This unprecedented approach risks transforming the Convention into a 'fourre-tout'; a receptacle in which all sorts of asserted rights may be stuffed. It may also turn the Convention into an all-encompassing instrument for those trying to establish the jurisdiction of the Court whenever other legal grounds cannot be found for that purpose.[81]

At the same time, there is the question of whether the parallels between the proceedings might have any procedural impact on the position of the two tribunals. The ICJ has not addressed the issue, while the ECtHR only seems to have only barely acknowledged it in the *Georgia v Russia (II)* case. Among its arguments Russia advanced for the inadmissibility of the claim was the potential conflict between the jurisprudence of the two courts and the consequent risks to legal certainty. In its Decision on admissibility of 13 December 2011, however, the Court rejected the argument both because overlapping jurisdiction did not constitute grounds for inadmissibility of inter-state claims and because the ICJ had already declared itself incompetent:

> The Court observes that in a judgment of 1 April 2011 the ICJ held that it did not have jurisdiction to entertain the application lodged with it by Georgia on 12 August 2008 under the ICEFRD … It is undisputed between the parties that the procedure before that international court has accordingly come to an end. Besides that, it is clear from the explicit wording of Article 35 § 2 of the Convention that it applies only to individual applications.[82]

As has been pointedly observed, the question remains as to whether the Court's position would have been different if the ICJ had reached a judgement on the merits.[83]

6. Some Reflections on Improving Prospects and Overcoming Difficulties

Armed conflicts between Eastern European states have put the ECtHR on new ground by reopening debates over certain aspects of the European protection system – first and

[80] Joint dissenting opinion of Vice-President Al-Khasawneh and Judges Ranjeva, Shi, Koroma, Tomka, Bennouna and Skotnikov, paras 7–10 (*Application of the International Convention on the Elimination of all Forms of Racial Discrimination (Georgia v Russian Federation), Provisional Measures, Order of 15 October 2008,* ICJ Reports 2008, 401–02).

[81] Dissenting Opinion of Judge Yusuf, para 1 (*Application of the International Convention on the Elimination of All Forms of Racial Discrimination (Armenia v Azerbaijan), Provisional Measures, Order of 7 December 2021,* ICJ Reports 2021, 395).

[82] Application no. 38263/08, Former Fifth Section Decision, para 79.

[83] Petit de Gabriel (n 5) 212.

foremost the question of jurisdiction – and bringing to light other issues that have previously received less attention– such as the Court's regard for IHL and growing awareness that the current regulation of interim measures is insufficient. The latest conflicts have also apparently incentivised states to bring simultaneous cross-claims before various international tribunals.

Taking the perspective of the ECtHR, the progression of such cases it is increasingly obliged to address give rise to reflection. The first observation is that the Court is not currently well equipped to adjudicate disputes arising in the context of international armed conflict. Their factual complexity is one challenge; another is the Court's incapacity to render judgment within a minimally reasonable timeframe. Recall that the only case decided so far was Georgia's application filed on 11 August 2008 for which the judgment is dated 21 January 2021.

This makes another issue all the more relevant: close to 11,000 individual claims have been brought in the context of the armed conflicts that are the heart of the inter-state claims. Clearly, this represents a very large increase in the Court's workload, which could diminish its efficiency. Also relevant is the practice of the Court to defer decisions on individual claims relating to the same issue or arising from the same circumstances when an inter-state case is pending[84] which, however much sense it makes, inevitably prolongs the resolution of individual cases beyond a reasonable period.

All the above considerations explain why serious, thought-out proposals for reform are being elaborated,[85] which enjoy overall support from both the Court and the Council of Europe. As far as the Court is concerned, it identified the main factors that it believes need to be addressed in its Memorandum in view of the 4th Summit of Heads of State and Government of the Council of Europe that took place in Reykjavik on 16 and 17 May 2023. Among those are the increased workload due to the increase in inter-state cases related to international conflicts and their legal and factual complexity, as well as the high number of individual applications linked to these conflicts. In this regard, the Memorandum states that

> inter-State cases, due to their nature, are extremely demanding in terms of resources. The Court has reorganised internally to be able to deal more quickly with pending interstate applications. Priority has been accorded to the cases pending in relation to Crimea, Eastern Ukraine and the 2022 invasion. It is essential that the Court's crucial mission of processing and adjudicating inter-State cases in good time to ensure accountability should not be endangered by insufficient resources.[86]

[84] This practice was echoed in the Copenhagen Declaration of April 2018; see para 45. On the relationship between individual and inter-state applications in the practice of the ECtHR, see A Cannone, 'Ricorsi individuali e casi interstatali nella pratica passata e recente della Corte Europea dei Diritti dell'Uomo' (2022), *Ordine Internazionale e Diritti Umani* 581.

[85] See, eg A Nußberger, 'The Way Forward', *Inter-State Cases under the European Convention on Human Rights. Experiences and Current Challenge* (n 11) 50–3; ibid, 'The Way Forward. A Pragmatic Approach in Addressing Current Challenges of Inter-State Cases', *Völkerrechtsblog*, 26 April 2021, voelkerrechtsblog.org/the-way-forward.

[86] Para 23, www.echr.coe.int/documents/d/echr/memorandum_summit_reykjavik_2023_eng.

While the Court focused on the specific issues at hand, the report prepared by the CDDH, in addition to suggesting specific measures, takes a broader approach, underscoring the unavoidable dilemma involving the political dimension:

> The response to large-scale violations is a responsibility for the Council of Europe as a whole. While the Court addresses legal questions pertaining to the Convention, the political dimension is left to political authorities and the existing European bodies and mechanisms. The Convention system relies on the collective responsibility of the Council of Europe to address the root causes and consequences of those violations and explore avenues for dialogue including through ad hoc mechanisms.[87]

The Declaration adopted by the Committee of Ministers on 5 April 2023 echoes this call, declaring that it

> Commits itself to reviewing the political tools at its disposal in relation to interstate disputes, with the potential contribution of other Council of Europe bodies such as the Parliamentary Assembly, as well as the Secretary General and the Commissioner for Human Rights.[88]

Addressing the political dimension is indispensable because, if the Convention mechanism's success is great in relation to individual claims, the same can never be said for inter-state claims related to international armed conflict because the Convention did not contemplate that eventuality, although it can play a relevant role. Ultimately, however, the magnitude of the conflicts exceeds the capacity of judicialisation and requires responses from the institutionalised international community. Most importantly, the convulsive situation in this part of Europe must end as soon as possible and with it the serious violations of the human rights of the concerned populations. In addition, making a virtue of necessity, the unfortunate period that we are living through has brought to our attention a list of issues to address in order to deepen and improve ECHR protections.

Bibliography

Burbano-Herrera, C, 'The Inter-American Court of Human Rights and Its Role in Preventing Violations of Human Rights through Provisional Measures' in Y Haeck et al (eds), *The Inter-American Court of Human Rights: Theory and Practice, Present and Future* (Cambridge, Intersentia, 2015) 353.

Burbano-Herrera, C and Haeck, Y, 'Provisional Measures: Inter-American Court of Human Rights (IACtHR)' in H Ruiz-Fabri (ed), *Max Planck Encyclopedia of International Procedural Law* (Oxford, Oxford University Press, 2019).

Burgorgue-Larsen, L, 'Interims measures in the European system of Human Rights' (2009) 2, *Inter-American and European Human Rights Journal* 99.

Cannone, A, 'Ricorsi individuali e casi interstatali nella pratica passata e recente della Corte Europea dei Diritti dell'Uomo' (2022), *Ordine Internazionale e Diritti Umani*, 581.

Dzehtsiarou, K, 'Can the European Court of Human Rights prevent war? Interim measures in inter-states cases' (2016), *Public Law* 254.

—— 'Conversations with friends: "friends of the Court" interventions of the state parties to the European Convention on Human Rights' (2023) 43, *Legal Studies* 381.

[87] n 15, para 70.
[88] n 16, para 7.

—— 'Georgia v Russia (II)' (2021) 115, *American Journal of International Law* 288.
Dzehtsiarou, K and Tzevelekos, VP, 'Interim Measures: Are Some Opportunities Worth Missing?' (2021) 2, *European Convention on Human Rights Law Review* 1.
—— 'The Aggression Against Ukraine and the Effectiveness of Inter-state Cases in Case of War' (2022) 3, *European Convention on Human Rights Law Review* 165.
Gentile, G and Sartori, D, 'Interim Measures as "Weapons of Democracy" in the European Legal Space' (2023), *European Human Rights Law Review* 18.
Haeck, Y and Burbano Herrera, C, 'The Use of Interim Measures Issued by the European Court of Human Rights in Times of War or Internal Conflict' in A Buyse (ed), *Margins of Conflict. The ECHR and Transitions to and from Armed Conflict* (Antwerp, Intersentia, 2010) 77.
Haeck, Y, Burbano Herrera, C and Zwaak, L, 'Strasbourg's Interim Measures Under Fire: Does the Rising Number of State Incompliances with Interim Measures Pose a Threat to the European Court of Human Rights?' (2011) 11, *European Yearbook on Human Rights* 375.
Janer Torrens, D, *Conflictos Territoriales y Convenio Europeo de Derechos Humanos* (Pamplona, Aranzadi, 2023).
Keller, H and Marti, C, 'Interim Relief Compared: Use of Interim Measures by the UN Human Rights Committee and the European Court of Human Rights' (2013) 73, *Heidelberg Journal of International Law* 325.
Leach, P, 'On Inter-State Litigation and Armed Conflict Cases in Strasbourg' (2021) 2, *European Convention on Human Rights Law Review* 27.
Longobardo, M and Wallace, S, 'The 2021 ECtHR Decision in *Georgia v Russia (II)* and the Application of Human Rights Law to Extraterritorial Hostilities' (2022) 55, *Israel Law Review* 145.
Meier, S, 'Reconciling the Irreconcilable? – The Extraterritorial Application of the ECCHR and its Interaction With IHL' (2019) 9, *Goettingen Journal of International Law* 395.
Mondré, A, 'Studying the Increase in Inter-State Applications' in *Inter-State Cases under the European Convention on Human Rights. Experiences and Current Challenges, Proceedings of the Conference organised under the aegis of the German Presidency of the Committee of Ministers (Berlin, 12–13 April 2021)* (Council of Europe, March 2022), 47.
Okowa, P, 'The International Court of Justice and the Georgia/Russia Dispute' (2011) 11, *Human Rights Law Review* 739.
Petit de Gabriel, EW, 'Georgia, Rusia, la CIJ y el TEDH. Límites jurisdiccionales, complementariedad y protección vicaria de los derechos humanos' in S Torrecuadrada García-Lozano and C Espósito (eds), *Los desafíos de la Corte Internacional de Justicia frente a los Derechos Humanos* (Las Rozas, Madrid, Wolters Kluwer Legal & Regulatory España, 2022) 199.
Risini, I, *The Inter-State Application under the European Convention on Human Rights: Between Collective Enforcement of Human Rights and International Dispute Settlement* (Leiden/Boston, Brill Nijhoff, 2018).
Saccucci, A, 'Interim Measures at the European Court of Human Rights: Current Practice and Future Challenges' in FM Palombino, R Virzo, G Zarra (eds), *Provisional Measures Issued by International Courts and Tribunals* (The Hague, TMC Asser Press, Springer, 2021) 215.
Steininger, S and Deitelhoff, N, 'Against the Masters of War: The Overlooked Functions of Conflict Litigation by International Courts' (2021) 84, *Law and Contemporary Problems* 95.
Tan, F and Zwanenburg, M, 'One step forward, two steps back? Georgia v Russia (II), European Court of Human Rights, Appl No 38263/08' (2021) 22, *Melbourne Journal of International Law* 136.
Vaiter-Romain, N, 'La Cour Européenne des Droits de l'Homme, juge du "provisoire": effet de miroir ou réalité?' (2012) 89, *Revue trimestrielle des droits de l'homme* 71.
Watthée, S, *Les mesures provisoires devant la Cour européenne des droits de l'homme. La protection préventive des droits conventionnels en puissance?* (Brussels, Anthemis, 2014).

PART II

The Court of Justice of the European Union: Managing the Challenges of Primacy and Pluralism

4

The Primacy of European Union Law: Fit for Purpose?

DANIEL SARMIENTO

1. Introduction

Is the principle of primacy of European Union (EU) law in crisis? Do recent rulings from several national high courts confirm the suspicion that the notion of primacy was only a mirage, an optical illusion created by an enthused case law of the Court of Justice of the European Union (CJEU) and a choir of loud supporters, blind to the crude national reality that surrounded the European project and its legal order?

Several developments point in the direction of constantly eroding primacy as a tool capable of guaranteeing the uniformity and effectiveness of EU law in the Member States. From rulings of national courts challenging the authority of the CJEU to the rule of law backsliding evident in some Member States, it appears as if the primacy of EU law has lost force, displaying inherent limitations for all to see. However, this narrative runs in contradiction with the growing role of the EU and the expectations that citizens have put in its abilities and powers to solve the most pertinent existential challenges of our time: from fighting a global pandemic to supporting a war in a neighbouring country, or overcoming a climate and an energy crisis, it is the EU that its citizens (and national governments) entrust to deal with such matters. An organisation mandated with safeguarding the very existence of its Member States and their way of life can hardly be defined as a failed project.

In this chapter I will argue that the principle of primacy, as a fundamental criterion that ensures the uniformity and effectiveness of EU law, is indeed under significant stress. However, the argument that will be made does not point towards an existential crisis of primacy and the EU legal order, but rather to the need of modifying its physiognomy to match the current reality of the European project. In contrast with the voices that rely on pragmatic solutions to the challenges currently faced by the principle of primacy, this chapter advocates a different approach towards the principle of primacy, one which includes proposals of Treaty amendments to reinforce it in a way that reflects the specificities of the EU whilst preserving the federal spirit that undergirds the European project.

2. Primacy thus Far: As Good as it Gets?

The principle of primacy emerged in the 1960s as a corollary of the direct effect of European Economic Community law.[1] The two principles act as the two sides of the same coin, direct effect allowing individuals to invoke EU rules directly before national authorities, and primacy acting as a sword that empowers those authorities to set aside national rules that contradict the EU rules invoked in the case. Both principles combine in an original, pragmatic construction that empowers individuals to bolster the private enforcement of EU law, indirectly contributing to improve the effectiveness of European rules in the national legal order while primarily defending their own individual interests.[2]

To conceive primacy statically as some 'conflict rule' that simply confirms the preference of one legal rule over another shortsightedly leaves out the broader complexities that the principle embraces. Primacy is a highly complex, multifaceted principle that requires constant development, as the case law of the CJEU has shown since the principle's inception in the seminal 1964 case *Costa/Enel*.[3] First, the primacy of EU law vis-à-vis national law is not a hierarchical criterion that determines validity in accordance with a predetermined rank. In contrast with what the optical impression of the word might convey, primacy does not determine validity based on hierarchy, but on a criterion of *competence*. National law must give way to EU law merely because the EU has exercised its competences in a field of EU policy agreed by the Member States in accordance with the procedures established by the Treaties.[4] Once the EU gains competence in an area of policy also within its competence, its rules prevail over national law, due to the conferral of that power to the EU by the Member State, either through primary or secondary EU law. The primacy of EU law reflects the competence of the EU and, at the same time, the lack of competence of the Member States. If national rules contradict EU rules, their existence undermines the competence of the EU to act in whichever field. Such is the context in which the principle of primacy operates, in which it guarantees the correct allocation of powers between the EU and the Member States according to an arrangement previously reached by the Institutions and Member States involved.

Second, the principle of primacy also has a dynamic dimension. Whilst the principle can be wielded in strictly static terms in order to settle situations when rules conflict, the reality is more complex. Together with the seminal judgment in *Costa/Enel*, the Court has handed down a broad array of rulings that have paved the way for the applicative dimension of primacy, navigating a path to help national judges deal with the consequences of incompatibility between EU and national rules. If a national court lacks the power to annul a rule of national law, it has no duty to do so. In such cases, according to *Simmenthal*,[5] the national court's duty is to *set aside* the conflicting rule. However, if the

[1] See B De Witte, 'Direct Effect, Primacy and the Nature of the Legal Order' in P Craig and G De Búrca (eds), *The Evolution of EU Law* (Oxford, Oxford University Press, 2011).

[2] M Dougan, 'When worlds collide: competing visions of the relationship between direct effect and supremacy' (2007) 4 *Common Market Law Review* 44.

[3] Case 6/64 *Costa/Enel*, EU:C:1964:66.

[4] JHH Weiler and U Haltern, 'The Autonomy of the Community Legal Order – Through the Looking Glass' (1997) *Harvard International Law Journal* 37.

[5] Case 106/77 *Amministrazione delle Finanze dello Stato v Simmenthal SpA*, EU:C:1978:49.

national court has the power to annul, annul it must, to preserve the effectiveness of EU law and the principle of legal certainty. Parallelism among jurisdictions is another eventuality, as is 'double preliminarity', which occurs when national courts are duty-bound to refer the case to both the CJEU and to its Constitutional Court.[6] Even more delicate issues arise when national courts find that setting aside or annulling the national rule in question could cause significant harm, in which cases courts are often inclined to limit the duration of the effects of their judgments.[7] In sum, primacy is not merely a conflict rule that determines the outcome when one provision clashes with another, but rather a complex array of criteria for the accommodation of distinct legal orders that each deploy directly effective rules and grant rights to individuals with a legitimate claim to justice in a court of law.

Third, even in its most straightforward dimension, which has previously been called the 'static' dimension of primacy, the principle's status is far from settled. The primacy of EU law extends over the entirety of the national legal order, including its constitutional provisions and any decision of a national authority, including its courts. This maximalist understanding of the scope of primacy has been rejected by most of the Member States' constitutional courts, which refuse to surrender their prerogative to rule in the last instance on the proper allocation of competence between the two political entities: the EU and the Member State. In some jurisdictions this scrutiny has extended beyond competence control, entering the terrain of 'identity control' in a more substantive and value-oriented type of review of EU action. This tension in determining the exact scope of EU law and its primacy has kept the CJEU and constitutional courts busy for decades, resulting in a status quo of stable instability, in which each of the players has the ability to destabilise, and even do away with, the coherence and unity of the current terms of cohabitation between EU and national law.

This situation unfortunately devolved into open hostility in 2020, when the German Federal Constitutional Court declared a ruling of the CJEU 'objectively arbitrary' and inapplicable, which it reinforced by following the same logic and reaching the same outcome in reviewing a Decision of the European Central Bank (ECB).[8] Shortly afterwards, the Romanian Constitutional Court followed suit, refusing to enforce rulings of the CJEU that had declared prior case law of the Romanian court in breach of EU law.[9] The Polish Constitutional Court followed the same path, although in a different context, to challenge the CJEU's response to the rule of law crisis that emerged after 2015.[10] At that point, it was difficult to see any end to the unravelling of the stable instability that had kept the EU's legal order in peaceful coexistence with national law.

Following the initial shock caused by these national rulings, tensions seemed to lower, particularly in the Court's relations with the German Federal Constitutional Court and the Romanian Constitutional Court. However, the lasting memory of the shock and its fallout demonstrates the limits of the principle of primacy and its inherent

[6] Cases C-188/10 and C-189/10 *Melki and Abdeli*, EU:C:2010:363.
[7] Case C-379/15 *Association France Nature Environnement*, EU:C:2016:603.
[8] BVerfG, Judgment of the Second Senate of 5 May 2020 – 2 BvR 859/15.
[9] See the press release of 23 December 2021, www.ccr.ro/comunicat-de-presa-23-decembrie-2021.
[10] Judgment of 7 October 2021 (case K 3/21).

weaknesses, including the remedial shortcomings of the judicial system.[11] In the absence of a clear, explicit rule imposing the primacy of EU law, constitutional courts feel entitled to uphold their national constitution, even against the EU. The principle of primacy has been humbled at a time while other major developments continue to gradually but resolutely change the face of the EU itself, an evolution that raises doubts as to whether the principle of primacy, as we currently understand it, suits its purpose.

3. The Changing Face of Evolving EU Law

The erosion of the principle of primacy contrasts sharply with the success of the EU project of integration. The past 20 years, particularly in the wake of the financial crisis that erupted in 2008, have witnessed an impressive transformation of the EU as a political and economic project. With very little amendment to its Treaties, the EU has undergone a process of transformation that equals, and in some respects even surpasses, the 1992 reforms of the Maastricht Treaty. These changes have been effectuated not only through legislative, executive or international means, but also as a result of social change in the European polity. The result is a stronger and more ambitious EU, having received from its citizens a broad array of tasks to handle, tasks that the Member States are powerless to address on their own. The paradox lies in attaining a stronger EU at a time when the primacy of its law is weakened, questioned and challenged by the same Member States that rely on the EU to protect them from existential challenges. These changes in the EU are tectonic shifts that, although taking place silently, gradually or both, are transforming the very visage of the European project.

First, the transformations are clearly visible in the array of new powers being exercised by the EU. These powers are not necessarily new, but they have been articulated in unprecedented manners that set the EU on course towards an endless accumulation of powers that reinforce its role vis-à-vis the Member States and its citizens. Most of the novel policy arrangements were prompted by serious crises caused by external shocks, namely the COVID-19 pandemic, climate change and the invasion of Ukraine by the Russian Federation. These shocks triggered unprecedented initiatives that collectively deploy the EU's prerogative as an instrument to ensure protection of existential interests of the Member States and its citizens. Hence joint purchases of vaccines or gas,[12] the Green New Deal[13] and an unprecedented stimulus package under a novel fiscal arrangement (NextGenerationEU), each of which use the EU as a financial shield and purveyor of financial stability for the Member States.[14] The trend continued following the energy

[11] On 22 December 2021 the European Commission launched infringement proceedings against Poland as a result of the judgment of the Constitutional Court of 7 October 2021. Earlier in the year, the Commission had also launched infringement procedures against Germany as a result of the ruling in *Weiss*, but these were withdrawn once the Constitutional Court found compliance with its judgment.

[12] FS Della Corte, 'The EU Vaccines Strategy: A Missed Opportunity for EU Public Health?' (2023) *European Journal of Risk Regulation*, 25 January.

[13] J Jendrośka, M Reese, and L Squintani, 'Towards a new legal framework for sustainability under the European Green Deal' *The Opoloe Studies in Administration and Law*, DOI: 10.25167/OSAP.4274.

[14] F Fabbrini, 'Next Generation Eu: Legal Structure and Constitutional Consequences' (2022) *Cambridge Yearbook of European Legal Studies* 23.

crisis caused by the invasion of Ukraine, which also occasioned developments in the field of defence, including the use of EU funds to finance the provision of military assistance to a neighbouring country. Never before had areas of policy been implemented in these ways.[15] The outcome of this trend is a considerably stronger EU, given the mandate it has received from the Member States and its citizens to ensure subsistence in the face of existential challenges. The EU has moved from an instrument to ensure peace among the Member States through an internal market and borderless zone to an instrument to guarantee the conditions for the *subsistence* of its Member States.

Second, the institutional design of many of its policies is increasingly federal. The traditional division of tasks between a EU that legislates and Member States that handle executive implementation and judicial oversight is fading. It is evolving towards a more robust, federal-like system of enforcement, in which EU authorities play a growing role in the decision-making and EU courts in dispute resolution. The Banking Union case provides a telling example in which a federal-like composite system has been established for prudential bank supervision and resolution.[16] The creation and institutional design of the European Public Prosecutor is another example of this trend,[17] as is the latest anti-money-laundering reform, which sees the emergence of new bodies in line with the same federal-like design.[18] This shift has forced a new approach in the case law towards the way in which Member States interact with EU authorities, but also to the division of tasks between national and EU courts. The traditional role of national courts as protagonists in the interpretation and enforcement of EU law in the Member States has shifted as more centralised, federal-like institutional arrangements favour the EU courts, responding to the perceived need of strong centralised powers to attain the EU's goals.[19]

Third, the dynamics of integration have altered the signification of fundamental rights and EU citizenship. In the case of fundamental rights, what used to be a generic array of principles is now enshrined, with the same rank as primary law, in the Charter of Fundamental Rights of the European Union. The difference between recognising fundamental rights solely in case law and enshrining them in primary law is of great consequence. Since the entry into force of the Charter, the CJEU has received a growing number of questions for preliminary reference on points of fundamental rights, gradually turning it into a fundamental rights court. The importance of the questions referred to it have forced the Court into elaborating an increasingly sophisticated approach, further reinforcing its authority as an arbiter of fundamental rights. The importance of fundamental rights goes hand in hand with the growing role played by EU citizenship, a status that seemed modest at first, but which is now destined to become the

[15] T Hamilton, 'Defending Ukraine with EU weapons: arms control law in times of crisis'(2022) 1 *European Law Open* 635 doi:10.1017/elo.2022.35.

[16] Regulation (EU) No 468/2014 of the European Central Bank of 16 April 2014 establishing the framework for cooperation within the Single Supervisory Mechanism between the European Central Bank, competent national authorities and designated national authorities (SSM Framework Regulation) [2014] OJ L 141/1.

[17] Council Regulation (EU) 2017/1939 of 12 October 2017 implementing enhanced cooperation on the establishment of the European Public Prosecutor's Office ('the EPPO') [2017] OJ L 283/1.

[18] Proposal for a Regulation of the European Parliament and the Council establishing the Authority for Anti-Money Laundering and Countering the Financing of Terrorism and amending Regulations (EU) No 1093/2010, (EU) (094/2010, (EU) 1095/2010) (COM/2021/421 final).

[19] C-414/18 *Iccrea Banca* Case, EU:C:2019:574 and Case C-219/17 *Berlusconi*, EU:C:2018:502.

'fundamental status of nationals of the Member States'. The status of EU citizenship is no longer limited to the succinct list of rights enumerated in Article 20 TFEU, but also reaches the overall protection granted by the 'substance of the rights attached to the status' of EU citizenship.[20] This development has drawn EU law closer to the very core of nationality law, to the extent of setting limits on Member States' authority to withdraw nationality,[21] or even determine the conditions of access and recognition.[22]

Fourth, the EU is not only an economic project, but is also based on values. Article 2 of the Treaty on the European Union enumerates those foundational values in terms that set the core identity of the EU. The terms in which the values are expressed might have seemed declarative but, over the course of time and due to repeated retrocession in the standard of rule of law in some Member States, the values now stand as normative tools that warrant protection through law.[23] This transformation of the function of EU values stands behind the development of an 'identity' of the EU, a set of normative benchmarks that act as backstops on Member State action and international law alike. The introduction of the EU's 'identity' based on those values offers tools with practical implications. For example, the Member States can no longer invoke their national identities when their actions compromise the EU's 'identity'.[24] In symbolic terms, the EU's 'identity' provides a countermeasure to the Member State's 'constitutional cores' or 'constitutional identities', as defined in the case law of the apex national courts. This new approach towards EU values has yielded surprising outcomes, such as the CJEU becoming an active defender of the independence of national courts, including supreme or constitutional courts.[25] Judicial dialogue in Europe is not only a matter of reaching optimal interpretations of EU law, but also a question of safeguarding basic institutional infrastructure, including the judicial standards of the EU and of its Member States.

In sum, the EU of 2025 is an organisation that has evolved substantially from the project outlined back in 1964 when *Costa/Enel* was handed down. The building blocks of the EU comprise constitutional principles and values with the force of law, giving rise to autonomous categories of citizenship, rights and democracy with a decisive impact on the everyday lives of its citizens. An organisation of this nature promotes and implements political agendas whose impact is significant and transformative. For this EU to achieve its aims, the availability of a robust normative toolbox capable of ensuring the project's effectiveness is essential. In contrast to its present state, where the EU has achieved an unprecedented degree of ambition and sophistication, the challenge to its central principle of primacy seriously undermines the narrative described thus far.

The current crisis did not unfold in isolation. The German Constitutional Court's judgment in *Weiss* declaring a judgment of the CJEU 'objectively arbitrary' and an ECB decision ultra vires, only represents the tipping point of a trend that has become increasingly grave over time. While true that a pragmatic solution was eventually found for the crisis provoked by *Weiss*, the ruling sent a clear message to all national jurisdictions

[20] Case C-34/09 *Ruiz Zambrano*, EU:C:2010:560.
[21] Case C-135/08 *Rottmann*, EU:C:2009:588.
[22] Case C-369/90 *Micheletti*, EU:C:1992:295.
[23] Case C-157/21 *Poland/Parliament and Council*, EU:C:2022:98.
[24] Case C-357/19 *Euro Box Promotion*, EU:C:2021:1034.
[25] See L Pech, P Wachowiec, and D Mazur, 'Poland's Rule of Law Breakdown: A Five-Year Assessment of EU's (In)Action' (2021) 13 *Hague Journal on the Rule of Law* 1.

inclined to depart from the common criteria set by the CJEU. If recognition of the principle of primacy only derives from the case law and a Declaration annexed to the Treaties, the frailty of the EU's legal order becomes obvious for all to see. For a EU that intends to play a transformative role in promoting societal change in times of existential challenges, such frailty is too high a price to pay.

4. Living with Fragile Primacy in an Invigorated EU

It is tempting to affirm that challenges to the principle of primacy are inherent to integration, and that the EU should be willing to tackle them pragmatically. To an extent, the entire history of European integration is marked by various challenges of the kind, generally solved through a combination of political compromise and discrete manoeuvring. Just as the EU has struggled through many crises by focusing on problem-solving rather than problem-raising, the challenges to primacy could be approached similarly, relying on the goodwill of all the stakeholders to reach a reasonable compromise. This approach is tempting, and could be even considered the correct way forward. However, it is a strategy that gambles on the successful management of previous crises, whilst the current crisis of primacy is taking place in an entirely different context. This becomes evident from depictions of different scenarios that arise in the context of fragilised primacy at the core of its legal order.

A fractured primacy is not an acceptable normative premiss on which essential policy measures like NextGenerationEU, joint purchases of vaccines or energy supplies, or measures of support in the field of defence while a deathly war is taking place in a neighbouring country. The list of external shocks shaking the foundations of the EU is growing longer, now including climate change as an additional and long-term risk for the Member States and its citizens. These challenges are not internal shocks provoked by a Member State or group of Member States. On the contrary, they are external shocks that affect the EU and its Member States as a whole. The response of the EU to these shocks has an existential dimension, inasmuch as failure risks the collective failure of all the Member States, including the risk of their very existence. Whilst fragilised primacy grew out of traditional concerns with the internal market, the new and invigorated EU has hardly any margin of error, and the far-reaching implications of a compromised primacy that entitles national stakeholders to depart from the uniform implementation of EU law could prove lethal.

The same applies to the current federal-like institutional arrangements, which demand a high degree of cooperation among the EU and the national authorities. As entire policy fields turn towards mechanisms and other forms of highly integrated administration, this model can only operate on the premiss of robust principle of primacy accepted by all the players, particularly national authorities. A supervisory mechanism for credit institutions cannot be effective if the decisions of the ECB do not have primacy over the decisions of national authorities, particularly when a discrepancy in the interpretation of EU law arises. The European Public Prosecutor must rely on the uniform interpretation provided by the CJEU, not on the various interpretations that national high courts may provide. As the EU navigates towards increasingly integrated administrative action, the principle of primacy must act as a firm foundation accepted by all the stakeholders, for otherwise the structure becomes unstable, fragile and doomed to fail along with its policy aims.

As the EU becomes more rights-centred and the status of citizenship evolves, questions of values and principles will emerge in which a variety of views will create divergences among the Member States. Values-based reasoning in the case law of the Court or in the legislative process will trigger even more complex conflicts whose resolution will certainly leave some stakeholders unsatisfied. Religion in the workplace, the protection of privacy and its conflicts with public security, the protection of animals and balancing that protection with entrenched cultural practices, and so on; the EU is called to stake a position in many current societal debates that were for a long time alien to the discussions over the internal market. However, these debates are now, directly or indirectly, part of EU policy, and the EU's legislative and judicial institutions cannot be held to a position in these matters while the highest courts of the Member States question the principle of primacy. For the EU to strike a robust fundamental rights policy, it requires an authoritative criterion to navigate the complexity of a highly diverse Europe. Such a criterion is imperative, once the policy is set, for the principle of primacy to deploy its full force.

Seen in this light, the current crisis of the principle of primacy is not just another bump in the road comparable to other recent crises. The current challenges to primacy are much more unsettling and threatening EU efforts to provide robust responses to existential challenges. For that reason, pragmatic, ad hoc responses will not solve the problem. The crack that has emerged is not like a chip in a porcelain vase that can be repaired with glue; it is a crack that will eventually make its way to the heart of a gigantic concrete dam holding a river back.

5. A Future for the Principle of Primacy

The alternatives to pragmatic solutions for the crisis of primacy are not self-evident. They run from idealistic and politically naïve proposals to highly complicated proposals whose chances of success are uncertain. In any event, a quick review is worthwhile, as idealistic and politically challenging options deserve attention. What seemed impossible a decade ago in terms of European integration has become the norm today (NextGenerationEU was hardly conceivable in the midst of the euro-crisis in 2012); a lesson on the importance of keeping an open mind when exploring options to overcome the primacy crisis.

A first proposal takes the classic approach: introducing a primacy clause in the Treaties whose force of law is binding on all the Member States. This option was contemplated in Article I-6 of the 2004 Constitutional Treaty, according to which 'the Constitution and law adopted by the institutions of the EU in exercising competences conferred on it shall have primacy over the law of the Member States'.[26] The argument

[26] Draft Treaty establishing a Constitution for Europe [2003] OJ C 169/1.

could be attempted that such a provision is currently in force today through the indirect means of Declaration no 17, concerning primacy, but that argument does not hold. Declaration no 17 is a non-binding act annexed to the Treaties, introduced to confirm that the non-enactment of the Constitutional Treaty and its Article I-6 in no way affect the status of the primacy principle in EU law. Furthermore, Declaration no 17 represents a restatement of the Court's case law through a legal opinion of the Council, not a solemn declaration by the Member States. Even in its quality as a multilateral Declaration, its construction belies the efforts of the Member States to avoid throwing off the balance between EU law's unilateral and broad conception of primacy and the limits set on it by the national apex courts.[27]

Would introducing a provision like Article I-6 resolve the primacy crisis? Probably not. To a certain extent, the current law, as it stands, has already incorporated a primacy clause through the authoritative interpretation of the Treaties as elaborated by the CJEU. Almost 60 years since *Costa/Enel*, the Member States have arguably had plenty of opportunities to amend the scope of this doctrine by way of a Treaty amendment, but nothing of the kind has transpired. On the contrary, in amendment after amendment the Member States have proved eager to expand the competences of the EU upon the understanding that EU law held primacy over national law, including constitutional law. This tacit acceptance of primacy by the parties to the Treaties, together with the CJEU's clear and unconditional case law, has not stopped the high courts of the Member States from setting a benchmark limiting the scope of EU law's primacy. An explicit recognition of the principle in the articulated text of the Treaties would likely maintain the *status quo* at its current level, irrespective of the clarity of the message conveyed by incorporating such a provision.

One variant to this classic option might, however, alter the proposal's fate: explicitly recognising the primacy clause in both the Treaties and, in identical fashion, in the constitutions of all Member States would significantly improve the chances of settling the principle on robust and stable ground for the long term. From enshrining a principle of primacy in this dual fashion, in both the Treaties and national constitutions, would ensure a firm commitment from all legal orders ensues, setting a conflict rule that provides clear guidance on which legal order (and jurisdiction) prevails over the other. National courts could no longer claim the final word on the interpretation of the Treaties, or the distribution of competencies, even exceptionally. The mandate that the authority of EU law prevails would be clear. A similar technique has been used in the past, namely in the Treaty on Stability, Coordination and Governance (also known as 'The Fiscal Compact'), signed on 2 March 2012 by the Member States (with the exception of the United Kingdom and the Czech Republic).[28] This Treaty establishes in Article 3(2) the duty of Member States to introduce rules on fiscal discipline and stability, 'preferably constitutional rules'.

[27] See F Weber, 'The Identity of Union Law in Primacy: Piercing Through Euro Box Promotion and Others' (2022) 7 *European Papers* 2.

[28] Treaty on Stability, Coordination and Governance in the Economic and Monetary Union (2012) (Document 42012A0302(01).

Despite the robustness of such a solution, and irrespective of the feasibility of undertaking 27 constitutional amendments, in truth this proposal would not dispel the risk of constitutional conflict or, eventually, other challenges to primacy. Whilst such a clause would contribute to preventing conflicts, mostly in the field of competence (granting the CJEU the ultimate word in determining the scope of the EU's jurisdiction), it would not stop national constitutional courts from invoking their own constitutional identities, particularly in areas that touch on points close to values and principles that require balancing. Also, any interference of EU law would run into red lines in constitutions that admit 'eternal clauses' or provisions that are not subject to amendment, irrespective of the scope and terms provided in the primacy clause. These matters will be for national constitutional courts to resolve, giving them sufficient leeway to continue to claim the last word in the ongoing discussion over the authority of EU law in the Member States.

The limitations of the previous proposals explain the procedural angle of the discussions on the ways to overcome the crisis of primacy, the part that focuses not so much on the substance of the primacy clause itself, but on the procedures that allow the EU to claim its authority and that of its legal system. Procedural solutions do not solve the very crux of the matter, but they act as buffers to prevent constitutional conflict from escalating into crisis. To this end, these proposals represent a middle ground between the maximalist option of constitutional reform and the pragmatic approach.

A first procedural option is the creation of a mixed chamber in the CJEU, composed of judges sitting on the CJEU and also some who sit on national constitutional and supreme courts.[29] The mixed chamber could be a last-instance jurisdiction to hear actions against a decision of the CJEU on a point of EU competence. Its jurisdiction could also extend to cases on fundamental rights. But above all, the role of the mixed chamber would be to settle a claim of primacy coming from the EU legal order and a national legal order. In conflicts upon which both jurisdictions have had the chance of ruling, either the EU or the Member State concerned could bring the case to the mixed chamber. The mixed chamber would decide the matter and rule with a voice whose legitimacy is compounded by the chamber's joint composition, thus providing a robust decision with sufficient authority to overrule either the CJEU or the national high court. Rather than a blanket confirmation of the primacy of one legal order over the other, the result provides a composite means for adjudicating specific disputes with a degree of added legitimacy until the next is raised.

There are several procedural guarantees to ensure that the mixed chamber would fulfil its role with the balance necessary for added legitimacy. Its composition would be made up of 13 judges, of which seven seats would rotate among the judges sitting on the CJEU, whilst six would come from national supreme and constitutional courts, also upon rotation. Although decisions based on consensus of all the sitting members of the mixed chamber could be made, an *in dubio mitius* voting rule should also apply: a decision validating a contested EU act should be supported by at least eight judges. This rule would avoid situations where the judges of the CJEU could unanimously side with the

[29] D Sarmiento and JHH Weiler, 'The EU Judiciary After Weiss' *Verfassungsblog*, 2 June 2020 and 'The EU Judiciary After Weiss – A Reply to our Critics' (2020) *EU Law Live*, 6 July 2020.

EU for primacy by requiring at least the support of one judge of the national high courts to validate the contested decision.

Another procedural proposal focuses on the US technique of 'certification', a means federal courts in that country use to get clarification from state courts about the interpretation of state law.[30] Extended to the EU legal context, a 'certification' procedure would empower the CJEU to refer questions of national law, on constitutional points of principle, to the Member States' highest courts. Doing so would indeed facilitate dialogue among the CJEU and the highest courts of the Member States, but more specifically it would also provide the Court with binding guidance about provisions concerning national identity, national competence or constitutional limits that risk colliding with EU law. Implementing this course of action, like the mixed chamber, would require specific rules, but probably not a reform of the Statute. At present, Article 24 of the Statute provides that the Court may 'require the Member States and institutions, bodies, offices and agencies not being parties to the case to supply all information which the Court considers necessary for the proceedings'. This provision could find further development in some future reform of the Rules of Procedure, entitling the CJEU to request guidance on a point of interpretation of national law from a court of that Member State.

Like the mixed chamber, a European 'certification' procedure would not solve the challenges raised by constitutional conflicts between the EU and its Member States. However, it would mitigate the chances of further conflict by opening a formal channel of communication between the CJEU and the Member States' highest courts, even in circumstances in which no prior preliminary reference articulated between the two jurisdictions has been requested. 'Certification' would be a tool to facilitate a mutual understanding whose eventual content is unknown in advance. The tool would also depend on the willingness of the CJEU to make use of it, and there are a fair number of procedural options in the Statute and Rules of Procedures that have become obsolete or forgotten as a result of lack of use by the Luxembourg judges. Procedural solutions are buffers that contribute either to prevent constitutional conflict or to help in reaching an acceptable final outcome, but they do not solve the inherent tension between two colliding and legitimate claims of authority coming from the EU and one or several of its Member States.

6. Conclusion

The doubts relative to the principle of primacy of EU law have reached a tipping point. At the stage of European integration in which we currently stand, in which the EU's institutions have been delegated unprecedented authority to address existential challenges, the risk of fragmenting the unity of the EU's legal order has become too high. The Member States cannot confer that level of responsibility to the EU while empowering their internal authorities to question the uniform implementation of EU law in their territory. The EU's institutional organisation provides

[30] A Nicòtina and E Martini, 'From Monologues to Dialogue: The US "Certification" Procedure as a Source of Inspiration for EU Cooperative Judicial Federalism' (2022) *European Yearbook of Constitutional Law*.

sufficient guarantees of democratic accountability and legitimacy for Member States and their national jurisdictions to accept that the common rules enacted by the EU are uniform standards that supersede national law in its areas of competence. The control over the exercise of EU competence is a task that is well performed by the CJEU, a jurisdiction with seven decades of experience in adjudicating disputes in the EU's jurisdiction. At the present stage of European integration, undermining primacy is self-destructive. The practice not only harms the overall project, but its individual members too. Considering the relevance of the existential challenges at stake, it is hard to understand the ongoing popularity of the defence of an indeterminate 'constitutional identity', solely defined by a court of law, capable of rallying its defenders to the point of jeopardising policies put in place to deal with some of society's existential challenges.

Behind the curtain of the notion of constitutional identity lies nationalism and its many faces, a force that eludes capture or rationalisation when it touches the core of identity politics in the Member States. The history of Europe, including its most recent history, is ample proof of the propensity of nationalism to obscure the real problems of the people in favour of discourses that turn to be self-destructive in the long term. The challenges currently faced by the Member States, whether a global pandemic, energy crises or climate change, come head-to-head with their share of vaccine sceptics, climate change deniers and conspiracists who question solutions proposed and often even the existence of the problem itself. Against this backdrop, it becomes less surprising to come across primacy-deniers who still refuse to accept the power of EU law to supersede national law. Primacy denialism can be as destructive a force as nationalism, for both embrace core values in the name of ethereal goals whilst sacrificing the edifice that holds society together in order to address common challenges.

Nationalism is likely here to stay, however, but it can be interiorised and channelled through the democratic process. Similarly, the sceptics of the primacy of EU law should also be able to make their case. For that reason, attempts to settle the matter by introducing a strict primacy clause in the Treaties or in the Constitutions of the Member States are destined to fail. As long as primacy deniers continue to haunt the EU and its legal order, primacy clauses duly elaborated in writing will not repel the ideology underlying the attacks. The way forward is to channel those claims and prove them invalid through appropriate procedures, such that all the interests at stake are reflected and the balance eventually tips in favour of a European majority. The mixed chamber is an example of how to proceduralise a primacy clause, refusing to eradicate the concerns of primacy sceptics, but embracing them and giving them voice in a composite procedure in which a decision must finally emerge. Nothing will stop a national court or a Member State from refusing to comply with a decision of the mixed chamber, but at such point it will be obvious that the only way forward for that Member State is to exit the European project. After a ruling of the CJEU followed by a decision of a body representing not only all the Member States, but also the voices of constitutional courts, the dissenting opinion must face a choice: to carry on with its European journey or take a different path. Procedures are helpful in fleshing out such outcomes, providing the necessary steps so that the final decision is acceptable and considered to be legitimate by all the stakeholders that wish to have a European future.

Bibliography

De Witte, B, 'Direct Effect, Primacy and the Nature of the Legal Order', in P Craig and G De Búrca (eds), *The Evolution of EU Law* (Oxford, Oxford University Press, 2011).

Della Corte, FS, 'The EU Vaccines Strategy: A Missed Opportunity for EU Public Health?' (2023) *European Journal of Risk Regulation*, 25 January.

Dougan, M, 'When worlds collide: competing visions of the relationship between direct effect and supremacy' (2007) 4 *Common Market Law Review* 44.

Fabbrini, F, 'Next Generation Eu: Legal Structure and Constitutional Consequences' (2022) *Cambridge Yearbook of European Legal Studies* 23.

Hamilton, T, 'Defending Ukraine with EU weapons: arms control law in times of crisis' (2022) 1 *European Law Open* 635. doi:10.1017/elo.2022.35.

Jendrośka, J, Reese, M and Squintani, L, 'Towards a new legal framework for sustainability under the European Green Deal', *The Opoloe Studies in Administration and Law*, DOI: 10.25167/OSAP.4274.

Nicòtina, A and Martini, E, 'From Monologues to Dialogue: The US "Certification" Procedure as a Source of Inspiration for EU Cooperative Judicial Federalism' (2022) *European Yearbook of Constitutional Law*.

Pech, L, Wachowiec, P and Mazur, D, 'Poland's Rule of Law Breakdown: A Five-Year Assessment of EU's (In)Action' (2021) 13 *Hague Journal on the Rule of Law* 1.

Sarmiento, D and Weiler, JHH, 'The EU Judiciary After Weiss' (2020) *Verfassungsblog*, 2 June and 'The EU Judiciary After Weiss – A Reply to our Critics' (2020) *EU Law Live*, 6 July 2020.

Weber, F, 'The Identity of EU Law in Primacy: Piercing Through Euro Box Promotion and Others' (2022) 7 *European Papers* 2.

Weiler, JHH, and Haltern, U, 'The Autonomy of the Community Legal Order – Through the Looking Glass' (1997) *Harvard International Law Journal* 37.

5

The Obligation to Interpret National Law, Including National Constitutions, in Conformity with European Union Law

JUAN IGNACIO UGARTEMENDÍA ECEIZABARRENA

1. Introduction

One interesting indicator when observing and assessing the role of national courts in the process of European integration can be found in the judicial obligation to interpret national law in conformity with European Union (EU) law, which is the subject of this chapter. This obligation ('conforming interpretation' with EU law) has been created and developed through the case law of the Court of Justice of the European Union (CJEU) as a mechanism to discipline national application of EU law, an instrument or technique at the service of its efficiency and effectiveness and, notably, as an instrument to alleviate deficiencies arising from national implementation of the directives. However, without denying that the obligation continues to perform successfully its function in favour of the efficiency and effectiveness of EU law, this obligation also functions, especially in the last decade, as an important mechanism for the legal control of national law in the service of the primacy of EU law. The doctrine has been used as an instrument to control the legality (in terms of EU law) not only of the national provisions, but of the meanings of these national provisions, that is, of the interpretation of national law adopted in application of EU law.

In this respect, we should note that the obligation to interpret in conformity with EU law extends to all national laws adopted in application of EU law and, it may be said, to all national provisions which fall within the scope of EU law, even those not intended to apply EU law directly. Interpreting and applying EU law in a way that is contrary to EU law is not permitted. This prohibition applies regardless of the rank of the national provision, even provisions that have constitutional standing. Thus, to the extent that constitutional provisions must be interpreted in accordance with EU law, this exegetical obligation becomes an instrument of control over constitutional interpretation.

I will structure the analysis of this topic in three parts. First, I will briefly describe the main features of the 'conforming interpretation' mechanism and its instrumental character for interpretative control. Second, I will draw attention to the issue of consistent or conforming interpretation in relation to the Constitution, that is, the obligation to interpret national constitutions themselves in accordance with EU law, which, as I have already stated, implies a reading of consistent interpretation that makes it an instrument for the control of constitutional interpretation, even in matters of fundamental rights. Finally, I will briefly point out some of the constitutional implications of the (compulsory) use of this instrument.

2. The Judicial Duty to Interpret National Law in Conformity with EU Law

2.1. Origin, Development and General Characteristics

Conformity interpretation means that any authority responsible for applying EU law in the domestic sphere must interpret national law in accordance with EU law. This obligation is imposed by EU law itself and binds in particular the national court responsible for its application. It is a requirement that, as the CJEU has consistently held,

> is inherent in the system of the Treaty on European Union, since it enables the national courts, in respect of matters within their jurisdiction, to ensure the full effectiveness of Union law when they adjudicate on disputes brought before them.[1]

Regarding content and scope, it should be noted that, since the introduction of this mechanism 40 years ago, it has evolved without cease. Its evolution has always, since its origins and in its subsequent development, been guided by the CJEU. During the first three decades, the coordinates and basic features of the mechanism were configured, almost always in relation to the directives. It was established in 1984 with the *Von Colson and Kamann* judgment, the requirement that national courts 'interpret their national law in the light of the wording and the purpose of the directive in order to achieve the result referred' in the directive.[2] The *Marleasing* judgment then extended this obligation of coherent interpretation to the application of both national law subsequent to the directives and pre-existing law.[3]

The subsequent *Pfeiffer* case widened the frame of reference by requiring national courts to consider the 'national law as a whole' (in order to assess to what extent it may be applied so as not to produce a result contrary to that sought by the directive),

[1] See, among many others, the following judgments of the Court of Justice: Case C-282/19 *MIUR* ECLI:ECLI:EU:C:2022:3, para 122a; Joined Cases C-397/01 to C-403/01, *Pfeiffer and others* ECLI:EU:C:2004:584, [2004] ECR 8835, paras 113 and 114; Case C-282/10 *Dominguez* ECLI:EU:C:2012:33, para 24; Case C-554/14 *Ognyanov II* EU:C:2016:835, para 59; Case C-579/15 *Popławski I* EU:C:2017:503, para 31; Case C-573/17 *Popławski II* EU:C:2019:530, para 55. On the subject, *ex plurimis*: A Bernardi (ed), *L'interpretazione conforme al diritto dell' Unione europea. Profili e limiti di un vincolo problemático* (Napoli, Jovene, 2015); S Haket, *The EU Law Duty of Consistent Interpretation in German, Irish and Dutch Courts*, (Cambridge, Intersentia, 2019).

[2] Case 14/83, ECLI:EU:C:1984:153, [1984] ECR 1891, para 26.

[3] Case C-106/89 ECLI:EU:C:1990:395 [1990] ECR 4135, para 8. See also Case C-456/98 *Centrosteel* ECLI:EU:C:2000:402, [2000] ECR 6007, para 16; or Case C-188/07 *Commune de Mesquer* ECLI:EU:C:2008:359, para 84.

encompassing all the standards and all their 'interpretation methods'.[4] Another crucial moment arose in 2005 when the *Pupino* judgment of the CJEU extended this obligation to the entire field of existing framework decisions for the now defunct third pillar of the Union, and therefore to the field of police and judicial cooperation in criminal matters within the EU.[5]

Over the last decade, the CJEU has continued to specify various elements and aspects of the scope of this instrument. Thus, the *Domínguez* judgment made clear that the techniques for ensuring the full effectiveness of EU law must follow a staggered order of application, giving priority to interpretation in conformity with the directive over verification of its direct effect/direct application.[6] Thus, non-application of the opposing national provision will only be possible if that interpretation fails and, in addition, the EU law provision is directly invocable or has direct effect (a point which seems to find definitive confirmation in *Popławski II*).[7] Finally, if this non-application fails because the opposing EU law rule lacks direct effect (or because it cannot be established in a horizontal or *inter privatos* relationship, as is the case with directives), it would still be possible to invoke, where appropriate, the state's financial liability for damages caused in breach of EU law.[8] Similarly, the CJEU's *Dansk Industri* decision and its jurisprudential progeny have more recently insisted that 'the requirement to interpret national law in conformity with EU law entails the obligation for national courts *to change its established case-law*, where necessary, if it is based on an interpretation of national law that is incompatible' with EU law.[9]

Another crucial feature of this mechanism involves its limits, for it cannot be used in an absolute manner. On the one side, it must be interpreted in a way that respects the general principles of law which are part of Community/EU law and, in particular, the principles of legal certainty and non-retroactivity, as well as fundamental rights.[10] On the other side, as the CJEU has emphasised on a number of occasions since its *Pupino* decision, an interpretation in conformity with EU law cannot go so far as to interpret

[4] ibid para 115. See also Cases: C-176/12 *Association de Médiation Sociale* EU:C:2014:2, para 38; C-573/17 *Popławski II* (n 1) paras 73 and 77; or C-183/18 *Bank BGŻ BNP Paribas* EU:C:2020:153, para 66.

[5] Case C-105/03 *Pupino* EU:C:2005:386, [2005] ECR 5285, para 42 et seq; other examples: Case C-554/14 *Ognyanov II* (n 1) para 67; *Popławski II*, ibid, paras 71–72; Case C-105/21 *IR* ECLI:EU:C:2022:511, paras 82, 84; Case C-396/22 *Generalstaatsanwaltschaft Berlin* ECLI:EU:C:2023:1029, para 47.

[6] Case C-282/10 *Domínguez* (n 1) para 22 et seq; Case C-306/12 *Spedition Welter* EU:C:2013:650, para 28; Case C-316/13 *Fenoll* ECLI:EU:C:2015:200, para 48; Case C-573/17 *Popławski II* (n 1) para 58 et seq; Case C-140/20 *Commissioner of An Garda Síochána and others* ECLI:EU:C:2022:258, para 118; Joined Cases C-339/20 and C-397/20 *VD and SR* ECLI:EU:C:2022:703, para 97.

[7] C-573/17 (n 1) paras 62 and 68.

[8] Case C-282/10 *Domínguez* (n 1) paras 22, 23 et seq; Case C-306/12 *Spedition Welter* (n 6) para 28; Case C-573/17 *Popławski II* (n 1) paras 58 et seq; Case C-140/20 *Commissioner of An Garda Síochána and others* (n 6), para 118.

[9] Case C-441/14 *Dansk Industri* (also known as *Ajos*) ECLI:EU:C:2016:278, para 33 (emphasis added); Case C-414/16 *Egenberger* ECLI:EU:C:2018:257, paras 72 and 73; Case C-68/17 *IR and JQ* ECLI:EU:C:2018:696, paras 64–65; Case C-55/18 *Federation of CCOO Services* ECLI:EU:C:2019:402, para 70; Case C-44/21 *Phoenix Contact* ECLI:EU:C:2022:309, para 52; Case C-287/22 *Getin Noble Bank* ECLI:EU:C:2023:491, para 57; Case 511/23, *Caronte & Tourist Spa* ECLI:EU:C:2025:42, para 80. Regarding framework decisions, inter alia: Case C-579/15 *Popławski I* (n 1) para 35; Case C-554/14 *Ognyanov II* (n 1) para 67.

[10] Case C-80/86 *Kolpinghuis Nijmegen* ECLI:EU:C:1987:431, [1987] ECR 3969 para 13; Case C-168/95 *Arcaro* ECLI:EU:C:1996:363, [1996] ECR I-04705 para 42; Case C-573/17 *Popławski II* (n 1) para 75; Case C-278/20 *Commission/Spain* ECLI:EU:C:2022:503, para 142; or Case C-397/21 *Humda* ECLI:EU:C:2022:790, para 43.

national law *contra legem*; that is, it must not read the national legislation in a sense that is incompatible with the literal meaning of the (interpreted) text. There can thus be no interpretation *contra litteram*.[11]

2.2. The Duty of Conforming Interpretation with EU Law as a Mechanism for Controlling the Interpretation of National Law

The obligation of conforming or consistent interpretation is based on the principle of loyal cooperation, the principle of effectiveness and, perhaps in more obvious or visible fashion, the principle of primacy of EU law. Indeed, the CJEU has on numerous occasions pointed out that, 'in order to ensure the effectiveness of all provisions of EU law, the *primacy principle* requires, *inter alia*, national courts to interpret, to the greatest extent possible, their national law in conformity with EU law' when adjudicating the case before them.[12]

However, this duty to carry out a compliant reading or exegesis is not only an obligation linked to the primacy of EU law, but is in fact the first mechanism at its service whenever EU law has to be applied through national law. Like primacy, conforming exegesis presupposes, in the vast majority of cases, (possible) legal conflicts between national law or provisions and EU legal provisions, and also provides the solution to such conflicts: EU law prevails. But this solution is configured, and here is the interesting aspect, in the most subtle and benign way possible for national law, for it consists of applying the national provision in question such that it becomes compatible with EU law, in other words by allowing national courts to discard the controversial meanings, that is, the rules (understanding 'rule' as the sense or meaning of a 'provision') that created the conflict or contradiction with that law, thus preserving the national provision.

In reality, the use of conforming interpretation does not imply the ruling out or non-application of a provision, but of some interpretation or rule of the provision that is contrary to EU law. As the CJEU has repeatedly observed, it is only when the incompatibility is insurmountable or cannot be hermeneutically reduced that the second mechanism comes into play: the disapplication of the incompatible national provision (and the state's obligation to remove it from the legal system).[13] It should

[11] Case C-105/03 *Pupino* (n 5) para 47. See also Case C-98/09 *Sorge* ECLI:EU:C:2010:369, [2010] ECR I-05837, para 52; Case C-294/16 PPU *JZ* EU:C:2016:610, para 33; Case C-573/17 *Popławski II* (n 1) para 76; Case C-232/20 *Daimler* EU:C:2022:196, para 77; Case C-426/20 *Luso Temp* ECLI:EU:C:2022:373, para 57; Case C-528/21 *M.D.* ECLI:EU:C:2022:933, para 99; Case C-78/22 *Ald Automotive* ECLI:EU:C:2023:379, para 40; Case 196/23 *Plamaro* ECLI:EU:C:2024:596, para 43.

[12] See, inter alia, Case C-573/17 *Popławski II* (n 1) para 57; Case C-183/18 *Bank BGŻ BNP Paribas* (n 4) para 60; Case C-882/19 *Sumal, S. L.* ECLI:EU:C:2021:800, para 70; or Case C-261/20 *Thelen Technopark Berlin* ECLI:EU:C:2022:33, para 26. Thomas Von Danwitz recalls that the primacy rule 'does not pursue a norm-hierarchical end in itself, but has been instrumental because it determines the scope of Union law to be observed by Member State institutions and in particular by the judiciary, either for the purpose of a conform interpretation of national law or for the application of provisions of Union law with direct effect' ('Uniform Interpretation and Primacy of Union Law in the Dialogue of the Courts' *VerfBlog* 4 November 2022).

[13] As the CJEU usually recalls, it should be pointed out that any national court, hearing a case within its jurisdiction, has, as an organ of a Member State, 'the obligation to disapply any provision of national law which is contrary to a provision of EU law with direct effect in the case pending before it' (Case C-573/17

therefore be recalled that disapplication implies displacing a legislative provision, that which is contrary to EU law, because it does not contain any meaning compatible with EU law. In contrast, exercising conformity interpretation implies displacing some meaning or significance of the legislative provision, that which is contrary to EU law, but without displacing that provision in so far as it contains some compatible meaning or rule.

In order to gauge the true dimension or capacity of conforming interpretation as a mechanism of interpretative control of EU law, its extent or scope must be ascertained. To this end, it may be interesting to determine, on the one hand, how much or which part of EU law serves as a reference for the interpretation of national law (interpretative provision) and, on the other hand, which part of national law must be in conformity (consistent, accommodated, concurrent, coherent, compliant, compatible, non-contradictory, etc) with EU law or a provision thereof and with CJEU case law.

With regard to the first determination, it should be noted that the obligation of compliant exegesis applies whenever national law has to be applied in order to convey the effectiveness of Union law. That is to say, when the Member State measure being applied is itself the transposition or application of an EU law provision. The obligation thus would not come into play in the case of a pure and genuine EU regulation, whose full effectiveness depends solely on its simple and direct national application. Nevertheless, the scope of the compliant exegesis obligation remains immense. Consider the national law that must be applied to give effect to directives, framework decisions, decisions requiring internal transposition, various international agreements of the Union, and even a number of regulations (note that some of them sometimes require measures of national transposition despite their status as 'directly applicable' rules).[14] Moreover, it should not be forgotten that a national provision must not only be interpreted in accordance with the EU law provision which it is intended to apply, but also that its interpretation must be consistent with, or at least not contradict, anything else in the Union legal order, including EU provisions that the national provision is not directly intended to apply.

At the other end, it should be noted that the obligation to interpret national law in conformity with EU law, as understood by the CJEU in accordance with its concept of the principle of the primacy of EU law, applies to all national law, irrespective of the rank of the legal provision interpreted, and is binding on all national authorities (judicial or otherwise) responsible for applying EU law. In this respect, there is also an obligation to interpret the national Constitution in conformity with EU law, in so far as its provisions fall within the scope of EU law. We will consider this issue further in the next section.

Popławski II (n 1) para 61; Joined Cases C-357/19, C-379/19, C-547/19, C-811/19 and C-840/19 *Euro Box Promotion EA* ECLI:UE:C:2021:1034, para 252).

[14] It is also interesting to note that, with regard to European legal acts that serve as a reference for interpretation, the CJEU has recently confirmed that conforming interpretation can also have an impact, albeit to a lesser extent, in relation to the Union's soft law. Thus, in Case C-911/19 *Fédération Bancaire Française* ECLI:EU:C:2021:599, para 71, or in Case C-501/18 *BT* ECLI:EU:C:2021:249, paras 80–81.

3. Constitutional Interpretation in Conformity with EU Law

3.1. The Interpretation of the Constitution in Conformity with EU Law in Accordance with the Case Law of the Court of Justice

The EU upholds a (nearly) absolute concept of primacy of EU law: the primacy of 'all' EU law, whether original or secondary, over any national rule, whatever its rank, even if it is a rule of constitutional rank. This primacy applies, but within the limits set by EU law itself, including the principle of the conferral of competences, the principle of equality of Member States before the Treaties and the principle of respect for the national identity of the Member States (Article 4.2 Treaty on European Union (TEU)).

Therefore, the obligation to interpret national law in conformity with EU law (in the national sphere of application of that law), as an obligation based on the principle of primacy, would apply to 'all' national law, including the national constitution. In other words, national constitutions should also be interpreted in accordance with EU law. Since this is an obligation designed to ensure the primacy (and effectiveness) of EU law, it is worth remembering, as the CJEU has stressed (recently with greater emphasis), that 'by virtue of the principle of primacy of EU law, rules of national law, *even of a constitutional order*, cannot be allowed to undermine the unity and effectiveness of EU law'.[15] Consequently, interpretations of national law that are contrary to EU law, *even if they have constitutional status*, must either be rejected or disregarded.

Moreover, such is the case even if the constitutional interpretation contrary to EU law is expressly endorsed by the constitutional court. Proof of this is found in the three judgments (2021/2022) of the CJEU related to decisions of the Romanian Constitutional Court in *Asociația 'Forumul Judecătorilor*, *Euro Box* and *RS*,[16] as well as in the CJEU judgment *YP and others* (2023) related to the Polish Constitutional Court's ruling in a case concerning effective remedies in Poland in areas covered by EU law.[17]

In the *Asociația 'Forumul Judecătorilor* judgment, for example, the CJEU held that the principle of the primacy of EU law

> must be interpreted as precluding legislation of a Member State having constitutional status, as interpreted by the constitutional court of that Member State, according to which a lower

[15] There are numerous judgments of the Court of Justice in this respect. Thus, among other cases, to mention the most recent ones: *Randstad Italia SpA*, to which the quotation belongs (Case C-497/20 ECLI:EU:C:2021:1037, para 52; emphasis added); Case C-430/21 *RS* ECLI:EU:C:2022:99, para 51; *Euro Box Promotion EA* (n 13) para 251; Case C-487/19 *WŻ* ECLI:EU:C:2021:798, para 157; C-564/19 *IS* ECLI:EU:C:2021:949, para 79; Joined Cases C-83/19, C-127/19, C-195/19, C-291/19, C-355/19 and C-397/19 *Asociația 'Forumul Judecătorilor din România'* ECLI:EU:C:2021:393, para 245; Case C-824/18 *AB and others* ECLI:EU:C:2021:153, para 148. Previously, eg: Case C-378/17 *Minister for Justice and Equality* EU:C:2018:979, para 49; Case C-416/10 *Križan and others* EU:C:2013:8, para 70; or Case C-399/11 *Melloni* EU:C:2013:107, para 59.

[16] See n 15 for case references.

[17] Joined Cases C-615/20 and 671/20, ECLI:EU:C:2023:562, para 89 et seq. See also the Case C-107/23 PPU *Lin* ECLI:EU:C:2023:606 as regards the rule that national rules on criminal prescription must allow effective prevention and repression in the fight against fraud affecting the EU's financial interests, and in which it is pointed out that national courts must in principle set aside national rules or case-law which create a systemic risk of impunity for such offences (see paras 98, 99, 109, 126 et seq and 137).

> court is not permitted to disapply of its own motion a national provision …, which it considers, in the light of a judgment of the Court, to be contrary to European Union Law.[18]

The judgment in *YP and others* will also state that the national court in the case should not take into account certain national provisions and certain case law of the Constitutional Court, as identified in the case at hand, 'in so far as those provisions and that case-law are liable to preclude that referring court from disapplying the resolution at issue and, consequently, from refraining from ruling on the case in the main proceedings'.[19]

3.2. Interpreting the Fundamental Rights Recognised in National Constitutions in Conformity with EU Law

It should be emphasised that the obligation to interpret the Constitution in accordance with EU law has become particularly evident in matters involving fundamental rights recognised in the national constitution as long as, however, the situation in which they are to be protected falls within the scope of EU law.

An entire body of CJEU case law regarding fundamental rights in the EU makes it clear that the national court must assess the compatibility of national measures (applying EU law) with EU fundamental rights, understood as general principles of EU law. This has been the case for over 30 years since cases such as *ERT*, *Kremzov*, *Roquette Frères* and many others.[20]

Once the Treaty of Lisbon entered into force, and the Charter of Fundamental Rights of the European Union (CFR) was recognised as possessing the same binding legal effect as the Treaties (Article 6(1) TEU), the need for national courts to review the coherence or conformity of national measures with the CFR became evident. Among the first decisions of the CJEU to establish this requirement are *Akerberg Fransson*[21] and *Melloni*[22] from 2013. These rulings inaugurated a whole body of subsequent case law along the same lines. Thus, to give one example among several, *Rendón Marín* (2016)[23] recalls the national courts' duty in relation to the right to respect for private and family life in Article 7 CFR (in connection with the protection of the child's best interests in Article 24.2), specifically with regard to the right of residence of a third-country national

[18] *Asociaţia 'Forumul Judecătorilor din România'* (n 15) para 252. The CJEU in *Euro Box Promotion EA* also stated that: 'the principle of the primacy of EU law is to be interpreted as precluding national rules or a national practice under which national ordinary courts are bound by the decisions of the national constitutional court and cannot, by virtue of that fact and without committing a disciplinary offence, disapply, on their own authority, the case-law established in those decisions, even though they are of the view, in the light of a judgment of the Court of Justice, that that case-law is contrary' to EU law (n 13, para 262). See, in a similar way, Case 430/21 *RS* (n 15) para 78.

[19] n 17 at para 92. See also the Opinion of Advocate General Manuel Sánchez-Bordona in Case C-107/23 PPU *Lin* (n 17) para 159. On the interpretation of national law, including constitutional provisions, in a manner consistent with EU law, I refer to my work: *La interpretación conforme al Derecho de la Unión Europea. Especial referencia al intérprete constitucional* (Pamplona, Aranzadi, 2023).

[20] Case C-260/89 *ERT* ECLI:EU:C:1991:254, [1991] ECR 2925, para 42; Case C-299/95 *Kremzow* ECLI:EU:C:1997:254, [1997] ECR 2629, para 15; Case C-94/00 *Roquette Frères* ECLI:EU:C:2002:603, [2002] ECR 9011, para 25.

[21] Case C-617/10 *Akerberg Fransson* ECLI:EU:C:2013:105.

[22] Case C-399/11 *Melloni* EU:C:2013:107.

[23] Case C-165/14 ECLI:EU:C:2016:675, para 6.

with a criminal record. In *Coman and Others* (2018), for its part, the judgment held that 'a national measure that is liable to obstruct the exercise of freedom of movement for persons may be justified only where such a measure is consistent with the fundamental rights guaranteed by the Charter'.[24] See also the judgments *Commission v Hungary* (both 2020) C-78/18[25] on transparency of associations and C-66/18[26] on higher education; or the recent *Inspectia Judiciara* (2023),[27] on the rights enshrined in Articles 47 and 48 CFR, particularly the right to defence.[28]

Because national law must be interpreted and applied in conformity with the fundamental rights of the EU (either as general principles or as rights recognised in the CFR), the question that follows concerns the role of national fundamental rights in this interpretative obligation. Or, to put the question another way, what happens in the event of a clash between different obligations of consistent interpretation concerning rights: one logically following from the fundamental rights established by the national constitution and the other consistent with the fundamental rights of EU law? The answer to this question lies in two key judgments delivered by the CJEU on 26 February 2013, the aforementioned *Akerberg Fransson* and *Melloni* cases.[29] These two judgments were delivered on the same day because the CJEU sought to distinguish between two situations or scenarios in the protection of EU fundamental rights at the national level, depending on the margin of national regulatory action of the Member States when applying EU law. As the Court stated in virtually identical terms in both judgments:

> [W]here a court of a Member State is called upon to review whether fundamental rights are complied with by a national provision or measure which, in a situation where action of the Member States is not entirely determined by European Union law, implements the latter for the purposes of Article 51(1) of the Charter, national authorities and courts remain free to apply national standards of protection of fundamental rights, provided that the level of protection provided for by the Charter, as interpreted by the Court, and the primacy, unity and effectiveness of European Union law are not thereby compromised.[30]

[24] Case of CJEU C-673/16 ECLI:EU:C:2018:385, para 47.

[25] ECLI:EU:C:2020:476, para 101 et seq, referring to Art 7 (right to respect for private and family life), Art 8.1 (right to protection of personal data) and Art 12.1 (freedom of association) CFR.

[26] ECLI:EU:C:2020:792, para 212 et seq, in conjunction with Art 13 (freedom of the arts and sciences), Art 14.3 (freedom to found educational establishments) and Art 16 (freedom to conduct a business) CFR.

[27] Case C-817/21, ECLI:EU:C:2023:391, para 40 et seq, esp para 48.

[28] See, in a similar way, the judgment of the CJEU Case C-64/16 *Associação Sindical dos Juízes Portugueses* ECLI:EU:C:2018:117, which analyses whether the EU law principle of judicial independence (based on Art 19.1(2) TEU and Art 47 CFR) precludes the application to members of the judiciary of a Member State (Portugal) of general salary reduction measures (adopted on the basis of State Law n 75/2014).

[29] The first concerns the *ne bis in idem* principle in cases of VAT fraud; the second deals with procedural guarantees in the event of a conviction in absentia in connection with the execution of a European arrest warrant, following the first preliminary ruling of the Spanish Constitutional Court (ATC 86/2011, ECLI:ES:TC:2011:86A).

[30] C-617/10 *Akerberg Fransson* ECJ para 29; and, similarly, C-399/11 *Melloni* ECJ para 60. This represents seminal jurisprudence then constantly reiterated by the CJEU. Thus, for example, in the Cases: *MAS and MB* (or *Taricco II*), with regard to the principle of legality of criminal offences and penalties under Art 49 CFR (Case C-42/17 ECLI:EU:C:2017:936, para 47); Case C-516/17 *Spiegel Online* ECLI:EU:C:2019:625, with regard to freedom of expression and information under Art 11 CFR (para 21); Case C-507/17 *Google LLC* ECLI:EU:C:2019:772, with reference to the protection of personal data in Art 8 CFR (para 72); Case *Euro Box Promotion* (n 13), with regard to the right to an effective judicial protection and judicial independence of Art 47 CFR, in connection with Art 19.1(2) TEU (para 211); or Case C-107/23 PPU *Lin* (n 17) paras 110, 123 and 124.

Consequently, when an act of EU law requires national measures for its implementation, because EU law does not fully exhaust the regulation on the matter (which was precisely the situation in *Akerberg*), it will never be possible, in the context of the national application of EU law, to interpret and apply national fundamental rights (the constitutional provisions on rights) in a way which is contrary to the Charter and the primacy of EU law; any interpretation not in conformity with it (such as, in *Akerberg*, an interpretation incompatible with the *ne bis in idem* principle recognised in Article 50 CFR) must be ruled out. National standards of fundamental rights, those of constitutional provisions, may be invoked, but only if they offer an equal or higher level of EU iusfundamental protection and do not restrict or contradict the rest of the Union's legal order.

If, on the other hand, the action of the Member States is entirely determined by EU law, without any national margin of discretion (which was the case in *Melloni*, with Article 4a of the Framework Decision on the European Arrest Warrant), then, according to the above-mentioned *Akerberg/Melloni* case law (*sensu contrario* deduction), in such a situation there is no other possibility than assessing and applying the CFR.[31] In other words, in these circumstances the national catalogues of fundamental rights are displaced by the CFR. This displacement occurs, moreover, as academics remind us,[32] 'regardless of any debate on the lesser or greater protection afforded' by the national catalogue.[33]

Moreover, there is an important operational element in relation to the requirement to interpret national law, whatever its rank. In accordance with the fundamental rights of the EU, this obligation of interpretation on the part of the national court is not normally limited to the mere verification of the adequacy of national law with these European fundamental rights. This exegetical activity of national law in accordance with the fundamental rights of the EU, when broken down, actually consists of two steps or elements: on one side is the obligation to interpret national law in accordance with the secondary law of the Union at stake; on another is the duty, in turn, to interpret this secondary law in accordance with primary law and the fundamental rights of the EU.

To use the CJEU's own words in the judgment *Ligue des droits humains*, which echoes 20 years of repeated jurisprudence:

> [W]hen a directive allows the Member States discretion to define transposition measures adapted to the various situations possible, they must, when implementing those measures,

[31] K Lenaerts, 'La protección de los derechos fundamentales en el ordenamiento jurídico de la UE: Un diálogo entre el Tribunal de Justicia y los Tribunales Constitucionales de los Estados miembros' (2022) 7 ff, www.tribunalconstitucional.es/NotasDePrensaDocumentos/NP_2022_041/FINAL_3_05_2022_KL_La_Proteccion_de_los_Derechos_Fundamentales_en_el_ordenamiento_juridico_de_la_UE%20(003).pdf.

[32] Inter alia: R Alonso García, 'El proceso de europeización del Tribunal Constitucional' (2022) 1 *Journal of Human Security and Global Law*, 14 and 19.

[33] This would be, in short, the reason that pushed the German Federal Constitutional Court, for situations or cases analogous to *Melloni*, to take the CFR as a direct parameter for the purposes of protection in *amparo*, ever since the two landmark decisions known as *Right to be forgotten I* and *II*, both of 6 November 2019 (of the First Senate of the Constitutional Court: 1 BvR 276/17 (*Recht auf Vergessen* I), and 1 BvR 16/13 (*Recht auf Vergessen II*); case law of the First Senate of the Constitutional Court later confirmed by the Second Senate in the Judgment of 1 December 2020, known as *Euroorden III*: 2 BvR 1845/18 and 2 BvR 2100/18). From these judgments, the protection of the 'remedy of *amparo*' has been extended to CFR rights (a guarantee limited to protection against judicial decisions, and not extended to the control of rules). On the subject, among others: P Cruz Villalón, 'Una forma de cooperación judicial no reclamada? Sobre la extensión del amparo a la Carta de Derechos Fundamentales de la UE' (2021) 25 *Anuario Iberoamericano de Justicia Constitucional* 71 ff.

> not only interpret their national law in a manner consistent with the directive in question but also ensure that they do not rely on an interpretation of the directive that would be in conflict with the fundamental rights protected by the EU legal order or with the other general principles recognised by EU law.[34]

As evidenced in the CJEU case law, this two-sided requirement for interpretative adequacy (compliance of national law with the secondary law of the case and both with the fundamental rights of the Union), following the Lisbon Treaty, now often refers to the fundamental rights guaranteed in the CFR.[35]

Additionally, as the CJEU reiterated in the aforementioned *Ligue des droits humains* judgment, it should be recalled that:

> [I]n accordance with a general principle of interpretation, an EU act must be interpreted, as far as possible, in such a way as not to affect its validity and in conformity with primary law as a whole and, in particular, with the provisions of the Charter. Thus, if the wording of secondary EU legislation is open to more than one interpretation, preference should be given to the interpretation which renders the provision consistent with primary law rather than to the interpretation which leads to its being incompatible with primary law.[36]

4. Constitutional Implications of the Obligation to Interpret National Law in Conformity with EU Law

At this point, it may be helpful to explore some possible constitutional implications from the developments examined. First of all, it should be stressed that this mechanism of exegesis or reading of national law in accordance with EU law is configured not only as an instrument for articulating the effectiveness of EU law, but also as a technique of regulatory control of the Europeanness of national law. Strictly speaking, it is not a question of controlling the regulatory 'provisions' or the 'texts' of the national legal system, but rather the content or meaning derived from these provisions, ie the norms derived from these provisions.

Conformity interpretation is a sophisticated instrument meant to serve the principle of primacy of EU law which, in the event of contradiction, does not imply necessarily the non-application or displacement of provisions 'contrary' to EU law, but rather, more mildly, requires 'only' the displacement of those rules or meanings of provisions which

[34] Case C-817/19 ECLI: EU: C: 2022: 491, para 87. Case law in line with its previous Cases: C-101/01 *Lindqvist* ECLI:EU:C:2003:596, [2003] ECR 12971, para 87; Case 275/06 *Promusicae* EU:C:2008:54, [2008] ECR 271, para 68; Joined Cases C-411/10 and C-493/10 *NS and others* EU:C:2011:865, [2011] ECR 13905, para 77.

[35] See Case C-817/19 *Ligue des Droits Humains* (n 34) para 87 et seq: Case C-601/15 PPU, *N* EU:C:2016:84, paras 60 and 82; Case C-270/17 PPU *Tupikas* EU:C:2017:628, para 60; Joined Cases C-133/19, C-136/19 and C-137/19 *Belgian State* (Regroupement familial – Enfant mineur) EU:C:2020:577, paras 33 et seq; Joined Cases C-793/19 and 794/19 *Spacenet* ECLI:EU:C:2022:702, paras 63 et seq, 117 and 131; or Case C-699/21 *EDL* ECLI:EU:C:2023:295.

[36] n 33 at para 86. In the same vein, the previous decisions: Case C-481/19 *Consob* EU:C:2021:84, para 50; or Joined Cases C-391/16, C-77/17 and C-78/17 *M and others* (Revocation of refugee status) EU:C:2019:403, para 77.

run contrary to EU law (non-application of the provision only being called for when it cannot howsoever be interpreted in conformity with EU law).

In other words, the requirement of conformity interpretation works as a mechanism of control over the interpretation of national law acting in application of EU law. It is a very powerful and incisive instrument of regulatory control, since the judicial obligation to apply conformity interpretation reaches as far as constitutional provisions themselves, in as much as their interpretation is also subject to the requirement. This is also the case with regard to fundamental rights, ie the interpretation of the provisions of the national constitution which recognise fundamental rights. This bears repeating: the requirement of conforming interpretation means that national constitutions and the constitutional rights they establish must be interpreted in accordance with EU law and thus in accordance with the CFR (in the context of the national application of EU law). This implies, of course, that when managing the different obligations of conforming interpretation in the event of a conflict between said obligations, the obligation to interpret national law (for example, of an Act) such that it remains compatible with EU law must take precedence over the obligation to interpret it in a way that is compatible or consistent with the national constitution and/or the fundamental rights recognised therein.

Second, the obligation to interpret national law in conformity with EU law binds the national court responsible for applying EU law. This is not without significant implications for the national courts, constitutional courts included. I would like to pause briefly on this point, homing in on the perspective of the CJEU case law:

(A) With regard to the national court responsible for applying EU law (ordinary jurisdiction), the following guidelines of the CJEU are worth recalling:

(A.1) The CJEU not only enjoins national courts (since the Court's Judgment in *Dansk Industri*) to depart from its settled case law if that case law is based on an interpretation of national law irreconcilable with EU law.[37] It also contemplates that, wherever a national court claims that it is impossible for it to interpret a provision of domestic law in compliance with a framework decision or other EU law on grounds of an binding interpretation of that national provision by the national apex court, said national court ought 'to ensure that the framework decision is given full effect, and if necessary to disapply, on its own authority, the interpretation adopted by the national Supreme Court, since that interpretation is not compatible with EU law'.[38]

(A.2) Regarding national courts' obligation of conformity interpretation, moreover, the CJEU has repeatedly reminded national courts, and more intensively of late, that they may request a preliminary ruling on previous judicial decisions of another national court which may bind it in the case if that first national court's ruling may lead it to apply national law contrariwise to EU law.

[37] See the *Dansk Industri* case law (n 9), which the CJEU continues to reiterate assiduously.

[38] Case C-579/15 *Popławski I* (n 1) para 36. See also: Case C-614/14 *Ognyanov I* ECLI:EU:C:2016:514, para 36; Case C-554/14 *Ognyanov II* (n 1) paras 68–70; Case 564/19 *IS* ECLI:EU:C:2021:949, para 81; Case 511/23 *Caronte & Tourist SpA* (n 9), para 80.

The *RS* judgment recalls, in this sense, that the national judge who has exercised the power to refer the preliminary ruling 'must therefore, if necessary, disregard the rulings of a higher national court if it considers, having regard to the interpretation provided by the Court, that they are not consistent with EU law, if necessary refusing to apply the national rule requiring it to comply with the decisions of that higher court'.[39] It concludes that 'it follows from the Court's case-law that that solution also applies where an ordinary court is bound, under a national procedural rule, by a decision of a national constitutional court which it considers to be contrary to EU law'.[40]

(B) The obligation to interpret national law and constitutions in conformity with EU law, under the limit of *contra litteram*, may also reach the Constitutional Court (or equivalent) in one way or another, at least insofar as it gives constitutional relevance to EU law when deciding the constitutional cases before it. Even though this court may not see itself as a 'national judge' of the application of EU law, experience shows that such a court is increasingly confronted with cases in which it has to consider the national application (jurisdictional or otherwise) of EU law when deciding on them. Experience also shows, in this regard, quite a few cases in which the constitutional tribunal ends up interpreting the national constitution in accordance with EU law. That is, the constitutional court often finds on its own a *pro Unione* interpretation that excludes the contents or meanings of a constitutional provision that are opposed to it.

Notwithstanding, it is true that, when this happens, it does so because the constitutional court self-imposes (directly or implicitly) the conformity interpretation obligation, basing it not on EU law, but on some constitutional clause such as the one that establishes the opening of the Constitution to international or supranational human rights law (for example: Article 10.2 of the Spanish Constitution; this was the case in the Constitutional Court's judgment 26/2014, issued after the European CJEU handed down its *Melloni* judgment).

Another example of explicit recognition of *pro Unione* interpretation of a national constitution is the Polish Constitutional Tribunal's ruling K 18/04 of 11 May 2005, issued when the country was in the process of ratifying the EU Accession Treaty. This is one of the earliest judgments of a constitutional court (or equivalent) of a Member

[39] Case C-430/21 *RS* (n 15) para 75, quoting in this respect the judgment of 5 October 2010, C-173/09 *Elchinov* EU:C:2010:581, [2010] ECR 8889, paras 30 and 31. See also Case C-497/20 *Randstad Italia* (n 15) para 54.

[40] Case C-430/21 *RS* (n 15) para 76 (which recalls, to that effect, the Case C-416/10 *Križan and Others* EU:C:2013:8, para 71). See also Case C-107/23 PPU *Lin* (n 17) para 133; or Case C-792/22 *Energotehnica* ECLI:EU:C:2024:788, paras 61–62 and 67. In this line, it will also be interesting to be attentive to what the CJEU decides in the preliminary ruling referred by the *Sąd Apelacyjny w Krakowie* (Krakow Court of Appeal) on 31 March 2022 (C-225/22 *'R' SA v AW 'T' sp z oo*), which is pending and in which the first of the three questions to be clarified is: 'Must the second subparagraph of Article 19(1), Article 2, Article 4(3) and Article 6(3) of the Treaty on European Union (TEU), in conjunction with Article 47 of the Charter of Fundamental Rights of the European Union ("the Charter") and Art 267 of the Treaty on the Functioning of the European Union (TFEU), and the principle of the primacy of EU law be interpreted as permitting a national court to disregard a decision of a constitutional court which is mandatory under national law, including constitutional law, in so far as that decision precludes an examination by the national court as to whether, having regard to the way in which the judges were appointed, the judicial body is an independent and impartial court previously established by law within the meaning of European Union law?'

State in which an interpretation of the national constitution in conformity with EU law was favoured, however paradoxical this may now seem in view of the current combative stance of this court. In K 18/04, regardless, the Polish Constitutional Court explicitly recognised 'the principle of interpreting domestic law in a manner "sympathetic to European law" as a mechanism for eliminating possible conflicts between EU law and the Polish constitutional text, although it also referred to "its limits"'.[41]

Yet another interesting and even clearer case of conformity interpretation of a national constitution is that of the Constitutional Court of the Czech Republic in its Judgment of 3 May 2006[42] regarding the constitutionality of the national implementation in the Czech Criminal Code of the Framework Decision on the European Arrest Warrant in relation to the Charter of Fundamental Rights and Freedoms integrated into the Czech Constitution, Article 14(4) of which states that 'No citizen may be forced to leave her homeland'. The Czech Constitutional Court will uphold the constitutionality of the above national legislation on the basis that from Article 1 para 2 of the Constitution ('The Czech Republic shall observe its obligations resulting from international law'), in conjunction with the principle of cooperation enshrined in Article 10 of the EC Treaty, 'follows a constitutional principle according to which national legal enactments, including the Constitution, *should whenever possible be interpreted in conformity with* the process of European integration and the cooperation between European and Member State organs'. In this respect, the Court states that,

> If the Constitution, of which the Charter of Fundamental Rights and Basic Freedoms forms a part, can be interpreted in several manners, only certain of which lead to the attainment of an obligation which the Czech Republic undertook in connection with its membership in the EU, then an interpretation must be selected with supports the carrying out of that obligation, and not an interpretation which precludes its.[43]

From a supranational perspective, it should be noted that the CJEU has not explicitly stated (as it has for the national courts responsible for applying EU law) the existence of a (European) obligation for constitutional judge to interpret the constitution in accordance with EU law (always up to the limit of *contra legem*). Nevertheless, as has been observed, the CJEU has provided a number of judicial guidelines that push towards an obligatory *pro Unione* reading of national constitutions by constitutional judges. Thus, mainly, on one side, the aforementioned *Akerberg/Melloni* case law on the use of national constitutional standards for fundamental rights in the field of application of EU law. Such case law, although it refers to the judge who applies EU law, is ultimately also binding on the constitutional judge who gives constitutional relevance to the fundamental rights of the EU and their national jurisdictional application. And on another side, recent CJEU case law (the above-mentioned *Asociația 'Forumul Judecătorilor,*

[41] A position later confirmed in other subsequent decisions of the Polish Constitutional Court such as decision K 32/09, on the occasion of the Treaty of Lisbon, of 24 November 2010 (para 108), or decision SK 45/09, of 16 November 2016, which analysed the compatibility of a provision of secondary law in relation to the fundamental right to a fair trial (para 97).

[42] Pl ÚS 66/04.

[43] Paras 81 et seq of the judgment. For a more recent case of (explicit) conforming interpretation by a constitutional court, the decision of the Portuguese Constitutional Court 268/2022 is very interesting, on the control of the constitutionality of the law transposing the Data Retention Directive 2006/24 into Portuguese law.

Euro Box, RS and *Energotehnica* judgments), emanating in relation to some rulings of the Romanian Constitutional Court, reaffirming that the principle of the primacy of EU law precludes national rules or practices that bind ordinary national courts to the decisions of the national constitutional court to the extent of not allowing them to disapply a national rule which they consider contrary to EU law, or not allowing them to review its compatibility with EU law.

In conclusion, the obligation to interpret national law in conformity with EU law is an obligation that is binding for any national authority responsible for the application of EU law, but particularly national courts. This obligation remains an appropriate mechanism for ensuring the effectiveness of national implementation of EU law. This said, the evolution of the CJEU case law also shows that this obligation is developing into a powerful technique or mechanism for normative control of national law in terms of its 'Europeanness' (the degree to which it aligns with the legal norms of the EU). It has become or is becoming an instrument of control for the interpretation of provisions of national law, including constitutional provisions, even those, notably, that establish fundamental rights. This is why it is possible to note that, since *Akerberg* and *Melloni*, CJEU case law has established the obligation of national courts to carry out a jurisdictional reading of these national provisions relating to fundamental rights in accordance or coherent with the CFR.

Bibliography

Alonso García, R, 'El proceso de europeización del Tribunal Constitucional' (2022) 1 *Journal of Human Security and Global Law* 12.

Bernardi, A (ed), *L'interpretazione conforme al diritto dell' Unione europea. Profili e limiti di un vincolo problemático* (Jovene, Napoli, 2015).

Cruz Villalón, P, 'Una forma de cooperación judicial no reclamada? Sobre la extensión del amparo a la Carta de Derechos Fundamentales de la UE' (2021) 25 *Anuario Iberoamericano de Justicia Constitucional* 57.

Haket, S, *The EU Law Duty of Consistent Interpretation in German, Irish and Dutch Courts*, (Cambidge-Antwerp-Chicago, Intersentia, 2019).

Lenaerts, K, 'La protección de los derechos fundamentales en el ordenamiento jurídico de la UE: Un diálogo entre el Tribunal de Justicia y los Tribunales Constitucionales de los Estados miembros', (2022) www.tribunalconstitucional.es/NotasDePrensaDocumentos/NP_2022_041/FINAL_3_05_2022_KL_La_Proteccion_de_los_Derechos_Fundamentales_en_el_ordenamiento_juridico_de_la_UE%20(003).pdf.

Ugartemendia Eceizabarrena, JI, *La interpretación conforme al Derecho de la Unión Europea. Especial referencia al intérprete constitucional* (Pamplona, Aranzadi, 2023).

Von Danwitz, T, 'Uniform Interpretation and Primacy of Union Law in the Dialogue of the Courts' *VerfBlog* 4 November 2022.

6

The 2024 Reform of the Statute of the Court of Justice of the EU and the Transformation of the EU Judicial System: Preliminary Rulings before the General Court of the EU

SARA IGLESIAS SÁNCHEZ*

1. Introduction

There is no doubt that the preliminary ruling procedure has been key in ensuring the success of legal integration in the European Union (EU). It has created a judicial space for dialogue in which the Court of Justice of the European Union (CJEU; 'the Court') has been able to foster the uniform interpretation of EU law in an increasingly complex legal environment. It has provided a channel of communication through which national courts infuse adjudication in Luxembourg with real-life practice to form a sort of backbone for judicial dialogue around the most crucial aspects of coexisting national and European legal orders. Notwithstanding, the preliminary ruling procedure is often portrayed as a victim of its own success, for this procedure accounts for the bulk of the Court's workload. To mitigate the risk of overwhelming the Court's capacity to engage in high-quality judicial dialogue, brave and radical proposals are needed.[1] One such option is transferring jurisdiction over preliminary rulings to the General Court.

The 2024 Reform of the Statute of the Court of Justice ('the Statute') brought about a transformation[2] deemed the most significant change in the judicial architecture of

* This is an updated and adapted text that draws on previous publications by the author: the Editorial to the *Revista General de Derecho Europeo* no 59 and the Long-Read 'Preliminary Rulings before the General Court. Crossing the last frontier of the reform of the EU judicial system?' (2022) 125 *EU Law Live Weekend Edition*, eulawlive.com/weekend-edition/weekend-edition-no125/. Supported by the Transform EU research project no. PID2023-148537NB-I00 (Agencia Estatal de Investigación, Spain), and IDEIR, UCM.

[1] See GC Rodríguez Iglesias, 'L'avenir du système juridictionnel de l'Union européenne' (1999) 35 *Cahiers de droit européen* 275.

[2] Regulation 2024/2019 of the European Parliament and of the Council of 11 April 2024Amending Protocol No 3 on the Statute of the Court of Justice of the European Union [2024] OJ L 2024/2019.

the EU since the creation of the Court of First Instance.[3] Preliminary ruling cases in 'specific areas' will now, for the first time, be adjudicated by the General Court. The reform also affects what is often called the 'filtering of appeals' mechanism of Article 58a of the Statute that has been in force from 1 May 2019, in order to include decisions of boards of appeals which already existed on that date but were not explicitly included under that provision, as well as decisions relating to arbitration clauses under Article 272 of the Treaty on the Functioning of the European Union (TFEU). This aspect of the reform, however, will not be addressed here.[4] This chapter is devoted, first, to the main lines of the 2024 Reform of the Statute whereby jurisdiction to adjudicate on preliminary ruling cases has been transferred to the General Court, and then to reflect on the potential impact of the reform on the overall design and future evolution of the EU judiciary.

2. The Background to the Court of Justice's Request

In discussions predating the Nice reform, the CJEU itself brought up the transfer of preliminary rulings to the General Court as one of the potential solutions for managing the steady increase in workload that this procedural avenue has occasioned.[5] The possibility of such a transfer, which was explicitly excluded when the Court of First Instance was created,[6] was included in the Treaty of Nice[7] but remained dormant for more than 20 years. This occurred because, despite its formal insertion in the Treaty, transferring preliminary ruling jurisdiction to the General Court was still considered problematic,[8] and was contemplated only as a backup plan if all the other possible avenues for reform failed to enable the Court to keep up with its workload. As the Court itself explained in its request, priority was given to other measures, such as establishing the Civil Service Tribunal; transferring most direct actions to the General Court; and, more recently, setting up a system to filter appeals. Although the preliminary rulings procedure itself has also undergone significant modification, those reforms were always

[3] T Tridimas, 'Breaking with Tradition: Preliminary Reference Reform and the New Judicial Architecture' *EU Law Live*, 26 June 2024, eulawlive.com/op-ed-breaking-with-tradition-preliminary-reference-reform-and-the-new-judicial-architecture.

[4] See on this matter, K Bradley, 'The Court of Justice appeal filter mechanism and effective judicial protection: throwing out the baby with the bathwater?", *EU Law Live*, 01/07/2024, https://eulawlive.com/the-court-of-justice-appeal-filter-mechanism-and-effective-judicial-protection-throwing-out-the-baby-with-the-bathwater. On the filtering mechanism, see C Oró Martínez, The Filtering of Appeals by the Court of Justice: Taking Stock of the First Two Orders Allowing an Appeal to Proceed' (2022) 112 *EU Law Live Weekend Edition*.

[5] Court of Justice, 'Document de réflexion de la Cour de justice et du Tribunal de première instance sur l'avenir du système juridictionnel de l'Union européenne', 11 May 1999, Council Document 8208/99 as well as 'Contribution de la Cour de Justice et du Tribunal de première Instance à la Conférence intergouvernementale' CONFER/VAR 3964/00, 28 February 2000.

[6] See Art 168A Treaty establishing a Constitution for Europe (TCE), inserted by the European Single Act [1987] OJ L 169/1.

[7] Previously Art 225(3) TCE, now Art 256(3) TFEU.

[8] eg A Johnston, 'Judicial Reform and the Treaty of Nice' (2001) 38 *Common Market Law Review* 499.

aimed at streamlining the procedure within the CJEU and left its exclusive jurisdiction untouched.

The discussion was rekindled in 2015 with the reform of the Statute that revamped the General Court by doubling its number of judges and repealing the Civil Service Tribunal.[9] Even though no decision was made to entrust the General Court with preliminary rulings at the time, the CJEU re-examined the option – in accordance with its legislative mandate[10] – and determined in 2017 that the General Court reform remained incomplete, making the activation of Article 256(3) TFEU premature.[11] The Court cautiously depicted the potential transfer as 'an extremely delicate undertaking' and openly expressed reluctance to relinquish its exclusive preliminary rulings jurisdiction *at that time*, thus leaving itself the option to reconsider the matter in the future.

Barely five years later, the CJEU deemed reconsideration necessary. Although the risks and problems were arguably largely unchanged, in 2022 the Court's perspective of the situation had shifted. First, it noted the increase in preliminary requests and the impact of that increase on the length of proceedings, which from an average of 15 months in 2016 gradually increased to around 17 months in 2022.[12] Several authors have since, however, pointed out that the numbers of preliminary ruling requests does not seem to have increased dramatically in the last period.[13] Instead, the preoccupation seems to stem from the higher complexity and constitutional character of the requests – which involves motives that may well be more qualitative than quantitative.[14] A second aspect of the Court's shift was the message it conveyed considering that the reform of the General Court could be seen as accomplished. Here lies, however, another critical point of the motives underlying the reform: in a way, the 2024 Reform can be perceived as an inevitable collateral effect of the 2015 reform (Regulation 2015/2422), which doubled the size of the General Court and suppressed the Civil Service Tribunal.[15]

3. The 2024 Reform in a Nutshell

Before examining the main lines of the reform, it must be noted that the Reform Regulation also introduces important novelties concerned with the transparency of

[9] See on this matter, G Butler, 'An Interim Post-Mortem: Specialised Courts in the EU Judicial Architecture after the Civil Service Tribunal' (2020) 17 *International Organizations Law Review* 586.

[10] Article 3 of Regulation (EU, Euratom) 2015/2422 of the European Parliament and of the Council of 16 December 2015 amending Protocol No 3 on the Statute of the Court of Justice of the European Union [2015] OJ L 341/14.

[11] Report submitted pursuant to Art 3(2) of Regulation (EU, Euratom) 2015/2422 of the European Parliament and of the Council amending Protocol No 3 on the Statute of the CJEU.

[12] See fn 6 of the report.

[13] M Bobek, 'Preliminary rulings before the General Court: What judicial architecture for the European Union?' (2023) 60 *Common Market Law Review* 1515.

[14] R Alonso García, 'The Persian Jurist in Luxembourg. On the Decentralisation of the Preliminary Ruling Procedure' (2024) 195 *EU Law Live Weekend Edition*, eulawlive.com/weekend-edition/weekend-edition-no195.

[15] Regulation (EU, Euratom) 2015/2422 of the European Parliament and of the Council of 16 December 2015 amending Protocol No 3 on the Statute of the Court of Justice of the European Union [2015] OJ L 341/14.

judicial proceedings: these novelties were not contemplated by the 2022 request of the Court, but were included into the final text mostly because the European Parliament insisted on them.[16] Even though these new features will not be examined in this chapter,[17] they are worth mentioning as they entail a historical change towards enhancing the openness and transparency of EU courts.

The reform adds a new paragraph to Article 23 of the Statute, which foresees that the written observations submitted in preliminary ruling procedures shall be automatically published (without any need for a separate request) on the curia.eu website. This is quite revolutionary compared to the CJEU's previous practice, which had already become the object of discussion[18] and is striking given the opposition expressed by some Member States.[19] The transparency rule is in any case subject to two provisos. First, the publication is to occur 'within a reasonable time after the closing of the case'. Second, publication will be the rule, but exceptions will be fairly easy to trigger if the person having submitted the observations 'raises objections to the publication of that person's own written submissions'.[20]

Another novelty 'democratises' participation in Court procedures and extends it to institutions other than the Commission. An amendment to Article 23 of the Statute now provides that the Parliament, the Council and the European Central Bank will be entitled to submit statements 'where they consider they have a particular interest in the issues raised by the request'.

Leaving aside these important developments, and focusing on the transfer of jurisdiction over preliminary rulings in certain areas to the General Court, the Reform follows the proposals contained in the Request by the Court of Justice. The Court proposal carefully designed a cautious but ambitious reform along four main lines. First, it identified suitable 'specific areas' which, according to Article 256 TFEU, could be transferred to the General Court (section 6.3.1 below). Second, it proposed a *guichet unique* system for the allocation of cases, the responsibility for which remains with the CJEU (section 6.3.2 below). Third, the Court advanced key procedural arrangements to ensure uniformity in the preliminary ruling proceedings in both Courts (section 6.3.3). Fourth, even though the proposal did not address the review procedure, the silence on the subject not only conveys the CJEU's acceptance of the review procedure, the procedure also plays a crucial role in the future system (section 6.3.4).

[16] See, on the decision-making procedure, S Iglesias Sánchez, 'Moving forward towards the Preliminary Ruling's Reform: Hearing before the Legal Affairs Committee of the European Parliament' *EU Law Live*, 22 May 2023, eulawlive.com/insight-moving-forward-towards-the-preliminary-rulings-reform-hearing-before-the-legal-affairs-committee-of-the-european-parliament-by-sara-iglesias-sanchez. See the Report on the draft regulation of the European Parliament and of the Council amending Protocol No 3 on the Statute of the Court of Justice of the European Union 27 September 2023, A9-0278/2023, 2022/0906(COD), www.europarl.europa.eu/doceo/document/A-9-2023-0278_EN.html.

[17] See generally, J Martín y Pérez de Nanclares, 'La reforma del Tribunal de Justicia de la Unión Europea: La ruptura de un tabú' (2024) 90 *Revista Española De Derecho Europeo* 21.

[18] See, eg the discussion in C-213/15 P Opinion of Advocate General Bobek in his Opinion of 21 December 2016, Commission/Breyer, EU:C:2016:996.

[19] Declaration by Austria, Cyprus, France, Greece, Italy and Malta, Council Document 7296/24 ADD 1, 8 March 2024, data.consilium.europa.eu/doc/document/ST-7296-2024-ADD-1/en/pdf.

[20] See, for an analysis of the implications of this new rule, P Dermine, 'Transparency and Openness at the Court of Justice – Towards ex post Publicity of Parties' Observations' *EU Law Live*, 19 July 2024, eulawlive.com/op-ed-transparency-and-openness-at-the-court-of-justice-towards-ex-post-publicity-of-parties-observations.

3.1. The Choice and Delimitation of the Specific Areas Transferred

According to Article 256(3) TFEU 'the General Court shall have jurisdiction to hear and determine questions referred for a preliminary ruling under Article 267 [TFEU], in specific areas laid down by the Statute'. This means that a general transfer of the preliminary ruling jurisdiction is precluded by primary law and that criteria must be established to identify the 'specific areas' to which the Treaty refers.

The term 'areas' is not defined in the Treaties and is extremely vague. It can range from very concrete and delimited material spheres of EU law to vast material fields of EU law, such as competition law, environmental law, migration law, consumer law or even the 'area' of freedom, security and justice. The approach adopted by the CJEU and embodied by the 2024 Reform represents the first delimited meaning, as the 'specific areas' are very concrete aspects of broader material fields. New Article 50b of the Statute lists them: a) the common system of value added tax; b) excise duties; c) the Customs Code; d) the tariff classification of goods under the Combined Nomenclature; e) compensation and assistance to passengers in the event of denied boarding or of delay or cancelation of transport services; and f) the system for greenhouse gas emission allowance trading.

This delimitation of specific areas is in line with the language used by the Court in its contribution to the Nice intergovernmental conference, which spoke of '*contentieux spécifiques*'. The method through which the Court has distilled these five specific areas was carefully designed by applying four parameters: the specific areas must be clearly identifiable in the text of the request for a preliminary ruling and severable from other areas (encapsulation requirement); they must be areas where litigation does not generally give rise to issues of principle (absence of constitutional relevance); there must be a substantial body of case law to guide the General Court (established case law); and there must be a sufficiently high number of references in the area in question (numeric relevance). According to the Request of the Court, this last criterion means that cases in the selected areas would amount to 20 per cent of the preliminary rulings in the period of reference (the last five years).

Interestingly, the Court has opted for a pragmatic determination of the areas subject to transfer, avoiding the traditional areas of 'expertise' of the General Court (ie, competition, state aid, intellectual property, common foreign and security policy, staff regulations, commercial policy, access to documents, EU funding or banking union). Structural reasons that do not surface in the request of the Court or in the Reform Regulation may explain the perceived need for 'parallelism between direct actions and preliminary rulings in the overall system of "saying the law"'.[21] This parallelism may arguably seek to minimise the risk of divergent interpretation by ensuring that the General Court does not decide preliminary rulings (which can only be subject to review in exceptional cases) in areas where direct actions can be subject to

[21] K Lenaerts, 'The Unity of European Law and the Overload of the ECJ – the System of Preliminary Rulings Revisited' in I Pernice, J Kokott and C Saunders (eds), *The Future of the European Judicial System in a Comparative Perspective* (Baden Baden, Nomos, 2006) 211–39, 235.

a full-fledged appeal before the CJEU. Pushing the parallelism further would amount to admitting no inconvenience in transferring preliminary jurisdiction in those areas where the General Court already virtually functions as an appellate court (ie in the areas covered by the filter system for appeals),[22] since the Court possesses similarly limited opportunities to review cases on appeal (albeit according to different and more flexible criteria).[23] The areas to which the 'filtering of appeals' mechanism applies did not, however, make it onto the selected list of 'specific areas', which seems to make sense: the combined effect of the filtering of appeals and the transfer of preliminary jurisdiction to the General Court would virtually exclude the CJEU from the interpretation of EU law in areas where an previously established body of case-law is disputed or even, clearly absent.

It is in light of these considerations that the Court's choice is understandable. The mechanism allows identification of material areas based on objective criteria to guide the first experimental phase of transferring preliminary jurisdiction to the General Court. It must, however, be noted that the methodology behind the choice of areas was far from arithmetic. The second criterion for selection – a virtual lack of litigation bringing up issues of principle – amounts to a selection criterion based on the 'constitutional' significance of an area not only because of the absence of Grand Chamber rulings but also having into account the complexity and sensitiveness of the subject matter itself. The parameters that form the basis of the system of transfer designed by the Court provide solid ground for justifying the identification of specific areas on the basis of effectiveness and also offer significant guarantees for the uniformity of the case law. The parameters' relevance goes well beyond the identification of the five concrete areas of this first request by establishing a system suitable to be applicable to future developments.

3.2. Case Allocation – The *Guichet Unique* System

One of the main arguments against the decentralisation of preliminary jurisdiction involves the 'unseverability of EU law'. As the Court itself acknowledged in its 2017 Report, cases that appear technical may hide interpretative questions that impinge upon fundamental issues or transversal questions.[24] The Reform Regulation addresses that concern through a combination of safeguards. The first safeguard has already been mentioned, namely, one of the parameters requires, for the identification of specific transferable areas, that the area be sufficiently self-contained. Additionally, for a case

[22] Today the system of Art 58a of the Statute applies to decisions of: the boards of appeals of the EU Intellectual Property Office; the Community Plant Variety Office; the European Chemicals Agency: the European Union Aviation Safety Agency. The request of the Court proposes including in that system: the EU Agency for the Cooperation of Energy Regulators; the Single Resolution Board; the European Banking Authority; the European Securities and Markets Authority; the European Insurance and Occupational Pensions Authority; the EU Agency for Railways.

[23] According to Art 58a of the Statute, an appeal shall only proceed if 'it raises an issue that is significant with respect to the unity, consistency or development of Union law'.

[24] The Court recalled, as an example, the landmark judgment of 26 February 2013, C-617/10 *Åkerberg Fransson*, EU:C:2013:105.

to be assigned to the General Court, it must 'exclusively' concern one of the specific areas. Indeed, the new Article 50b of the Statute establishes that the General Court's jurisdiction will only extend to preliminary rulings that 'come exclusively within one or several' of the specific areas mentioned above. Furthermore, the responsibility for case allocation will exclusively fall upon the CJEU itself, which is for reasons linked to legal certainty and expedition.[25] Article 50b therefore explicitly establishes that all requests under Article 267 TFEU are to be submitted to the CJEU, which will verify the 'exclusivity' criterion.

During the legislative procedure, different clarifications were added to the 'exclusivity' criterion at the request of the different institutions that participated in the legislative procedure.[26] It soon became apparent that one of the main challenges of the new system of allocation of cases would be distinguishing cases that 'purely' pertained to the specific areas from those raising horizontal matters. To provide more clarity, first, a new paragraph was inserted into Article 50b:

> [T]he Court of Justice shall retain jurisdiction to hear and determine requests for a preliminary ruling that raise independent questions relating to the interpretation of primary law, public international law, general principles of Union law or the Charter of Fundamental Rights of the European Union.

The interpretative problem is therefore shifted to the determination of the meaning of an 'independent question'.

Second, the recitals of the Reform Regulation offer more hints, albeit of purely interpretative value. The CJEU retains jurisdiction in preliminary rulings that also concern areas not listed in Article 50b (Recital 12). Issues of jurisdiction or admissibility are not considered horizontal questions and are to be decided upon by the General Court (Recital 1). Finally, the Regulation indicates, in its Recital 13, that the 'clear' determination of the type of issues that remain under the jurisdiction of the CJEU is understood as forming part of the guarantee of Article 47 of the Charter – the right to a fair and public hearing within a reasonable time by an independent and impartial tribunal previously established by law. The obligation of the Court and the General Court to 'briefly provide reasons' justifying their competence in a given case is also mentioned in Recital 15. Again, it is noteworthy that the legislature has only established such important modulations and requirements through recitals, which significantly dilutes their legal force.

Despite these clarificatory efforts, the exclusivity criterion raises a plethora of questions that are eventually expected to materialise. Tridimas has provided a quite complete and interesting account of some of these issues in a recent article,[27] and other unexpected scenarios will surely emerge as well. What if the questions of admissibility and

[25] Article 50b(2) of the proposed Regulation.

[26] See, on the vicissitudes of the legislative procedure, Martín Pérez de Nanclares (n 17). See also, S Iglesias Sánchez, 'Moving forward towards the Preliminary Ruling's Reform: Hearing before the Legal Affairs Committee of the European Parliament' *EU Law Live*, 22 May 2023, eulawlive.com/insight-moving-forward-towards-the-preliminary-rulings-reform-hearing-before-the-legal-affairs-committee-of-the-european-parliament-by-sara-iglesias-sanchez.

[27] Providing other interesting examples from the case-law, see T Tridimas, 'Sharing uniformity: A new era beckons' (2024) 1 LCEL Research Paper Series 2, www.lcel.uni.lu.

jurisdiction raise issues of principle?[28] Could these issues be rebranded as matters appertaining to primary law/Article 267 TFEU and therefore remain within the CJEU's purview? What about horizontal questions related to remedies and procedural issues? What about general principles whose effects particularly unfold in the realms of the specific areas, eg the principle of 'neutrality of VAT', or the interpretation of abuse of law in the VAT realm?

At first sight, it appears that the criterion of exclusivity, when combined with the rule of retained jurisdiction incorporated into Article 50b, does not amount to a rule of 'absolute purity' in the sense that only cases which are absolutely encapsulated in specific areas and presenting no link whatsoever with other elements of EU law are transferable. This solution may defeat the purpose of the reform, since truly 'pure' cases may be exceedingly scarce. Rather, a more reasonable approach to the exclusivity rule might employ a test based on the centre of gravity of the case which offers a solid proxy for identifying 'independent questions'. Only cases raising questions whose centre of gravity is clearly located elsewhere shall – from the point of view of the core object of the preliminary questions – reverse the rule of transfer.[29] The consolidation of this test will prove crucial for the future practice of the *guichet unique* system, since the *sole* criterion for allocation of preliminary rulings to the General Court is that of material exclusivity.

A connected discussion concerns, of course, how the 'exclusivity requirement' may affect the General Court's task of interpreting EU law, keeping in mind the CJEU's traditional freedom to reformulate questions and step aside from the specific wording of the requested order of references and provisions cited therein, when, for example, other potentially relevant areas for the solution of the case were not identified by the national referring court. Because such elements may only come up at a later stage of the procedure, the General Court itself will play a major role in the interpretation of the 'exclusivity requirement' by deciding which cases it needs to refer back to the CJEU. At this point, it is unclear how the exclusivity requirement fits with the possibility enshrined in Article 256(3) TFEU, according to which 'where the General Court considers that the case requires a decision of principle likely to affect the unity or consistency of Union law, it may refer the case to the CJEU for a ruling'.

A final remark on the role of national judges. Of course, national courts can easily circumvent the allocation system by superfluously citing different legal instruments and/or horizontal principles or fundamental rights in their order for reference. The risk of tampering with the allocation of jurisdiction by national jurisdictions that add horizontal or connected questions is real and may persist until the General Court gains the trust of its new interlocutors. The scrutiny to be carried out at the point of allocating cases promises to be both a delicate and vital task, most of all because the interconnection of EU law with fundamental rights and principles is ubiquitous and the impact of

[28] See, eg, the issues decided by the Grand Chamber in C-274/14 *Banco Santander*, EU:C:2020:17; C-132/20, *Getin Noble bank*, EU:C:2022:235; or C-718/21, *LG v Krajowa Rada Sądownictwa* EU:C:2023:1015.

[29] Besides *Åkerberg Fransson*, many other cases come to mind, such as the judgments of 8 September 2015, C-105/14 *Taricco and Others* EU:C:2015:555; of 5 December 2017, C-42/17 *MAS and MB*, EU:C:2017:936; of 2 May 2018, C-574/15 *Scialdone* EU:C:2018:295; or of 9 November 2017, C-298/16 *Ispas* EU:C:2017:843.

the many sources of EU law in a given case may well be genuine instead of a merely cosmetic addition. Given the difficulties raised by the very early stage at which the allocation will be done in the proceedings, good faith cooperation of national courts will also undoubtedly be key for the new system's success.[30]

3.3. Procedural Safeguards and Procedural Transplants

The Reform Regulation includes procedural guarantees deemed essential for the smooth functioning of the new system. The modifications of the Statute aim to ensure that both EU Courts treat preliminary rulings in the same manner. The guarantees thus seek to adapt the traditional functioning of the General Court by transplanting some of the essential elements that traditionally ensured the quality of preliminary ruling decisions at the Court,[31] a transplant that was effectuated by the amended Rules of Procedure of the General Court.[32] Two of those elements deal with the internal organisation of the General Court. The first is specialisation: according to Article 50b of the Statute, the General Court is to assign the preliminary rulings to 'chambers designated for that purpose'. The second is the addition of a new Court 'formation': Article 50 of the Statute is amended so the General Court may also sit 'in a chamber of an intermediate size between the chambers of five Judges and the Grand Chamber'. A third element inserted in Article 49a consists of systematically designating an Advocate General in all the preliminary cases to be treated by the General Court.

These measures should be welcomed. The designation of specific chambers within the General Court may facilitate specialisation and the introduction of the new procedural rules for preliminary rulings in the jurisdictional organisation of the body, whose judicial culture has been strongly influenced by the rather different needs of adjudicating direct actions. Designating special chambers is also, as the CJEU noted in its request, a practice with which the General Court is familiar, as it has already been implemented in the areas of staff cases and intellectual property law. By concentrating preliminary ruling proceedings in a limited number of chambers within the General Court, the reform therefore seeks to lay a foundation for consistency on both the procedural and material planes. Concentrating preliminary jurisdiction may mitigate the risk of poor consistency intrinsic to 'a jurisdiction with nine five-judge chambers and a tendency to solve cases in chambers of three judges'.[33] Moreover, in this system there is no recourse to appeal as a matter of principle (and only very limited possibilities of review). Restricting preliminary rulings to specific chambers may also lead to organisational practices that

[30] See, for the role of national courts, C Wissels, and T Boekestein, '"The Proof is in the Pudding": Some Thoughts on the 2024 Reform of the Statute of the Court of Justice from a Highest National Cour' *EU Law Live*, 9 July 2024, eulawlive.com/op-ed-the-proof-is-in-the-pudding-some-thoughts-on-the-2024-reform-of-the-statute-of-the-court-of-justice-from-a-highest-national-court.

[31] See C Amalfitano, 'The Transplant of Procedural Rules from the Court of Justice to the General Court' *EU Law Live*, 24 July 2024, eulawlive.com/op-ed-the-transplant-of-procedural-rules-from-the-court-of-justice-to-the-general-court.

[32] Amendments to the Rules of Procedure of the General Court of 10 July 2025 [2024] OJ L 2024/2095.

[33] Pointing at this risk, D Sarmiento, 'The Reform of the General Court: An Exercise in Minimalist (but Radical) Institutional Reform' (2017) 19 *Cambridge Yearbook of European Legal Studies* 236, 248.

help rationalise the internal allocation of cases, even though important differences with the CJEU would remain (such as the lack of a general meeting similar to the one that takes place weekly at the CJEU).[34]

After the essential elements transplanted from the Court, the second most notable novelty is making it possible for the General Court to sit in a chamber of intermediate size. One of the reasons why the Court esteemed the General Court is ripe for this new challenge is precisely due to the experience it acquired ruling in chambers of extended composition, which involve five judges rather than the traditional three-judge formation. The introduction of an intermediate-sized chamber seems in this context meant to avoid needing recourse to the Grand Chamber of the General Court (even if, in the amended rules of procedure this possibility is not excluded, and in the latest times, the General Court has increased the use of the Grand Chamber). The underlying argument, however, is that, when issues of principle emerge, the five-member panel would assess devolving the case to the CJEU rather than to the Grand Chamber of the General Court. As the Court noted in the request

> it should not be necessary to convene the Grand Chamber of the General Court in order to rule on questions transmitted to the General Court for a preliminary ruling since, first, cases requiring a decision of principle such as those that usually come within the jurisdiction of the Grand Chamber should be referred to the Court of Justice … and second, on account of the number of Judges in the Grand chamber, Judges who are not in the chambers designated for that purpose could be led to rule in preliminary ruling cases, which would be such as to undermine the guarantee referred to in the first sentence of Article 50b(3) of the Statute.

This assumption is debatable. First, that a case deserves the attention of the Grand Chamber does not necessarily mean that it raises a matter of principle affecting the unity and consistency of EU law in the sense of Article 256(3) TFEU. This is all the more apparent when the role of Grand Chambers is not even defined within EU courts.[35] Second, by eluding recourse to the Grand Chamber, the full legitimacy that Grand Chamber decisions confer is taken away, depriving the General Court of one important instrument for asserting its authority in the transferred areas, most of all, if it wished to deviate from established case-law even on a technical matter – which does not necessarily amount to a matter of principle in the sense of Article 256(3) TFEU. The introduction of a 'mini-Grand Chamber' in the form of a chamber of intermediate size also risks introducing an impression of hyperspecialisation and lack of jurisdictional unity within the General Court, creating a bipolar division or even a hierarchy between the preliminary ruling chambers and the rest. Let us not forget that the issue at stake is not just material specialisation but also, and above all, circumscribing to some chambers a specific jurisdictional avenue that goes beyond the application of specific procedural rules. Last but not least, this trend that seems to foster the encapsulation of the preliminary ruling procedure in the specialised chambers of the General Court cannot avoid that the jurisdiction as a whole gets involved in the operation of

[34] ibid 241.
[35] On the role of Grand Chambers, M Bobek, 'What Are Grand Chambers for?' (2021) 23 *Cambridge Yearbook of European Legal Studies* 1.

the new jurisdictional tasks. After all, crucial decisions, such as the decision to refer a case back to the CJEU under Article 256(3) TFEU, are to be taken by the Plenum of the General Court.[36]

The third crucial procedural safeguard (and transplant) is the assignment of every preliminary ruling case to an Advocate General. The possibility of appointing a judge of the General Court as an Advocate General is already foreseen in Article 49 of the Statute,[37] but its use has been extremely sparse.[38] The proposal of the Court ensures that this will change now that every preliminary ruling case will be assigned to an Advocate General at the General Court. As is the case in the CJEU, having an Advocate General does not necessarily mean that there will be an Opinion in every case. Indeed, according to Article 20 of the Statute, Opinions are reserved for cases raising new points of law. That the selected areas already benefit from an established body of case law will in practice limit the number of Opinions.[39] However, the role of Advocates General at the CJEU goes well beyond the drafting of opinions. It is crucial when it comes to resolving different procedural questions all along the judicial procedure. Besides, as the Court itself points out, the added value is an extra pair of eyes: an Advocate General will 'usefully supplement, qualify or enrich the analysis carried out by the Judge-Rapporteur in his or her preliminary report'. The main challenges for this legal transplant come from the different statutory regime of Advocates General at the CJEU and at the General Court, where the judges designated to be Advocates General will remain, at the end of the day, judges, perpetuating, at least to some extent, the 'double personality' challenge that led the General Court to abandon the practice of designating Advocates General at that Court in the past.[40]

3.4. The Review Procedure

The review procedure, which seemed dead and buried after the elimination of the Civil Service Tribunal, is primed for reappearance, and moreover to play a central or at least more crucial role than it had in its previous period of application. And yet, the review procedure remains almost untouched. The reform does not substantially modify the review procedure, which has been available since Nice, and Article 256(3) TFEU already sets itself that

> decisions given by the General Court on questions referred for a preliminary ruling may exceptionally be subject to review by the CJEU, under the conditions and within the limits laid down by the Statute, where there is a serious risk of the unity or consistency of Union law being affected.

[36] Article 207(3)–(4) of the amended Rules of Procedure of the General Court.

[37] See also Arts 30–31 of the Rules of Procedure of the General Court.

[38] So far, this possibility has been only used in four cases in the 1990s: T-24/90 *Automec v Commission* EU:T:1992:39; T-120/89 *Stahlwerke Peine-Salzgitter v Commission* EU:T:1991:6; T-51/89 *Tetra Pak Rausing v Commission* EU:T:1990:15 and T-1/89 *Rhône-Poulenc v Commission* EU:T:1991:88.

[39] In fact, fewer than half of the cases in the selected areas in the last five years have had an Opinion, according to the data in Annex 3 to the Request.

[40] J Wildemeersch, 'The (new) role of the Advocate General at the General Court' *EU Law Live*, 16 July 2024, eulawlive.com/op-ed-the-new-role-of-the-advocate-general-at-the-general-court/4.

The basic tenets of the review procedure, laid down in Articles 62 to 62b of the Statute, also remain in place. The reform request submitted by the CJEU did not contemplate any changes and merely recalled that review should be exceptional, since the main proceedings remain at the national level. The rule of principle should be, by consequence, that the decisions of the General Court are final.[41] The amendments to the Rules of Procedure of the Court of Justice currently only contemplate a minor modification in the review procedure, one that responds to pragmatic concerns. The modification clarifies that the Registrar will inform the General Court, the parties and the referring court when no proposal to review has been made by the First Advocate General, so communication that the General Court's decision has become final is transparent.[42]

Continuity in the review procedure seems to be the rule, at least, procedurally speaking. All preliminary decisions by the General Court will be scrutinised by the First Advocate General, on whose proposal the Court will decide whether or not to carry out a review.[43] In the absence of such a proposal for review, the answers of the General Court will take effect after a maximum period of two months.[44] The Court will have to rule by means of an urgent procedure, with the intervention of the parties of Article 23 of the Statute as well as those parties to the proceedings before the General Court.[45] The effects of the answers subject to review will only take effect after that procedure, but the Court can decide otherwise. Finally, if found that 'the unity and consistency of Union law' has been affected, then the answers of the Court will supersede those of the General Court.[46]

The interpretation of what may affect the unity and consistency of EU law will likely take inspiration from past application of the same criteria, but the obvious differences of the new situation (taking into account the broader interpretative effects of preliminary rulings, as well as the wider areas of law in which the procedure is to apply) may lead the CJEU to reconsider the strictness with which such criteria have been applied in the past. How the future interpretation of those criteria will unfold in the light of the growing practice within the system of filtering of appeals also remains to be seen, in particular because these criteria also partly rely on the preservation of unity and consistency albeit using a lower standard (not the 'serious risk' standard, but that of 'raising an issue which is significant', not only for the unity and consistency, but also for the 'development of Union law').

For the reform to fulfil its objective, in any case, the workload inevitably entailed by the review procedure must be offset by the benefits of the transfer of preliminary rulings, meaning that review needs to be truly exceptional.

[41] Page 6 of the Request.

[42] Amendments to the Rules of Procedure of the Court of Justice [2024] OJ L 2024/2094.

[43] Article 62 of the Statute.

[44] According to the second paragraph of Art 62b. The first AG may make the proposal after one month of delivery of the decision; and within one month of receiving the proposal of the first AG, the Court shall decide. That means that were no proposal made by the first AG, the ruling of the General Court may already have effect after the first month.

[45] Article 62a of the Statute.

[46] Second paragraph of Art 62b of the Statute.

4. The Future of the Preliminary Ruling Procedure

The reform proposed by the CJEU marks a new chapter in the history of the EU judicial architecture. The impact of the reform will be difficult to gauge if its success is measured only in terms of numerical effectiveness. Indeed, the estimation of the number of cases to be transferred is based on retrospective projection without any grounds for predicting the numbers will remain constant. Except in the VAT area, the numbers of cases in the rest of the 'specific areas' remain modest. The real impact of this reform, however, resides in its groundbreaking character as a matter of principle: once the system is decentralised and reticence progressively fades away, the regime could be extended to more areas. The 2024 Reform Regulation therefore represents the spearhead of preliminary jurisdiction at the General Court: the ultimate raison d'être of the reform lies in devising a testing ground for reconfiguration of the preliminary ruling procedure in a future where the CJEU will be able to concentrate on its constitutional role by virtue of the partial 'deconstitutionalisaton' of the preliminary ruling procedure.[47] In this context, some broader systemic considerations are worth mention.

First, the transfer of preliminary rulings to the General Court will affect the identity of the different actors in the EU judicial system. The long-standing reticence towards transferring jurisdiction over the instrument, paradigmatically heralded by AG Ruiz-Jarabo in *de Coster*,[48] is related to the perceived constitutional role of the preliminary ruling procedure. It is true that the procedure was inspired at inception by the procedures of control of constitutionality through questions of unconstitutionality to national constitutional courts. However, the scope of preliminary rulings goes far beyond the scope of constitutional matters, as *Pyjamas*, *Toilet paper*[49] and many other cases make abundantly clear. While the CJEU has been characterised as a non-specialised court that rules on constitutional matters and other cases,[50] the reform proposal certainly frees it from part of its general preliminary jurisdiction so it can devote more resources to its constitutional function.[51]

Second, the transfer of preliminary rulings to the General Court consolidates a trend that began in the days of the Civil Service Tribunal, and that continued with the setting

[47] See S Iglesias and D Sarmiento, 'A new model for the EU judiciary: decentralising preliminary rulings as a paradoxical move towards the constitutionalisation of the Court of Justice' *EU Law Live*, 8 July 2024, eulawlive.com/insight-a-new-model-for-the-eu-judiciary-decentralising-preliminary-rulings-as-a-paradoxical-move-towards-the-constitutionalisation-of-the-court-of-justice-by-sara-iglesias-a.

[48] Opinion of 28 June 2001, C-17/00 *de Coster* EU:C:2021;366, pts 73–74, as well as his extrajudicial writings cited in fn 95 of that Opinion.

[49] See judgment of 20 November 1997, C-338/95 *Wiener SI* EU:C:1997:552 and the Opinion of AG Jacobs in that case, as well as judgment of 10 November 2016, Joined Cases C-313/15 and C-530/15 *Eco-Emballages SA* EU:C:2016:859.

[50] M Rosenfeld, 'Comparing Constitutional Review by the European Court of Justice and the U.S. Supreme Court] in I Pernice, J Kokott and C Saunders (eds), *The Future of the European Judicial System in a Comparative Perspective* (Baden Baden, Nomos, 2006) 33–63, 40.

[51] D Sarmiento, 'On the Road to a Constitutional Court of the European Union: The Court of Justice After the Transfer of the Preliminary Reference Jurisdiction to the General Court' (2023) 19 *Croatian Yearbook of European Law and Policy* 7.

up of the system of filtering of appeals. The General Court shares with the CJEU an apex court role in specific areas of law[52] where cassation before the latter is only possible in exceptional circumstances 'in the interest of the law'. The reform will therefore not only mark the coming of age of the reformed General Court, but also a considerable transformation in its own perception and identity. The General Court will have to adapt its working methods and internal organisational structure. Even more importantly, it will have to hone its style as a new interlocutor in the otherwise already well-established world of judicial dialogue with national courts.

The ensuing interaction between the two EU judicial bodies will progressively approach the relationship between a constitutional and a supreme court, without neglecting, notwithstanding, the additional complexity and the peculiarities of the EU judicial system. As is often the case in the institutional architecture of the EU, the competences, responsibilities and functions of EU bodies are unique and do not correspond to a predetermined model or national framework of reference. Both EU Courts will be, in principle, supreme, in their respective areas of preliminary ruling jurisdiction. Both Courts will also in part be constitutional for that matter, because the General Court is not barred from interpreting Treaty provisions that fall within the exclusive realm of the specific areas under its jurisdiction. The risk of diverging interpretations – to which we are accustomed in the European constitutional space – must be avoided, even if some divergence is inevitable. Although such a scenario may not immediately sound the preliminary ruling procedure's death knell,[53] both EU Courts shall be extremely careful. The review system, the last resort safety valve, will play a much more paramount role than ever before. The criteria for the interpretation of what constitutes a risk for the unity and consistency of EU law may have to be clarified or even revisited, keeping in mind the particularly intense effects of preliminary rulings for the uniform interpretation of EU law.

Finally, another – not as obvious – element in the background of this reform is the ongoing discussion on the allocation of roles in the preliminary ruling procedure. The Court is repeatedly seized by cases where it faces both questions relating to the application and the interpretation of EU law, with different voices pointing to the need to concentrate the Court's role in interpretation, whereas application should remain with national courts. In this context, proposals to reconsider *CILFIT*[54] have emerged as part of an attempt to return some responsibility to national courts,[55] even though the main pillars of that landmark ruling still hold.[56] In this broader debate on the rationalisation of the role of the CJEU in the preliminary ruling procedure, an implicit connection is made between the Court's refusal to limit national court 'input' and its capacity to keep its own level of 'output' up to match it. The implicit choice is for a concentrated

[52] In this sense, Martín y Pérez de Nanclares (n 17). On this debate, S Iglesias Sánchez, 'Shared Jurisdiction of EU Courts over Preliminary Rulings: One procedure. Two Courts. One Interpretation?' (2024) 3–4 *Review of European Administrative Law* 75.

[53] As announced by AG Ruiz-Jarabo in *de Coster* (n 48).

[54] Judgment of 6 October 1982, C-283/81 *Srl CILFIT and Lanificio di Gavardo SpA v Ministry of Health* EU:C:1982:335.

[55] See the proposal in this sense in the Opinion of Advocate General Bobek of 15 April 2021 in C-561/19 *Consorzio Italian Management* EU:C:2021:291 and the Opinion of Advocate General Emiliou of 18 June 2024 in C-144/23 *Kubera* EU:C:2024:522. On this debate, see FX Millet, 'Cilfit still fits' (2022) 18 *European Constitutional Law Review* 533.

[56] Judgment of 6 October 2021, C-561/19 *Consorzio Italian Management* EU:C:2021:799.

interpretative model that avoids sharing interpretative tasks with last instance national courts, opting instead for deconcentration at the level of EU courts. As Tridimas points out, with the transfer to the General Court:

> The risk of fragmentation is more contained as the GC is part of the same judicial structure, owes no allegiance to any national legal order, and poses no risk of rebellion. It is a managed delegation that is designed not to challenge the CJ.[57]

This reform entails therefore a significant choice not only for the division of tasks among EU courts, but probably most importantly, although perhaps less visibly, for the interaction between those courts and their national interlocutors. Ensuring the survival and pre-eminence of the preliminary ruling procedure as a means for uniform interpretation requires not only preserving but also enhancing its output in terms of effectiveness and quality at the central level. The reform, even at the expense of internal decentralisation, reflects a strong commitment to a centralised system of interpretation.

Bibliography

Alonso García, R 'The Persian Jurist in Luxembourg. On the Decentralisation of the Preliminary Ruling Procedure' (2024) 195 *EU Law Live Weekend Edition*, eulawlive.com/weekend-edition/weekend-edition-no195.

Amalfitano, C 'The Transplant of Procedural Rules from the Court of Justice to the General Court', *EU Law Live*, 24 July 2024, eulawlive.com/op-ed-the-transplant-of-procedural-rules-from-the-court-of-justice-to-the-general-court.

Bobek, M, 'Preliminary rulings before the General Court: What judicial architecture for the European Union?' (2023) 60 *Common Market Law Review* 1515.

—— 'What Are Grand Chambers for?' (2021) 23 *Cambridge Yearbook of European Legal Studies* 1.

Bradley, K, 'The Court of Justice appeal filter mechanism and effective judicial protection: throwing out the baby with the bathwater?" *EU Law Live*, 1 July 2024, eulawlive.com/the-court-of-justice-appeal-filter-mechanism-and-effective-judicial-protection-throwing-out-the-baby-with-the-bathwater.

Butler, G, 'An Interim Post-Mortem: Specialised Courts in the EU Judicial Architecture after the Civil Service Tribunal' (2020) 17 *International Organizations Law Review* 586.

Dermine, P, 'Transparency and Openness at the Court of Justice – Towards ex post Publicity of Parties' Observations' *EU Law Live*, 19 July 2024, eulawlive.com/op-ed-transparency-and-openness-at-the-court-of-justice-towards-ex-post-publicity-of-parties-observations.

Iglesias Sánchez, S, 'Moving forward towards the Preliminary Ruling's Reform: Hearing before the Legal Affairs Committee of the European Parliament' *EU Law Live*, 22 May 2023, eulawlive.com/insight-moving-forward-towards-the-preliminary-rulings-reform-hearing-before-the-legal-affairs-committee-of-the-european-parliament-by-sara-iglesias-sanchez.

—— 'Preliminary Rulings before the General Court. Crossing the last frontier of the reform of the EU judicial system?' (2022) 125 *EU Law Live Weekend Edition*, eulawlive.com/weekend-edition/weekend-edition-no125.

[57] T Tridimas, 'Sharing uniformity: A new era beckons' (2024) 1 LCEL Research Paper Series 2, www.lcel.uni.lu.

S Iglesias Sánchez, 'Shared Jurisdiction of EU Courts over Preliminary Rulings: One procedure. Two Courts. One Interpretation?' (2024) 3–4 *Review of European Administrative Law* 75.
Iglesias S and Sarmiento D, 'A new model for the EU judiciary: decentralising preliminary rulings as a paradoxical move towards the constitutionalisation of the Court of Justice' *EU Law Live*, 8 April 2024, eulawlive.com/insight-a-new-model-for-the-eu-judiciary-decentralising-preliminary-rulings-as-a-paradoxical-move-towards-the-constitutionalisation-of-the-court-of-justice-by-sara-iglesias-a.
Johnston, A, 'Judicial Reform and the Treaty of Nice' (2001) 38 *Common Market Law Review* 499.
Lenaerts, K, 'The Unity of European Law and the Overload of the ECJ – the System of Preliminary Rulings Revisited' in I Pernice, J Kokott and C Saunders (eds), *The Future of the European Judicial System in a Comparative Perspective* (Baden Baden, Nomos, 2006) 211–39.
Martín y Pérez de Nanclares, J, 'La reforma del Tribunal de Justicia de la Unión Europea: La ruptura de un tabú' (2024) 90 *Revista Española De Derecho Europeo* 21.
Millet, FX 'Cilfit still fits' (2022) 18 *European Constitutional Law Review* 533.
Oró Martínez, C, 'The Filtering of Appeals by the Court of Justice: Taking Stock of the First Two Orders Allowing an Appeal to Proceed' (2022) 112 *EU Law Live Weekend Edition*.
Rodríguez Iglesias, GC, 'L'avenir du système juridictionnel de l'Union européenne' (1999) 35 *Cahiers de droit européen* 275.
Rosenfeld, M, 'Comparing Constitutional Review by the European Court of Justice and the U.S. Supreme Court' in I Pernice, J Kokott and C Saunders (eds), *The Future of the European Judicial System in a Comparative Perspective* (Baden Baden, Nomos, 2006) 33–63.
Sarmiento, D, 'On the Road to a Constitutional Court of the European Union: The Court of Justice After the Transfer of the Preliminary Reference Jurisdiction to the General Court' (2023) 19 *Croatian Yearbook of European Law and Policy* 7.
—— 'The Reform of the General Court: An Exercise in Minimalist (but Radical) Institutional Reform' (2017) 19 *Cambridge Yearbook of European Legal Studies* 236.
Tridimas, T, 'Breaking with Tradition: Preliminary Reference Reform and the New Judicial Architecture' *EU Law Live*, 26 June 2024, eulawlive.com/op-ed-breaking-with-tradition-preliminary-reference-reform-and-the-new-judicial-architecture.
—— 'Sharing uniformity: A new era beckons' (2024) 1 LCEL Research Paper Series 2, www.lcel.uni.lu.
Wildemeersch, J, 'The (new) role of the Advocate General at the General Court' *EU Law Live*, 16 July 2024, eulawlive.com/op-ed-the-new-role-of-the-advocate-general-at-the-general-court/4.
Wissels, C and Boekestein, T, '"The Proof is in the Pudding": Some Thoughts on the 2024 Reform of the Statute of the Court of Justice from a Highest National Cour' *EU Law Live*, 9 July 2024, eulawlive.com/op-ed-the-proof-is-in-the-pudding-some-thoughts-on-the-2024-reform-of-the-statute-of-the-court-of-justice-from-a-highest-national-court.

7

The Jurisdiction of the Court of Justice of the European Union in the Field of Common Foreign and Security Policy

JAVIER DÍEZ-HOCHLEITNER

1. Introduction*

According to Article 24.1 of the Treaty on European Union (TEU) and the first paragraph of Article 275 of the Treaty on the Functioning of the European Union (TFEU), the jurisdiction of the Court of Justice of the European Union (CJEU) does not cover Common Foreign and Security Policy (CFSP). However, both provisions establish two exceptions; one when affirming the jurisdiction of the CJEU to ensure respect for Article 40 TEU; and another to review the legality of decisions adopted by the Council that introduce restrictive measures against natural or legal persons. As its case law unfolds, however, the CJEU has been 'discovering' that its jurisdiction in the field of the CFSP actually extends beyond what is established, in a literal reading, by the Treaties.

More specifically, the CJEU has: (i) acknowledged the possible use of mechanisms other than that contemplated in Article 263 TFEU to question the validity of CFSP decisions that involve restrictive measures against individuals; or (ii) asserted its competence to control the legality of certain acts adopted within the framework of the CFSP that do not impose restrictive measures. As regards the first issue, the CJEU has not only admitted the validity of challenging acts imposing restrictive measures by means of the plea of illegality or by reference for a preliminary ruling, but has even maintained its jurisdiction to hear non-contractual liability actions seeking compensation from the Union for damages caused by such measures. As for the second issue – the precise boundaries of the objective scope of its jurisdiction – the CJEU has gone so far as to affirm on several occasions its jurisdiction to review the legality of acts adopted within the scope of the CFSP that do not impose restrictive measures but which, in the CJEU's opinion, do not 'genuinely' constitute CFSP acts, and to hear claims for damages arising from such acts as well.

* Author's note: this study does not refer to the judgments of the CJEU of 10 September 2024 in *News 77 Solutions* case (C-351/22) and *KS and KD* case (C-20/22 P and C-44/22 P), but only to the opinions of AG Capeta, because it was sent to print prior to that date. Consequently, the reading of this study should be completed with an analysis of said judgments.

In this chapter I will review the CJEU case law surrounding its jurisdiction in the field of the CFSP and explore how far its doctrine could – or should – evolve, with particular attention to Article 47 of the Charter of Fundamental Rights (CFR) (together with Article 6 of the European Convention on Human Rights; ECHR), as well as Article 41.3 CFR, according to which:

> Every person has the right to have the Community make good any damage caused by its institutions or by its servants in the performance of their duties, in accordance with the general principles common to the laws of the Member States.

2. Evolution of the Case Law of the CJEU as Regards its Jurisdiction to Review the Legality of CFSP Acts

2.1. Expansion of the Remedies Available to Challenge CFSP Acts Imposing Restrictive Measures against Natural or Legal Persons

In 2014, the General Court stated in the *National Iranian Oil Company* case that bringing a plea of illegality against a decision of general nature imposing restrictive measures was not excluded, arguing that the reference in Article 275 TFEU to Council decisions imposing restrictive measures against individuals does not distinguish between general and individual measures.[1] This possibility is irrespective of whether all natural persons or entities in a regulation providing for restrictive measures have standing to challenge the legality of the regulation since, according to well-established CJEU case law starting with the 2008 *Kadi and Al Barakaat* judgment, that act is equivalent to a set of individual decisions affecting each and all of them.[2]

With regard to the possibility of challenging the legality of CFSP acts imposing restrictive measures through requests for preliminary rulings, the CJEU broadened access to this mechanism in *Rosneft*,[3] and in doing so departed from the Opinions of several Advocate Generals.[4] The CJEU based its decision on three central arguments. First, the CJEU ruled, Article 24.1 TEU does not refer to Article 275 TFEU in order to determine the type of procedure under which the Court may review the legality of certain decisions (ie the action of annulment of Article 263 TFEU, to which Article 275 expressly refers), 'but rather the type of decisions whose legality may be reviewed by the Court, within any procedure that has as its aim such a review of legality'.[5] Second, per the CJEU, the review of the legality of acts of the Union is based on two complementary

[1] Case T-578/12 *National Iranian Oil Company v Council of the EU* EU:T:2014:678, para 93.

[2] Joined Cases C-402/05 P and C-415/05 P *Yassin Abdullah Kadi and Al Barakaat International Foundation v Council of the EU and Commission of the EC* (Grand Chamber) EU:C:2008:461, paras 241–44.

[3] Case C-72/15 *PJSC Rosneft Oil Company v Her Majesty's Treasury and Others* (Grand Chamber) EU:C:2017:236.

[4] I refer to the Opinion of AG J. Kokott in Opinion procedure 2/13 on the *Accession of the EU to the ECHR* EU:C:2014:2475, paras 89–103, to her Opinion in Case C-263/14 *European Parliament v Council of the EU* case (Agreement between the EU and Tanzania) EU:C:2015:728, fn 15, and to the Opinion of AG N. Wahl in Case C-455/14 P *H v Council of the EU and Others* case EU:C:2016:212, para 79. On the contrary, in *Rosneft*, AG M Wathelet favoured the decision finally adopted by the CJEU, Opinion in Case C-72/15 *Rosneft* ECLI:EU:C:2016:381, paras 61–66.

[5] Case C-72/15 *Rosneft* (n 3) para 70.

judicial procedures (the action for annulment and the reference for a preliminary ruling), being that:

> It is inherent in that complete system of legal remedies and procedures that persons bringing proceedings must, when an action is brought before a national court or tribunal, have the right to challenge the legality of provisions contained in European Union acts on which a decision or national measure adopted in respect of them is based, pleading the invalidity of that decision or measure, in order that the national court or tribunal, having itself no jurisdiction to declare such invalidity, consults the Court on that matter by means of a reference for a preliminary ruling, unless those persons unquestionably had the right to bring an action against those provisions on the basis of Article 263 TFEU and failed to exercise that right within the period prescribed.[6]

The CJEU's third argument focused on the principle of effective judicial protection enshrined in Article 47 CFR. This principle, the Court argued, calls for a restrictive interpretation of the clauses excluding the jurisdiction of the CJEU in the field of the CFSP (the 'carve-out' clauses contained in paragraph 1 of Article 24 TEU and Article 275 TFEU): 'Since', the judgment reads, 'the purpose of the procedure that enables the Court to give preliminary rulings is to ensure that in the interpretation and application of the Treaties the law is observed, in accordance with the duty assigned to the Court under Article 19(1) TEU, it would be contrary to the objectives of that provision and to the principle of effective judicial protection to adopt a strict interpretation of the jurisdiction conferred on the Court by the second paragraph of Article 275 TFEU'.[7] The CJEU thus offered an interpretation of the Treaties far removed from the wording of Article 275 TFEU in which, in addition to closely relating the action of annulment to the preliminary reference on validity, the fundamental right to effective judicial protection had indisputable weight.[8]

On this point, we cannot fail to point out that the CJEU has yet to rule on the *Neves 77* case,[9] which raises the question of the admissibility of references for preliminary rulings on interpretation in this field. In favour of a positive response might be the value of coherence and unity in the interpretation of the Treaties, for which the preliminary ruling on validity and the preliminary ruling on interpretation are intimately connected,[10] as well as, *a fortiori*, the maxim *a maiore ad minus*.[11] However,

[6] Ibid para 67.

[7] Case C-72/15 *Rosneft* (n 3) para 75.

[8] For an analysis of the *Rosneft* judgment, see: P Andrés Sáenz de Santamaría, 'Mejorando la lex imperfecta: tutela judicial efectiva y cuestión prejudicial en la PESC (A propósito del asunto Rosneft)' (2017) 58 *Revista de Derecho Comunitario Europeo* 871; C Martínez Capdevila 'La sentencia en el asunto Rosneft: el TJUE maximiza su jurisdicción en la PESC (a costa de la coherencia con su propia jurisprudencia)' (2018) 67 *Revista Española de Derecho Europeo* 95; P Koutrakos *Judicial Review in the EU's Common Foreign and Security Policy*, ICLQ no 67 (2018) 1, 16 ff; and S Poli, 'The Common Foreign Security Policy after Rosneft: Still imperfect but gradually subject to the Rule of Law' (2017) 54 *Common Market Law Review* 1799.

[9] Reference for a preliminary ruling from the *Tribunalul București* (Romania) lodged on 31 May 2022, Case C-351/22 *Neves 77 Solutions SRL v Agenția Națională de Administrare Fiscală – Direcția Generală Antifraudă Fiscală*.

[10] See J Martín y Pérez de Nanclares, 'El control jurisdiccional del TJUE en materia de medidas restrictivas adoptadas en el ámbito de la PESC: el equilibrio entre efectividad y legalidad' (2023) 75 *Revista de Derecho Comunitario Europeo* 91, 107; and C Breitler, 'Jurisdiction in CFSP Matters – Conquering the Gallic Village One Case at a Time?' *European Law Blog* 13 October 2022, 1.

[11] See, in this regard, Opinion of AG M Wathelet Case C-72/15 *Rosneft* (n 3) para 75.

Attorney General Capeta takes the opposite view in two of her Opinions, *Neves 77* and *KS and KD*,[12] although she does affirm the jurisdiction of the CJEU to interpret general principles of EU law and fundamental rights as expressed in the Charter (even if the Court's interpretation addresses a national court's assessment of the lawfulness of national measures that implement CFSP acts).[13]

2.2. Extending the Objective Scope of the Jurisdiction of the CJEU Beyond Restrictive Measures

The CJEU has not only gained more power to review acts of the CFSP that impose restrictive measures through its case law by expanding the mechanisms and means of appeal those measures can be challenged. It has also widened the very object of review (beyond such measures).[14] Thus, the CJEU, in its 2015 *Elitaliana* judgment, claimed jurisdiction to hear an action for annulment against measures taken by the EU Rule of Law Mission in Kosovo ('Eulex Kosovo') – which was established by Council Joint Action 2008/124/CFSP – involving the choice of tenderer for a public contract. The CJEU began its reasoning by pointing out, as it did in *Rosneft*, that Article 24.1 TEU and Article 275 TFEU, in so far as they introduce an exception to the rule of general jurisdiction that Article 19 TEU confers on the CJEU, must be interpreted restrictively.[15] Starting from that premise, the CJEU then referred to the specific nature of the measures in question, stressing that 'It follows from Article 16(2) of Joint Action 2008/124 that '[a]ll expenditure' of the Eulex Kosovo Mission 'shall be managed in accordance with the rules and procedures applicable to the general budget of the [EU]', and concluded that

> the measures at issue, whose annulment was sought on the basis of an infringement of the rules of EU public procurement law, related to the award of a public contract which gave rise to expenditure to be charged to the European Union budget. Accordingly, the contract at issue is subject to the provisions of the Financial Regulation.[16]

Moreover, in its 2016 *H v Council* judgment, the CJEU set aside an order of the General Court denying the General Court's jurisdiction to hear an action for annulment of two decisions of the Chief of Personnel of the EU Police Mission (EUPM) in Bosnia-Herzegovina through which the appellant, an Italian judge seconded to the EUPM in Sarajevo, had been reassigned. The CJEU ruled that the acts of personnel management in question did not fall within the scope of the 'carve-out' merely because they were part of an operational action of the Union adopted and carried out within the

[12] Opinions of T Capeta in Case C-351/22 *Neves 77* ECLI:EU:C:2023:907, paras 67–70, and in Joined Cases C-29/22 P and C-44/22 P *KS and KD v Council of the EU, European Commission and EEAS* ECLI:EU:C:2023:901, para 122.

[13] Opinion of AG T Capeta in Case C-351/22 *Neves 77* (n 12) para 48.

[14] For a critical analysis of the case law of the CJEU in this regard, see Koutrakos (n 8).

[15] Case C-439/13 P *Elitaliana SpA v Eulex Kosovo* EU:C:2015:753, para 43.

[16] Ibid paras 46–48.

framework of the CFSP. Starting from the finding that EU agents seconded to the EUPM remained subject to the Staff Regulations of the EU, the Court pointed out that:

> In those circumstances, the scope of the limitation, by way of derogation, on the Court's jurisdiction ... cannot be considered to be so extensive as to exclude the jurisdiction of the EU judicature to review acts of staff management relating to staff members seconded by the Member States the purpose of which is to meet the needs of that mission at theatre level, when the EU judicature has, in any event, jurisdiction to review such acts where they concern staff members seconded by the EU institutions.[17]

In this case, the *ratio decidendi* of the CJEU was also marked by the emphasis on carrying out a restrictive interpretation of the exception, derived from the fundamental right to effective judicial protection, to the general rule of Article 19 TEU in the field of the CFSP. Thus, the Court noted that:

> [A]s is apparent from both Article 2 TEU, which is included in the common provisions of the EU Treaty, and Article 21 TEU, concerning the European Union's external action, to which Article 23 TEU, relating to the CFSP, refers, the European Union is founded, in particular, on the values of equality and the rule of law ... The very existence of effective judicial review designed to ensure compliance with provisions of EU law is inherent in the existence of the rule of law ...[18]

Along the same line, in its 2020 *EU Satellite Centre* judgment, the CJEU stated, in more general terms, that the provisions of the Treaties relating to the CFSP 'must be interpreted restrictively and the scope of the derogation which they establish cannot be considered so extensive as to exclude the jurisdiction of the EU judicature to review acts of staff management'.[19]

However convincing, in none of the last three cases mentioned could the contested measures be considered as falling within the scope of the limited jurisdictional control that the second paragraph of Article 275 TFEU grants to the CJEU in the field of the CFSP (the 'claw-back'). The measures in question could in no way be assimilated to restrictive measures or qualified as decisions adopted in execution of restrictive measures. What then is the *rationale* underlying the CJEU doctrine in those cases?

By following the wording of the CJEU judgments, one way that some authors have proposed to make sense of them surmises that the contested acts 'are not "CFSP acts" in the strict sense, adopted on a CFSP legal basis, but are instead part of the EU's general administrative machinery, including in particular financial and personnel procedures' and, therefore, 'essentially pertains to rules within the CJEU's jurisdiction'.[20] This approach, however, does not fully convince me because, in the end, they imply considering – without a clear basis – that acts adopted in the field of the CFSP do not

[17] Judgment of the CJEU (Grand Chamber), Case C-455/14 P *H v Council* ECLI:EU:C:2016:569, paras 44–45. See T Verellen, 'H v. Council: Strengthening the Rule of Law in the Sphere of the CFSP, One Step at a Time' (2016) 1 *European Papers* 1041.

[18] Case C-455/14 P *H v Council* (n 17) para 41.

[19] Case C-14/19 P *European Union Satellite Centre v KF*, EU:C:2020:492, para 66.

[20] Cremona (2017), at p. 685 and 696.

comprise CFSP acts if their sole purpose is the administrative implementation that occurs subsequent to 'genuine' actions in foreing and security policy.

I find more persuasive the point of view that Advocate General Capeta advances in her recent *KS and KD* Opinion. Instead of denying the CFSP nature of such measures, the Advocate General proposes – following the position defended by the Council and the European External Action Service in their interventions – distinguishing between 'political or strategic decisions' and 'merely administrative CFSP measures' in order to make explicit a distinction that 'might reflect the intention of the authors of the Treaties to keep the EU Courts away from influencing policy choices in the area of foreign relations'.[21] In this regard, Advocate General Capeta argues that 'it is not the prerogative of courts to replace policy choices made by competent political institutions', warning that this is also true for any area of EU law.[22]

Apart from distinguishing 'political or strategic decisions' from 'merely administrative CFSP measures' when delimiting the scope of the CJEU 'cave-out' in the field of CFSP – a distinction that I share and believe better explains the *Elitriana* and *H v Council* judgments – Advocate General Capeta also argues in favour of an extensive interpretation of the second paragraph of Article 275 TFEU to include any CFSP measure which restricts the rights of individuals.[23] To back up this interpretation of Article 275 TFEU, Advocate General Capeta argues that second paragraph 'should not be interpreted as a "claw-back" provision, which restores the "normal" state of the EU Courts' jurisdiction in enumerated situations', but rather 'as a provision that informs the interpretation of the scope of the jurisdictional limitation under Article 24(1) TEU and the first paragraph of Article 275 TFEU', and that, as such, it must be interpreted broadly.[24] On the basis of this framing of the provision, the Advocate General claims that the reference to actions for annulment in respect of restrictive measures against individuals in the second paragraph of Article 275 TFEU can be understood 'in a broader sense as requiring that the jurisdiction of the EU Courts cannot be limited in respect of the legality review of CFSP measures which restrict the rights of individual'.

In this regard, Advocate General Carpeta argues that a 'plausible explanation for including verbatim only actions for annulment brought by individuals against restrictive measures is that at the time of the adoption of the Lisbon Treaty, due to the *Kadi* case law, possible breaches of individuals' rights by restrictive measures was an obvious example'.[25] In my view, an extensive interpretation of the second paragraph of

[21] Opinion of AG T. Capeta in Joined Cases C-29/22 P and C-44/22 P *KS and KD*, (n 12), paras 111-112.

[22] Ibid, paras 114-115. In contrast, in his Opinion in Case C-455/14 P *H. v Council*, AG N. Whal rejected – in response to an argument made by the European Commission – a possible distinction between "acts of sovereign foreign policy" (or "*actes de gouvernement*") and acts of implementation for the purpose of excluding only the former from the jurisdiction of the CJEU, claiming 'the absence of any reference in the Treaties or in the relevant case-law of the CJEU' to such a distinction; Opinion cited above at n 4, paras 60 and subsq.

[23] Opinion of AG T. Capeta Joined Cases C-29/22 P and C-44/22 P *KS and KD*, cited above at n 12, para 131.

[24] Ibid, paras 127 and 129.

[25] Ibid, paras 131–132. See in the same sense M Cremona 'Effective Judicial Review Is of the Essence of the Rule of Law: Challenging Common Foreign and Security Policy Measures Before the Court of Justice' (2017) 2 *European Papers* 671, 685 and 696.

Article 275 TFEU so as to include any CFSP measure restricting the rights of natural or legal persons, is required by Article 47 of the Charter.

Furthermore, Advocate General Carpeta also understands that the EU courts' jurisdiction covers the review of the legality of any CFSP act, even if it includes a political or strategic decision, when the act possibly infringes a fundamental right enshrined in the CFR. In this regard, Advocate General Carpeta emphasises that, according to CJEU case law, the values expressed in Article 2 TEU apply to the CFSP,[26] so that:

> If the purpose of the jurisdictional limitation in the CFSP is to prevent the EU Courts from intervening in political and strategic decisions in the area of the CFSP, such a purpose does not require the exclusion of jurisdiction to review alleged breaches of fundamental rights.[27]

I do not share this view. Nor do I agree that:

> In order to ensure the effective judicial protection of individuals who claim that their fundamental rights, as guaranteed by the EU legal order, have been infringed by EU institutions or bodies in the exercise of the CFSP, the EU Courts must, in principle, have jurisdiction to hear such claims.[28]

In my opinion, the effective judicial protection of natural and legal persons (Article 47 CFR) is ensured if we admit, as proposed above, that the second paragraph of Article 275 TFEU includes the control of legality of any CFSP measure which restricts the rights of individuals, at the request of persons directly and individually concerned.

On the other hand, asserting the jurisdiction of the CJEU over any CFSP act that may infringe a fundamental right goes far beyond the provisions of the Treaties and would entail: (i) not only admitting possible challenge by any Member State and by the EU Institutions referred to in Article 263 TFEU of CFSP decisions of a political nature (it would be difficult for an individual to prove being directly and individually affected by decisions of this nature); but also (ii) the admissibility of any action of appeal against any CFSP act when violation of a fundamental right is alleged (even if the claim would eventually be dismissed).

2.3. Decisions of the Council Concluding International Agreements in the Field of the CFSP

The 2014 CJEU judgment in *European Parliament v Council of the EU (Agreement with Mauritius)* deals with a different issue. In that case, the CJEU declared itself competent to hear an action for annulment against Decision 2011/640/CFSP – which the CJEU annulled – on the signing and conclusion of the Agreement between the EU and the Republic of Mauritius on the conditions of transfer of suspected pirates and associated seized property by the European Union-led naval force to the Republic of

[26] See Case C-455/14 P *H v Council* (n 17) para 41; Case C-72/15 *Rosneft* (n 3) para 72; and Case C-134/19 P *Bank Refah Kargaran v Council of the EU* EU:C:2020:793, para 35.

[27] Opinion of AG T Capeta in Joined Cases C-29/22 P and C-44/22 P *KS and KD* (n 12), paras 79 and 124.

[28] Ibid para 84.

Mauritius and on the conditions of suspected pirates after transfer, despite the fact that the Decision was adopted on the sole material basis of Article 37 TEU in the area of the CFSP.

The CJEU justified its decision to hear and uphold the annulment of the Decision on the ground that the challenge alleged violation of Article 218.10 TFEU, relating to the participation of the European Parliament in the process of concluding international agreements, the latter provision constituting the procedural legal basis of the contested act.[29] Consequently, the CJEU pointed out that

> it cannot be argued that the scope of the limitation, by way of derogation, on the CJEU's jurisdiction envisaged in the final sentence of the second subparagraph of Article 24(1) TEU and in Article 275 TFEU goes so far as to preclude the CJEU from having jurisdiction to interpret and apply a provision such as Article 218 TFEU which does not fall within the CFSP.[30]

Sensu contrario, we understand that if the ground on which the challenge to the act of approval by the EU of a CFSP international agreement is based is the violation of the material provisions of the CFSP Treaties, the 'carve-out' would apply.

3. Scope of the Jurisdiction of the CJEU to Hear Non-Contractual Liability Actions in the Field of the CFSP

3.1. The Evolution of the CJEU Case Law

Advocate General Mengozzi lamented in his Opinion in *Gestoras Pro Amnistía* that 'in the present state of Union law' the CJEU did not have jurisdiction to hear an action for non-contractual liability against the EU in the field of the then 'third pillar', ie, in matters of Police and Judicial Cooperation in Criminal Matters.[31] Specifically, he pointed out that the 'extended jurisdiction' sought by the appellants was alien to the Treaties, and warned that a reading extending the jurisdiction of the CJEU would constitute a *contra legem* interpretation of the Treaties. And so, faced with the obvious tension in the case between the right to effective judicial protection and respect for the principle of conferral, the Advocate General concluded that the appellants could seek compensation before national courts for damages caused by the national enforcement measures.[32] In its judgment, the CJEU echoed the Opinion of the Advocate General and confirmed its lack of jurisdiction to rule on the case.[33]

The case law of the CJEU as regards the non-contractual liability of the Union in the field of the CFSP has not followed the same path. Indeed, in *Elitaliana*, *H v Council*

[29] Case C-658/11 *European Parliament v Council of the EU*, EU:C:2014:2025, paras 71–72.

[30] Ibid para 73.

[31] Opinion of AG P. Mengozzi in Case C-354/04 P *Gestoras Pro Amnistía and Others v Council of the EU* EU:C:2006:667, paras 99 and 178.

[32] Ibid paras 156 ff.

[33] Case C-354/04 P *Gestoras Pro Amnistía* EU:C:2007:115, paras 61–62.

and *EU Satellite Centre*, the CJEU not only excluded the applicability of the 'carve-out' of Article 24.1 TEU and Article 275 TFEU, deciding that it had jurisdiction to review the legality of the CFSP acts at stake, but also concluded that it could hear actions for compensation against the Union for damages caused by such acts, based on Articles 268 and 340 TFEU and taking due consideration (once again) of both Article 19 TEU and Article 47 CFR.[34] In *Elitaliana*, the damage allegedly caused to the appellant was the income lost as a result of Eulex Kosovo awarding a contract to another firm; in the other two cases, the damages involved contested measures for selecting personnel.

The CJEU also opened the door to non-contractual liability claims related to CFSP acts according restrictive measures in its highly criticised[35] 2020 *Bank Refah Kargaran* judgment.[36] Despite the criticism, the doctrine established by this judgment was subsequently reaffirmed by the General Court[37] and marks a turning point in this matter. The case concerned an action for non-contractual liability brought by the Iranian bank *Bank Refah Kargaran*, which sought compensation for the damages allegedly suffered after it was included on the lists of individuals and entities whose funds and economic resources were frozen as a result of the CFSP decision and the regulation providing restrictive measures adopted in response to the Islamic Republic of Iran's nuclear programme. The Court began its judgment by stressing the general rule of jurisdiction that Article 19 TEU imposes 'in order to ensure that in the interpretation and application of the Treaties the law is observed', and noting that Article 24.1 TEU and Article 275 TFEU for CFSP contain an exception to the general rule and, consequently, those Articles are to be interpreted restrictively, as was already made clear in previous judgments.[38] Starting from this premise, the Court invoked classic case law to argue that the remedy of compensation must be examined with 'regard to the whole of the system established by the treaties for the judicial protection of the individual',[39] meaning, consequently, in light of: (i) the principle of the Rule of Law; (ii) the right to effective judicial protection; and (iii) the need for coherence in the interpretation and application of EU law.

Accordingly, the CJEU held that the right to effective judicial protection requires access to the protection of the courts for individuals whose rights and freedoms are violated, recalling that, as sustained in *Rosneft*, effective judicial review is inherent to the existence of the rule of law. On this basis, the Court concluded that, given its jurisdiction to hear claims for compensation in respect of regulations imposing restrictive measures based on Article 215 TFEU,[40] it also has the competence to adjudicate damages suffered as a consequence of restrictive measures imposed by CFSP decisions

[34] See, *per omnia*, C-455/14 P *H v Council* (n 17) paras 44 and 55.
[35] See, *per omnia*, T Verellen, 'In the Name of the Rule of Law? CJEU Further Extends Jurisdiction in CFSP (Bank Refah Kargaran)' (2021) 6 *European Papers* 17; and C Martínez Capdevila, 'El TJUE proclama su competencia para conocer de los recursos de indemnización vinculados con medidas restrictivas PESC (STJ de 6.10.2020, as. Bank Refah Kargaran, C-134/19 P): ¿maximización o extralimitación de su jurisdicción?' (2021) 53 *Revista General de Derecho Europeo* 209.
[36] Case C-134/19 P *Bank Refah Kargaran* (n 26).
[37] See Case T-455/17 *Naser Bateni v Council of the EU* EU:T:2021:411, paras 48–49.
[38] Case C-134/19 P *Bank Refah Kargaran* (n 26), para 32.
[39] Ibid para 34.
[40] The CJEU cited at this point its judgment in Case C-45/15 P *Safa Nicu Sepahan Co v Council of the EU*, EU:C:2017:402.

in order to ensure 'the necessary coherence of the system of judicial protection provided for by EU law' and to avoid a potential 'lacuna in the judicial protection of the natural or legal persons concerned'.[41]

3.2. Does the CJEU have Jurisdiction to Hear Non-Contractual Liability Actions Brought against the EU for CFSP Acts that are not Restrictive Measures?

We might now ask how far the jurisdiction of the CJEU extends. In particular, can the CJEU entertain claims for damages caused during the implementation of any CFSP decision (by, for example, Eulex, European External Action or the European Defence Agency)? The CJEU case law does not offer a clear answer. As we have seen, it can be argued that the criteria behind the *Elitaliana*, *H v Council* and *EU Satellite Centre* judgments to affirm the CJEU's jurisdiction was the distinction between political or strategic decisions in CFSP,[42] or, to use the terminology employed by Attorney General Nils Whal,[43] the distinction between CFSP sovereign foreign policy decisions and administrative or merely implementing acts. This is one of the criteria proposed by Advocate General Capeta in her Opinion in *KS and KD* to delimit the objective competence of the CJEU to review the legality of CFSP acts,[44] a criterion which I endorse, and which would equally apply to a decision to hear an action for damages brought by individuals.

However, in *KS and KD*, the Advocate General went further by stating that, just as the jurisdiction of EU courts includes, in her opinion, review of the legality of any CFSP act – including any act comprising a political or strategic decision – when a fundamental right might be infringed by it, it also covers any action for damages brought by individuals based on an alleged breach of fundamental rights by any type of CFSP measure.[45] Yet, just as I disagree with the first proposition,[46] neither can I subscribe to the second, as it lacks any basis in the Treaties. In any case, for a non-contractual liability action to succeed, the CFSP act in question must have, in and of itself, caused the appellant damages. However, in the case of a CFSP strategic or political decision, it is difficult to imagine one causing in and of itself actionable damages to individuals or entities (excluding third states).[47] It seems fair to assume that any damages will be caused by the measures adopted to carry out the strategic or political decision.

[41] Case C-134/19 P *Bank Refah Kargaran* (n 26), paras 35–43, particularly at para 39.
[42] See in this respect Koutrakos (n 8) 12 ff.
[43] Opinion of AG N Whal in Case C-455/14 P *H v Council* (n 4), para 60.
[44] See section 2.2 above.
[45] Opinion of AG T. Capeta in Joined Cases C-29/22 P and C-44/22 P *KS and KD* (n 12), para 154.
[46] See section 2.2 above.
[47] See Case C-872/19 P *Bolivarian Republic of Venezuela v Council of the EU* (Grand Chamber) EU:C:2021:507, in which the CJEU admitted, for the purposes of determining who has standing to bring actions for annulment against CFSP restrictive measures, that its case law on the concept of 'legal person', including third states, applies also in this area (paras 81 ff.).

3.3. Are National Courts Competent to Hear Non-Contractual Liability Actions Brought against the EU?

What seems inadmissible in any case is an interpretation of Article 24 TEU and Article 275 TFEU that denies the CJEU jurisdiction as well as the jurisdiction of any other court to hear actions for non-contractual liability brought by individuals or legal persons when a CFSP decision causes economically assessable damages. Of great interest in this regard is the *Tomanovic* judgment handed down by the High Court of Justice in London (Queen's Bench Division) in 2019. This case involves the same facts that are the subject of *KS and KD*, in which the victims claimed damages against the EU for the conduct of Eulex Kosovo in an investigation into crimes against Serbian nationals that it carried out.[48] In the appellants' view, Eulex Kosovo's actions violated numerous fundamental rights, including the right to life and the prohibition of torture.

It should be recalled that, before going to the High Court, the appellants initiated proceedings before the General Court claiming, inter alia, that the Council of the EU, the European Commission and the EEAS were 'ordered' to provide Eulex with funds to carry out its investigation and requesting that the CFSP decision establishing the Human Rights Review Panel (the body charged with overseeing Eulex's conduct in Kosovo) be annulled.[49] However, the General Court dismissed the claim because it considered that, according to the Treaties, it lacked jurisdiction to declare the CFSP act unlawful. Moreover, it found insufficient the applicants' argument that the General Court was required to assert its jurisdiction in order to preserve their right to effective judicial protection.[50] Whether or not the Court's ruling deserves criticism, it is quite clear, in my view, that the action brought by the appellants could not succeed.[51]

The question that ultimately arose before the High Court was whether national courts have jurisdiction to hear non-contractual liability actions brought against the Union or whether, on the contrary, only the CJEU can hear such actions (and, if so, when the 'carve-out' clause should operate in the field of CFSP). The wording of Article 24.1 TEU and Article 275 TFEU led Advocate General Kokott, in her 2/13 procedure Opinion, to affirm the jurisdiction of national courts in the area of CFSP.[52] The Advocate General began by asking 'whether the present competences of the EU are sufficient to ensure a level of legal protection in the common foreign and security policy that meets the requirements of Articles 6 and 13 ECHR'.[53] Attorney General Kokott then recalled the 'general rule' (in her words) of lack of jurisdiction of the Court in the field of the CFSP in order to question the proposal made by the European Commission to circumvent the problem by means of a 'a particularly broad interpretation of the second alternative in the second paragraph of Article 275 TFEU'. The Commission had intended – it should

[48] *Tomanovic et al v the European Union et al* [2019] EWHC 263 (QB).

[49] See, eg, Order of the GG in Case T-840/16 *KS v Council of the EU, European Commission and EEAS* EU:T:2017:938.

[50] ibid para 11.

[51] Namely because the General Court was asked to command different institutions to undertake a series of actions, not being the General Court competent to do so; Case T-269/13 P *Markus Brune v European Commission* EU:T:2014424, para 95.

[52] Opinion of AG J Kokott in the Opinion procedure 2/13 on the *Accession of the EU to the ECHR* (n 4).

[53] Ibid para 82.

be recalled that the Opinion dates from 2013 – for the CJEU to hear even references for preliminary rulings and actions for non-contractual liability.[54] Although this interpretation would prevail some years later, the Advocate General attempted to dismantle it and assert the jurisdiction of the national courts by invoking: (i) the literal wording of the Treaties; and (ii) the preparatory work.

Firstly, Advocate General Kokott argued that the interpretation proposed by the Commission directly clashed with the literal wording of the Treaties and the powers that the Member States had granted the CJEU, recalling that, in the area of CFSP and although the pillars were removed by the Lisbon Treaty, a desire to maintain the intergovernmental logic remained, which is consistent with the removal of powers from the CJEU in the scope of CFSP.[55]

Secondly, the Advocate General argued that the preparatory work on the Lisbon Treaty did not lead to the conclusion reached by the Commission, quite the contrary. She recalled that proposals to put forward a broader structuring of the powers and competences of the CJEU in the current Article 275 TFEU were rejected, which confirmed that Member States desired more restricted control in the field of CFSP.[56]

In these circumstances, the Advocate General recommended resolving the conflict between effective judicial protection and the principle of conferral by affirming the jurisdiction of national courts:

> [A]s Article 19(1) TEU shows, the system of legal protection established by the Treaties rests on two pillars, one of which is based on the Courts of the EU and the other on national courts and tribunals. Where, therefore – as is regularly the case in the CFSP – there is no direct recourse to the Courts of the EU, national courts or tribunals have, and will retain, jurisdiction. Ultimately this follows from the principle of conferral, according to which competences not conferred upon the EU in the Treaties remain with the Member States (Article 4(1) TEU, in conjunction with the first sentence of Article 5(1) and Article 5(2) TEU).[57]

Kokott favoured this solution despite the fact that, as she herself acknowledged, it does not ensure uniform interpretation and application of EU law. She seemed more concerned with upholding the compatibility of the system of judicial protection in the area of CFSP with Articles 6 and 13 ECHR. Moreover, at the beginning of her analysis, the Advocate General pointed out that this problem of compatibility would not only arise with the possible accession to the Convention, but that it was already on the table insofar as Article 52.3 CFR requires the rights contained in both instruments be given the same meaning and scope as those laid down by the Convention.[58]

Certainly, the Advocate General could not anticipate that the CJEU would expand its jurisdiction to review the legality of certain CFSP acts that are not restrictive measures, or to hear actions for damages brought against the Union in relation to such acts.

On the contrary, in his Opinion in *H v Council*, Advocate General Nils Wahl, while agreeing with Kokott's denial of CJEU jurisdiction in the field of CFSP outside the exceptions expressly provided for in the Treaties, pronounced himself in favour of the

[54] Ibid para 86.
[55] Ibid paras 86–89.
[56] Ibid para 90.
[57] Ibid para 96.
[58] Ibid para 85.

application also in the field of CFSP of the principle laid down in *Foto-Frost* according to which the CJEU has exclusive authority to declare acts of EU Law invalid.[59] However, in referring to the *Foto-Frost* judgment, Whal not only accepted the possibility that national courts might suspend an EU act as a precautionary measure (according to well established case law), even in the field of CFSP, but also indicated national courts could award compensation to the claimant, without further explanation.

Be that as it may, asserting the jurisdiction of national courts to hear non-contractual liability actions against the EU in the field of the CFSP does not seem a satisfactory solution, as it does not fit well with the essential objective of achieving uniform interpretation and application of EU law and would not improve the coherence of the EU's jurisdictional system. In the logic of the EU jurisdictional system and according to consistent case law,[60] the CJEU should have exclusive jurisdiction over any non-contractual liability action against the EU.

In this regard, in *Tomanovic*, the representative of the European Commission warned that 'it is a fallacy to conclude that if the Court of Justice does not have jurisdiction over a CFSP matter, it follows from the second sentence of Article 19(1) of the TEU that a national court must have jurisdiction', because 'That would lead to national courts having unlimited jurisdiction over CFSP matters, such that a national court could even annul the EULEX Joint Action', thus concluding that 'That would clearly be an absurd result and demonstrates why the jurisdiction of the national courts must necessarily be limited.'[61]

Moreover, if we grant jurisdiction to national courts, we should then also extend it to all the courts of the Member States and, consequently, it would be up to the claimant to choose the forum for resolution that most favours its position (*forum conveniens*).

3.4. The Judgment of the High Court in the *Tomanovic* Case

The main argument that led the High Court to exclude its jurisdiction was purely formal: the European Communities Act of 1972, by which the UK transposed what was then European Communities law into domestic law, did not include the provisions relating to CFSP. In the High Court's view, this posed an insurmountable obstacle preventing it from exercising jurisdiction over the case.[62]

Nevertheless, after recalling the system provided for in the Treaties as regards the CFSP, Judge Murray was inclined to consider that the CJEU was the competent judicial body for several reasons.

First, Judge Murray understood that, by restricting the jurisdiction of the Court in the field of CFSP, Article 275 TFEU was probably only aiming at CFSP acts involving

[59] Opinion of AG N Whal in Case C-455/14 P *H v Council* (n 4) para 34 ff., and para 102. In her Opinion, AG Kokott had openly ruled out the application of this principle in the field of CFSP; Opinion procedure 2/13 on the *Accession of the EU to the ECHR* (n 4) para 100.

[60] See Case C-377/09 *Françoise-Eléonor Hanssens-Ensch v EC*, EU:C:2010:459, para 26.

[61] See, to the contrary, S Øby Johansen, 'Suing the European Union in the UK: Tomanovic et. al. v. the European Union et. al.' (2019) 4 *European Papers* 345, 352.

[62] *Tomanovic et al* (n 48) para 94.

'sovereign policy choices'.[63] Indeed, referring to the submissions in the proceedings by Mr Nicholas Khan, on behalf of the Commission, Judge Murray noted that:

> 79. … The cases of *Elitaliana*, *H*, *KF* and *Rosneft* all demonstrate that the exclusion of the jurisdiction of the Court of Justice is to be narrowly construed and the mere fact that an issue arises in an CFSP context does not mean it is excluded from the jurisdiction of the Court of Justice.
>
> 80. It seems to me that there is a strong argument that a claim based on a violation by an EU institution, body, office or agency of human rights guaranteed by EU law falls outside the scope of the reference to CFSP provisions in Articles 24(1) TEU and 275 TFEU, provided that the claim, while arising in a CFSP context does not seek to annul or declare invalid the sovereign policy choice that gives rise to that context.
>
> 81. In this case, the claimants are not seeking to annul the EULEX Joint Action. They are seeking redress for failures in the carrying out of that sovereign policy choice that have led, if one accepts the findings of the HRRP, to the violation of their human rights. The CFSP is the context, but, as the cases of *Elitaliana*, *H* and *KF* demonstrate, that is not a sufficient basis for excluding jurisdiction where the nature of the claim is not itself concerned with a sovereign policy choice made by the Member States.
>
> 82. These arguments are reinforced, it seems to me, by Article 6 TEU, Article 19(1) TEU and Article 47 of the Charter and by the observations of the CJEU in the case of *Kadi* …

As seen, Justice Murray cited, among others, the CJEU judgments in *Elitaliana*, *H v Council* and *EU Satellite Centre* to point out that, although the contested acts in these cases were adopted in the framework of the CFSP, the CFSP context alone was not a reason to exclude the jurisdiction of the CJEU 'where the nature of the claim is not itself concerned with a sovereign policy choice made by the Member States'.

Second, citing Advocate General Wahl's Opinion in *H v Council* (and consciously departing from Advocate General Kokott's opinion), Judge Murray ruled in favour of applying the *Foto-Frost* doctrine in the area of CFSP:

> 88. In my view, the argument that the Court of Justice should have jurisdiction over these claims is strengthened by the Foto-Frost principle. The policy underlying the Foto-Frost decision must also apply in a CFSP context, as recognised by AG Wahl in his Opinion in the case of H. As neither his view on this question nor the contrary view of AG Kokott in her view on the ECHR Accession Opinion are binding upon this court, I will simply note that the Court of Justice does not appear to have ruled on this point. In the absence of authority to the contrary, I prefer AG Wahl's view, with all due respect to the view of AG Kokott and the academic commentaries to which I was referred.

Despite these and other less pertinent arguments, Judge Murray concluded that it was not possible to affirm beyond doubt the exclusive jurisdiction of the CJEU to hear claims for non-contractual liability in the CFSP field, and that any remaining doubts could only be dispelled by raising a reference for a preliminary ruling before the Court of Justice. However, the judge ruled out the possibility of raising one himself, given the United Kingdom's imminent exit from the Union.[64]

[63] Ibid paras 80–81.
[64] *Tomanovic et al* (n 48) paras. 90–93.

4. Conclusions

When deciding the scope of its jurisdiction over CFSP, the CJEU has opted for an interpretation of Article 24.1 TEU and Article 275 TFEU that is not only compatible with a systematic reading of the Treaties – taking particularly into account Article 19 TEU – but that is also consistent with the fundamental rights enshrined in the CFR – namely, the right to effective judicial protection (Article 47). However, in my opinion, the CJEU has not yet explored the full potential of this interpretative path, either in regard to the objective scope of its jurisdiction to control the legality of CFSP decisions or to the possibility of hearing actions for non-contractual liability for damages caused by EU acts.

As for the review of the legality of CFSP acts, in *Elitaliana*, *H v Council* and *EU Satellite Centre*, the CJEU has asserted its jurisdiction by resorting to a sort of legerdemain whereby the content of a CFSP act (if of administrative or financial nature) allows it to be considered as falling outside the domain of CFSP. I believe, however, that the Court will find it necessary – in cases such as *KS and KD* – to delve deeper into the interpretation of the 'carve-out' established in the Treaties and, in the light of Article 47 CFR, to decide whether the limit on its jurisdiction over CFSP should be restricted to the political or strategic decisions of the CFSP or whether natural and legal persons should be denied the possibility of challenging the legality of CFSP acts that, directly and individually, restrict their rights. Concerning non-contractual liability for damage caused by the EU in the field of CFSP, *Bank Refah Kargaran* and other judgments cited above (*Elitaliana*, *H v Council* and *EU Satellite Centre*) do not seem definitive.

Since the early 1990s, the CJEU has insisted that the general principle of state responsibility for compliance with EU law is inherent in the system of the Treaties.[65] Moreover, it has repeatedly held that the principle applies to any breach of EU Law, irrespective of the organ whose action or omission caused the breach.[66] As the principle of liability is a general principle rooted in the general logic of the Treaties – which practically admits no obstacles or impediments, and seeks to ensure at all times compensation for damages caused – how can it be argued that, when the EU acts within the framework of CFSP, the principle of conferral may be invoked in order to avoid assigning liability for damages arising from its own acts?

Denying both national court and CJEU jurisdiction cannot be the solution, which is what the General Court did in *Jannatian*.[67] The right to effective judicial protection not only justifies the path taken by the CJEU in *Elitaliana*, *H v Council* and *EU Satellite Centre*; it also requires further elaboration by providing a clear criterion to determine which acts are not covered by the 'carve-out' even if they have been adopted in the field of CFSP.

[65] See, inter alia, Joint Cases C-6/90 and C-9/90 *Andrea Francovich and Danila Bonifaci and others v Italian Republic*, EU:C:1991:428, para 35, and Case C-429/09 *Günter Fuß v Stadt Halle* EU:C:2010:717, para 45.

[66] See, inter alia, Joint Cases C-46/93 and C-48/93 *Brasserie du Pêcheur SA v Bundesrepublik Deutschland and The Queen v Secretary of State for Transport, ex parte: Factortame Ltd and others* EU:C:1996:79, para 32; and Case C-302/97 *Klaus Konle v Republik Österreic*, EU:C:1999:271, para 62.

[67] Case T-328/14 *Mahmoud Jannatian v Council of the EU* EU:T:2016:86, para 31.

In *Tomanovic*, Justice Murray concluded that only CFSP acts that involve 'sovereign' foreign policy choices lie outside the jurisdiction of the CJEU. The acceptance of this criterion – suggested by the Advocate General in *KS and KD*, and which, in my view, seems reasonable – would prevent the Court (or the ECtHR) from being one day forced to recognise that the EU's jurisdictional system in CFSP matters is contrary to Article 47 of the Charter (Articles 6 and 13 ECHR), as well as with Article 41.3 CFR. It should be noted that the prospect of success for a damage claim against the Union caused by a foreign policy choice also seems extremely low.[68]

Bibliography

Andrés Sáenz de Santamaría, P, 'Mejorando la lex imperfecta: tutela judicial efectiva y cuestión prejudicial en la PESC (A propósito del asunto Rosneft)' (2017) 58 *Revista de Derecho Comunitario Europeo* 871.

Breitler, C, 'Jurisdiction in CFSP Matters – Conquering the Gallic Village One Case at a Time?' *European Law Blog* 13 October 2022, 1.

Cremona, M, 'Effective Judicial Review Is of the Essence of the Rule of Law: Challenging Common Foreign and Security Policy Measures Before the Court of Justice' (2017) 2 *European Papers* 671.

Eckes, C, 'Common Foreign and Security Policy: The Consequences of the Court's Extended Jurisdiction' (2016) 22 *European Law Journal* 492.

Koutrakos, P, *Judicial Review in the EU's Common Foreign and Security Policy*, ICLQ no 67 (2018) 1.

Martín y Pérez de Nanclares, J, 'El control jurisdiccional del TJUE en materia de medidas restrictivas adoptadas en el ámbito de la PESC: el equilibrio entre efectividad y legalidad (2023) 75 *Revista de Derecho Comunitario Europeo* 91.

Martínez Capdevila, C, 'El TJUE proclama su competencia para conocer de los recursos de indemnización vinculados con medidas restrictivas PESC (STJ de 6.10.2020, as. Bank Refah Kargaran, C-134/19 P): ¿maximización o extralimitación de su jurisdicción?' (2021) 53 *Revista General de Derecho Europeo* 209.

—— 'La sentencia en el asunto Rosneft: el TJUE maximiza su jurisdicción en la PESC (a costa de la coherencia con su propia jurisprudencia)' (2018) 67 *Revista Española de Derecho Europeo* 95.

Øby Johansen, S, 'Suing the European Union in the UK: Tomanovic et. al. v. the European Union et. al.' (2019) 4 *European Papers* 345.

Poli, S, 'The Common Foreign Security Policy after Rosneft: Still imperfect but gradually subject to the Rule of Law' (2017) 54 *Common Market Law Review* 1799.

Verellen, T, 'H v. Council: Strengthening the Rule of Law in the Sphere of the CFSP, One Step at a Time' (2016) 1 *European Papers* 1041.

—— 'In the Name of the Rule of Law? CJEU Further Extends Jurisdiction in CFSP (Bank Refah Kargaran)' (2021) 6 *European Papers* 17.

[68] See C Eckes, 'Common Foreign and Security Policy: The Consequences of the Court's Extended Jurisdiction' (2016) 22 *European Law Journal* 492, 510.

PART III

Constitutional Courts: Navigating Integration and Autonomy

8

On the Guardians of the EU Member State Constitution: Redefining the Roles of the European and the National Judiciaries

PEDRO CRUZ VILLALÓN

1. Introduction

For the past 100 years, the question of the appropriate guardian of the Constitution has been a recurrent topic within European constitutional culture; for most of that period, the constitution alluded to has been the State Constitution, until recently, the only kind known in Europe.[1] The clear winner in this debate has been the judicial guarantee, to the detriment of a political guarantee of the Constitution, with the result that the notions of the guardian of the Constitution and constitutional adjudication have become broadly equivalent categories in Europe.[2] A remarkable evolution is nevertheless taking place in the European constitutional space. In the case of some European Union (EU) Member States, in addition to the national guardian of the Constitution,[3] another guardian makes itself increasingly present: the Court of Justice of the European Union (CJEU).[4] In particular, the European judiciary has in fact

[1] L Vincx, The Guardian of the Constitution. Hans Kelsen and Carl Schmitt on the Limits of Constitutional Law. Translation, introduction and notes by Lars Vinx (Cambridge, Cambridge University Press, 2015).

[2] See, J Collins, Democracy's Guardians: A history of the German Federal Constitutional Court (1951–2001) (Oxford, Oxford University Press, 2015).

[3] M Claes and B de Witte, 'The Role of Constitutional Courts in the European Legal Space' in A von Bogdandy, PM Huber and C Grabenwarter (eds), *Constitutional Adjudication. Common Themes and Challenges, The Max Planck Series in European Public Law*, vol IV (Oxford, Oxford University Press, 2023) 495–526; P Cruz Villalón, 'The Evolution of Constitutional Adjudication in Europe' in ibid 1–50.

[4] J Martín y Pérez de Nanclares, 'The Cooperation of Constitutional Courts in the European Legal Space' in A von Bogdandy, PM Huber and C Grabenwarter (eds), *Constitutional Adjudication. Common Themes and Challenges, The Max Planck Series in European Public Law*, vol IV (Oxford, Oxford University Press, 2023); J Zglinski, The new judicial federalism: the evolving relationship between EU and Member State Courts' (2023) 2 *European Law Open* 345.

assumed the role of guardian of the rule of law in several Member States, Hungary and Poland being the most salient cases.[5] Less prominent, at least for the moment, is the case of Spain where, due to a degraded political environment, public opinion frequently turns to 'Europe' to perform the function of ultimate guardian of its constitutional order.[6]

It should nevertheless be considered that this recent state of affairs in the European constitutional space has long been a possibility. The exceptional complexity of the European constitutional *aggregate*[7] makes it impossible for each constituent legal order to be exclusively responsible for its own guarantee. The complexity of the European constitutional structure entailed the complexity of the judicial guarantee of each component. Nevertheless, it is only now that the consequences of this complexity have become clear that the need for an explanation is unavoidable.[8]

In this direction, I will argue that there is a correspondence between the composite structure of the EU Member State Constitution (EUMSC) and the different ways in which the national and the European judiciaries engage in the judicial guarantee of the national constitution. I will argue that the structure of the Member State's constitution determines the identity of its guardian or, in the event, its guardians. Ultimately, the aim is to describe in assumedly schematic terms what is currently changing in the current debate over the classic question of the guardian of the Constitution as it was intensely debated in the 1920s. Accordingly, I will describe, in a first step, the composite structure of the EUMSC as a basic element of the complex European constitutional aggregate. In a second step, I will specify how the question of the guardian of the national Constitution is posed differently as applied to each of its components.

2. The EU Member State Constitution: A Three-Tiered Structure

The EUMSC[9] reveals in its very wording its quality as part of a broader entity, that of the European constitutional structure. To be precise, the EUMSC existed before the

[5] W Sadurski, *Poland's Constitutional Breakdown* (Oxford, Oxford University Press, 2019). The debate on 'guardians' is ever more present. See, Ondrej Hamulák, 'The Unbearable Lightness of being Guardian of the Constitution (Revolt and Revolution Dilemma in the approach of Czech Constitutional Court Vis-à-Vis EU and Supranational Legal Order)' (2014) 1 *European Studies* 119; T Kröll, 'The European Court of Justice, a guardian ("Hüter") of the Republican Principle of the Austrian Federal Constitution? Case Note on C-208/09, Sayn Wittgenstein' (2012) 6 *ICL Journal* 110; A Vincze, 'The ECJ as the Guardian of the Hungarian Constitution: Case C-286/12 Commission v. Hungary' (2013) 3 *European Public Law* 489.

[6] N Krisch, 'The Spanish constitutional crisis: Law, legitimacy and popular sovereignty in question', *Verfassungsblog. On matters constitutional*, 7 October 2017.

[7] As for the term I employ on this occasion: my apologies for contributing to the pervasive semantic creativity reigning on the discipline.

[8] Assumedly, this is not the occasion to enter into the matter with a minimum of accuracy. The fact remains that the alluded phenomenon is so attractive, both in urgency and conceptual richness, as to hazard the outline of a future exercise on the matter.

[9] See for previous attempts to confront the subject-matter, P Cruz Villalón, 'La Constitución del Estado miembro: Un intento de recapitulación' in L Gordillo (ed), *Spanish Constitution and European Integration. Treinta años de Derecho Constitucional de la integración. Actas del XIV Congreso de la Asociación de Constitucionalistas de España* (Valencia, Tirant, 2018) 19–29; P Cruz Villalón, 'Bemerkungen zu Begriff

European constitutional structure, and by consequence requires a reinterpretation according to the position it takes up within the larger constitutional entity. The constitutions of the Member States must thus be first addressed as a unitary category, despite the obvious diversity among the national constitutions.[10] This seems essential for the move from the plural *constitutions* to the singular *Constitution*. Only by treating the EUMSC unitarily will it be possible to address the question of the plurality of guardians away from its classic singular notion. Indeed, a category that seems to exist only in a diversity of configurations, the *constitutions* of the Member States, has witnessed an expansion and a deepening of their common features that justify postulating an abstract or autonomous conceptualisation of the category. In sum, this evolution permits us to approach the constitution of the EU Member State as a unitary normative figure that should be described in the singular, hence the use here of the acronym EUMSC.

Such an operation is particularly legitimate at a time when all EU Member States possess a written constitution, that is, a basic law in the most conventional sense of the word. In this respect, 'Brexit' has considerably simplified the endeavour, for it absolves the EU of the need to constantly consider the disturbing presence of the unwritten British constitution. Such formulae as the 'fundamental *political and constitutional* structures' in Article 4(2) of the Treaty on European Union (TEU), or even the allusions to the 'common constitutional traditions' in Article 51.4 of the Charter of Fundamental Rights (CFR), arguably conceived to accommodate the British singularity, make much less sense under the present circumstances.

My argument takes the following point of departure. What I will call here the *constitutionally relevant mandates* issued from the European legal order and addressed to the legal order of each Member State – and as a matter of principle in relation to its respective Constitution – will not be treated as mere *instructions* addressed to the national constituent power coming from outside the national legal order. Irrespective of their nature as EU primary law, I will address here their consequence, that is, their reception within the legal order of the Member State, presumably in its respective national constitution. The emphasis, in other words, will be put on the result, ie on the *internalisation* by the Member State's constitutional order of the constitutionally relevant mandates coming from the EU legal order. Crucially, this will allow shifting attention from the EU primary law to the national constitution inasmuch as it is determined by its condition as an EU-Member State Constitution. This should open a channel to transfer the tensions of constitutional relevance between the EU legal order and that of the Member State to the inner self of the national constitution in its quality as a basic component of the European constitutional *compositum*.[11]

und Funktion der Verfassung des EU-Mitgliedstates' in R Hofmann et al (eds), *Festschrift für Franz Merli* (Baden-Baden, Nomos, 2023) 671–83; P Cruz Villalón, 'La constitución (del Estado miembro de la UE) como logro evolutivo' in N Luhmann, *La constitución como logro evolutivo. Introducción, traducción y epílogo de Pedro Cruz Villalón* (Madrid, Tecnos, 2024) IL-LXXV.

[10] Out of the truly scant presentations of the matter, see, D Grimm, 'Zur Bedeutung nationaler Verfassungen in einem vereinten Europa' in D Merten and H-J Papier (eds), *Handbuch der Grundrechte*, Vol VI/2 (Heidelberg, CF Müller, 2009) 3–32, now in D Grimm, *Europa ja – aber welches? Zur Verfassung der europäischen Demokratie* (Munich, CH Beck, 2016) 147–81.

[11] Cruz Villalón (n 9).

The outcome is a composite three-tiered constitution of the EUMSC. Two basic magnitudes can be initially distinguished within it, a *Europeanised* or *hetero-determined* constitution and a *self-determined* or *original* constitution. To this, a third magnitude is to be added, a *debated* constitution (or constitution *of last resort*), which aims to restore the balance between the two previous magnitudes. Although all three are closely intertwined, I will present each as separately as possible.

2.1. The First Tier: The *Europeanised* Constitution

From the perspective of the European constitutional aggregate, the most apt description of the EUMSC should begin with the *Europeanised*, or *hetero-determined* constitution, in which the Member State's factual loss of constituent sovereignty comes to the fore. I begin with some brief remarks concerning the notion, material scope and normative position of the Europeanised or hetero-determined constitution. It relates to the sum of the contents of the constitution of the Member State which, since the accession of the concerned state to the EU, are a consequence of the already mentioned constitutionally relevant mandates coming from EU law.[12] This overlapping of the Europeanised constitution with EU law will have consequences for the binding force of the former.

In a matter where unanimity is required, the Member State is in no way alien to the original formation of EU primary law and singularly of these constitutionally relevant mandates.[13] The essential point is that, once the mandates are incorporated into the EUMSC, the concerned Member State, barring *exit*, loses its autonomous power of disposal of them. They become an integral part of its constitution. Furthermore, and always for our present purposes, the Europeanised constitution should be considered a faithful incorporation of the constitutionally relevant impulses emanating from EU law. Only this assumption will make possible subsequent attribution of its reinforced binding force. Put otherwise, the hypothesis of a contradiction between the Europeanised constitution and the relevant mandates coming from EU law should be at this moment excluded.

In this regard, it must be acknowledged that said mandates may or may not be reproduced in the text of the national constitution. In fact, it makes no difference from the perspective of EU law how each Member State incorporates and complies with those mandates, whether in its written constitution or elsewhere in its legal order: all that matters is that they are complied with. Nevertheless, in this circumstance, and in order to avoid unnecessary complication, I assume that these instructions emanating from EU law are reflected precisely in the constitution of the Member State, be it in its wording or by its authoritative interpretation. Finally, the entire edifice of this first tier of the EUMSC is subject to a resolutory condition: the activation of the right of the Member State to abandon, at any time, its status as such 'in accordance with its own

[12] A von Bogdandy, *Strukturwandel des öffentlichen Rechts. Entstehung und Demokratisierung der europäischen Gesellschaft* (Berlin, Suhrkamp, 2022).

[13] As D Grimm rightly points out in 'Die Rolle der nationalen Verfassungsgerichte in der europäischen Demokratie' in D Grimm, *Europa ja – aber welches? Zur Verfassung der europäischen Demokratie, Munich* (Munich, CH Beck, 2016) 200–03.

constitutional requirements' (Article 50.1 TEU) leads to the immediate abolition of the internal dichotomy of the national constitution. It is a return to the point of departure, that is, to the full constitutional sovereignty of the state.

In analysing the Europeanised constitution, it is worth distinguishing between its material and formal dimensions. As far as the former is concerned, it is hardly debatable that the mere reading of the founding Treaties together with the Charter, with the addition of the relevant case law, offers in and of its own a great deal of *information* pertaining to the kind of constitution the Member State is obliged to adopt. These already-mentioned instructions coming from EU law now reappear as a great many elements of the Europeanised national constitution:

(a) It is a *state* constitution. Statehood is the first feature of a constitution that relates to a state in the full sense of the word notwithstanding its voluntarily assumed status as a state integrated into a supranational community such as the EU. This is an essential requirement of the EU that as a matter of principle is a 'Union of States' (Article 4.2 TEU). In other words, the aforementioned instructions with constitutional relevance have 'States' as their immediate addressees, with the components that traditionally define them: power, territory and people. Both the power and the territory of the Member State are expressly mentioned in the second paragraph of Article 4.2 TEU. The former, through the references to the 'fundamental political and constitutional structures' and the 'essential functions' of the Member State. In equal terms, said provision mandates the EU respect the 'territorial integrity' of the state. Finally, the recognition of the citizenship of the Member State implicitly appears as a precondition for EU citizenship.

(b) It is a constitution *founded on values* (Article 2 TEU). The set of values listed in this article is meant to provide the foundation, in the first place, to the EU itself, but it is immediately added that these values are *common* to the Member States. In addition, other provisions of the TEU proclaim the imperative nature of these values, be it specifically for the Member States (Article 7) or for third European states intending to accede to the EU (Article 49). This has two basic equally decisive consequences: a functional one, insofar as it implies that the Constitution of the Member State has a prior normative basis that is to precede and to condition the exercise of its constituent power; and a substantive consequence: the EU is not founded on a religious, ideological, or ethnic basis, but on values, that is, it has a predominantly ethical foundation. As for the quality of the values, some correspond to generally accepted notions (freedom, equality, tolerance, justice), while others fit better into the category of the constituted political community's structural principles (rule of law, democracy, pluralism).

(c) It is a *conventional* constitution, in the sense that it is called to conform to the assumed scheme of a constitution as laid out in the proverbial Article 16 of the 1789 French Declaration of Rights: the guarantee of rights and the separation of powers, together with recognition of the principle of democracy or, in the classic terms of that Declaration, of the law as the expression of the general will (Article 6). As concerns the rights, beyond their mention in Article 2 TEU, it is the CFR that, since formally entering the EU legal order in 2009, represents the strongest element of this first tier of the EUMSC. For its part, the principle of separation of powers as mandated by EU law derives from the recognition of the 'essential functions' of the state in Article 4.2 TEU. Nevertheless, the element that best reflects the presence of the classic powers of the state is the role that each of them – legislative, executive and judiciary – performs in the EU's constitutional architecture itself: the EU organs and institutions require the collaboration of the powers of the Member State for both their structure and their functioning. The paramount case is represented by the judiciary, but no less vital are the legislative and executive powers of the Member States. In short, to properly function, the EU cannot dispense of the three state powers, which must respond to the conventional features assigned to each of them.

(d) Lastly, it is an *incomplete* or *torso* constitution. This condition results from several factors. To begin with, there is the implicit notion that the constituent power is one of the already mentioned essential functions of the state. EU law explicitly refers to the constitutional rules of the Member State in a variety of decisive moments: 'in accordance with its own constitutional requirements' is one recurrent expression (Article 49–50 TEU). The same applies to the reference to the aforementioned constitutional traditions common to the Member States (Article 52.4 CFR). It must be noted that the reference is not simply to the respective legal order, but precisely to its constitution, laying bare an awareness of the constitutional dimension of the Member State's legal order. Incidentally, this all prefigures the second tier of the EUMSC, the *self-determined* constitution. Still, before moving on from this point, the question of the binding force of this first tier must be addressed.

The hetero-determined EU constitution *participates* in the prevalent application that characterises the EU legal order.[14] With assumed caution, it is argued that it participates in the primacy of EU law since it is positively not EU law in and of itself, but Member State law *mirroring* EU law. Alternatively, this idea could be formulated by explicitly acknowledging that its primacy is not inherent (per se) but functional. Moreover, it should be remembered that the correspondence of the Europeanised constitution with EU law, as experience proves, requires an occasional process of adaptation.[15] Furthermore, the *Europeanised* constitution, in its condition as national constitutional law, is supreme in the national legal order, a character that it shares with the self-determined constitution. In its judgment of 14 March 2012, the Austrian Constitutional Court pointed out the different consequences for the effectiveness of the control carried out, depending on whether one or the other principle applies.[16]

[14] JL Requejo Pagés, 'Primacía de la Unión y soberanía nacional. Consideraciones sobre una posible solución normativa de un conflicto de principio' in J Urías Martínez and F Álvarez-Ossorio Micheo (eds), *Cultura constitucional en Europa. Encuentro hispalense en torno a la obra del profesor Pedro Cruz Villalón, Sevilla* (Seville, Publicaciones de la Universidad de Sevilla, 2022) 255–71, fn 1; C Izquierdo Sans, 'Preferencia aplicativa y diálogo judicial' (2019) 1 *InDret. Revista para el análisis del Derecho* 1.

[15] Constitutional reform of Art 13.2 of the Spanish Constitution, introducing the words 'and passive'. See also the final subsection of Art 23.1 of the German Basic Law: 'The establishment of the European Union, as well as changes in its treaty foundations and comparable regulations that amend or supplement this Basic Law or make such amendments or supplements possible, shall be subject to paragraphs (2) and (3) of Article 79.'

[16] U 466/11-18, 5.8. 'Charta-Erkenntnis'. *cf*, F Merli, 'Die Konstitutionalisierung der EU-Grundrechte: Das österreichische Beispiel' in PB Donath et al (eds), *Der Schutz des Individuums durch das Recht* (Berlin, Springer, 2023) 873–86.

2.2. The Second Tier: The Self-Determined Constitution

As in the previous case, denominating this second tier of the EUMSC is not straightforward. From a functional perspective, *self-determined, residual* (otherwise *original* constitution) are all proper alternative denominations. From a substantive perspective, it could also be called the *enucleated* constitution. From the perspective of the European constitutional aggregate, this second tier visualises the moment of plurality. It is a necessary consequence of the incompleteness of the Europeanised constitution. A correct understanding of this second tier requires an analysis in evolutionary terms. Thus, although I am dealing with it in a second moment, the fact is that *in the beginning it* was the self-determined, original constitution. At the same time, this second magnitude must be seen as the result of an ongoing intrusion of EU law in the domain of the EUMSC, an expansion that as a matter of principle takes place at the expense of the Member State's constitutional self-determination process, that is, in terms of its progressive erosion (hence the *residual* constitution). That is also why the Europeanised constitution appears now as a constitution *embedded* in the originally integral national constitution. This is also the reason why, in consideration of the already described scope of the Europeanised constitution, this second tier reveals itself as an *enucleated* constitution, ie a constitution which has lost the capacity to determine the core contents of the national constitution. Figuratively, the EUMSC must endure in its inner self the presence of a foreign body and do its best to repress consequential impulses to reject it.[17]

As for the material content of the self-determined constitution, it is defined as a matter of principle by reference to the scope of the Europeanised constitution. Here the affirmation that it is the constitution *by default* is sufficient, in the sense that the self-determined constitution embraces the domains not covered by the latter. There is no need to dwell at length on the variety of its contents. Whether the state is unitary or federal, monarchical or republican, presidential or parliamentary, whether its electoral system is majoritarian or proportional, its judicial review of legislation diffuse, concentrated or inexistent, etc, going all the way down to even more specific options, all these considerations continue to be topics that fall to the residual constituent power to determine.

As for the binding force of this second tier, it stems from its contrast with that of the first tier. The prevalent application formerly declared as related to the Europeanised constitution results here in a *subordinate* application of the residual constitution, meaning that it yields whenever necessary to the prevalent application of the former.

Consequently, the self-determined constitution exhibits a partial lack of differentiation with respect to the rest of the national legal order. There is differentiation between the two internal components (the constitution and the rest of the legal order) as concerns the internal supremacy of the former, but the differentiation is absent when it comes to their position vis-à-vis EU law. In other words, concerning the prevalent application of the Europeanised constitution, and generally of the whole of the

[17] JL Requejo Pagés, 'The Decline of the European Model of European Constitutional Jurisdiction' in A von Bogdandy, PM Huber and C Grabenwarter (eds), *Constitutional Adjudication. Common Themes and Challenges, The Max Planck Series in European Public Law, vol IV* (Oxford, Oxford University Press, 2023).

EU legal order, there is no difference between the two national magnitudes, the self-determined constitution and the rest of the national legal order.

2.3. The Third Tier: The *Disputed* Constitution (or Constitution *Of Last Resort*)

The composite structure of the EUMSC is completed by a third tier whose singular, even unique, character, as well as that of the European constitutional aggregate itself, stands out. Although the two previous components are present in the constitutions of federal states in all its variants, finding anything in them similar to this third tier of the EUMSC is arduous.

The complexity of this third component results from its dual nature. From a material perspective, it refers to an ultimate *space* that the Member State is under no circumstances ready to abandon, a space where the Member State *disputes* the prevalent application of EU law. From a functional perspective, it appears as a *device* conceived to counteract, as a measure of *last resort*, the expansive character of the constitutionally relevant mandates coming from the EU. In its present configuration, it is made up of two clauses that we may refer to for the present purposes as identity clauses. I will call them the EU constitutional identity clause and the Member State constitutional identity clause. Before taking them up, a couple of clarifications are needed.

First, this third tier is in no way determined by EU law, with which, on the contrary, it is in tension. This gives rise to major differences between the constitutional provisions of the various Member States. However, beyond these textual differences, and besides a couple of exceptions,[18] the basic attitude of the Member States does not vary greatly. The second clarification is the reminder that the content of this constitution competes with largely equivalent provisions of EU law in the form of a situation of *reciprocal metaconstitutionality*.[19]

As for the content of these constitutional identity clauses, the first of them refers to the incorporation of a specific provision into the EUMSC affirming the character and nature of the supranational community into which the Member State is integrated. The clause is conceived to ensure that the supranational community of which the Member State intends to be a part corresponds to the characteristics of a constitutional polity or, in sum, a guarantee relating to the Member State's commitment to the essential content of the constitutional order of the EU. The most relevant reference is Article 23.1 of the German Basic Law, which is important enough to give it autonomous value.[20] Moreover,

[18] See, G van der Schyff, 'EU Member State Constitutional Identity: A Comparison of Germany and the Netherlands as Polar Opposites' (2016) 76 *Zeitschrift für ausländisches öffentliches Recht und Völkerrecht (ZaoRV)* 167; P Faraguna, 'Constitutional Identity in the EU – A Shield or a Sword' (2017) 18 *German Law Journal* 1617.

[19] P Cruz Villalón, 'Constitución nacional y Constitución europea' in P Cruz Villalón, *La Constitución inédita. Estudios ante la constitucionalización de Europa* (Madrid, Trotta, 2004).

[20] 'With a view to establishing a united Europe, the Federal Republic of Germany shall participate in the development of the European Union that is committed to democratic, social and federal principles, to the rule of law and to the principle of subsidiarity ant that guarantees a level of protection of basic rights essentially comparable to that afforded by this Basic Law.'

the content of this provision could be found in the constitution of any other Member State. In short, the EU constitutional identity clause amounts to a *reverse* mandate of homogeneity of the genre frequently present in federal constitutions, in this case, a mandate intending to align the EU constitution with a constitution of the Member States. This guarantee fully coincides with the EU's assertion of its own principles and values set out in Article 2 TEU. The difference, however, is that on this occasion it is the Member State that proclaims in its own way the essential content of the EU 'constitution' as a precondition for its membership in the EU. For the rest, the circumstance that only a minority of Member States include this clause in their respective constitutions does not mean that they would be disposed to remain in a supranational union whose essential principles contradict its national constitution.

The second identity clause, the guarantee of the constitutional identity of the Member State, rounds off this third tier of the EUMSC. Its purpose is to safeguard the essential content of the national constitution in the ongoing process of European integration (the 'ever closer union').[21] Under one formulation or another, this feature of the EUMSC has predominantly materialised through constitutional case law rather than an express constitutional provision. The Italian category of *controlimiti* has been pioneering in this respect.[22] Similarly to the previous EU identity component of this third tier, it is conceived as a guarantee of last resort. Characteristic of this identity of the Member State is again its parallel recognition in Article 4.2 TEU (*national* identity).[23] While in the case of the EU constitutional identity, there is no single term that singles it out, the term *national* identity is enshrined in EU primary law. The value of this clause in illustrating the content of the Europeanised constitution was pointed out above. The difference is that, on that occasion, the clause is used as an expression of the 'Europeanisation' of the national constitution, whereas here it is used as a guarantee of it.

3. Redefining the Role of the European and the National Judiciaries as Guardians of the EUMSC

As I have observed from the outset, the three-tiered structure of the EUMSC has immediate impact on the identity of its guardian or guardians. Based on the previous description of each of the three identified tiers, it is now possible to examine using

[21] A von Bogdandy and S Schill, 'Die Achtung der nationalen Identität unter dem reformierten Unionsvertrag. Zur unionsrechtlichen Rolle nationalen Verfassungsrechts und zur Überwindung des absoluten Vorrangs' (2010) 70 *Zeitschrift für ausländisches öffentliches Recht und Völkerrecht (ZaoRV)*, 701; P Cruz Mantilla de los Rios, *La identidad nacional de los Estados miembros en el Derecho de la Unión Europea* (Madrid, Thomson Reuters Aranzadi, 2022); D Grimm, 'Three Meanings of Constitutional Identity and their Prospects in the European Union' in J de Poorter et al (eds), *A Constitutional Identity for the EU?* (2022) 4 *European Yearbook of Constitutional Law* 13; F-X Millet, L'Union Européenne et l'identité constitutionnelle des États membres (Paris, LGDJ, 2013).

[22] R Bifulco and D Paris, 'Der italienische Verfassungsgericht' in A von Bogdandy, C Grabenwarter and PM Huber (eds), *Handbuch Ius Publicum Europaeum, vol VI, Verfassungsgerichtsbarkeit in Europa: Institutionen* (Heidelberg, CF Müller, 2016) 271–356.

[23] P Cruz Villalón, 'La identidad constitucional de los Estados Miembros: Dos relatos europeos' (2013) 17 *Anuario de la Facultad de Derecho de la Universidad Autónoma de Madrid (AFDUAM)* 501.

differentiated treatment the generic question of the guardian of the Constitution in the case of the EUMSC.

3.1. The *Associated* Guardians of the Europeanised Constitution

As seen, the Europeanised constitution, alongside the national constitution, enjoys supremacy over the rest of the national legal order, by consequence of the mandates of constitutional relevance coming from EU law which at the same time participate in the primacy of application or prevalence of EU law. This gives rise to a situation in which the national Constitutional Court and the CJEU converge in guaranteeing this first tier, albeit ultimate responsibility lies with the CJEU.

Before proceeding, however, another preliminary clarification. EU law contains in Article 7 TEU an exceptional *political* guarantee of the Europeanised constitution, in the sense that it is entrusted, not to the CJEU, but to the political bodies of the EU which may adopt various measures against Member States that fail to comply with the values listed in Article 2 TEU. I will just mention the following points. First, by its very nature, it is a guarantee for situations of genuine exception, and therefore not a guarantee for normal circumstances. Secondly, because of the very high consensus required in the European Council, this guarantee has proven impracticable when it was required in recent years. This has led to a situation in which the CJEU has had to play the role of judicial guarantor and assume this responsibility with all the difficulties entailed. The final consideration is that, while a political guarantor is conceivable in a federal state or equivalent structure,[24] it runs into almost insurmountable difficulties in the context of a supranational community such as the EU.

This said, the confluence of the national constitutional jurisdiction and the CJEU in the guarantee of this first tier of the EUMSC is worth attention. The competence of each in this guarantee is unquestionable. What can be asked is how to organise the exercise of this competence in such a way as to avoid dysfunction. The best-known point of friction concerns the relationship between the preliminary ruling before the CJEU when questions of unconstitutionality come before the national constitutional court. The CJEU has famously emphasised the power of the ordinary national court to refer a question for a preliminary ruling at any time, along with its insistence that the CJEU interpretation of EU law is not contested.

The matter also raises the question of how the relationship between the two jurisdictional guarantees – that of the CJEU, as guarantor of primacy; and that of the Constitutional Court, as guarantor of supremacy – is articulated. This is a classic question in the dynamics of relations between two separate, largely self-referential legal systems, in particular whenever the Member State has a special constitutional jurisdiction. On this occasion, however, there are two jurisdictions called upon to guarantee

[24] See, for the Spanish case, P Cruz Villalón, 'Experiencia y jurisprudencia de la coerción estatal' (2020) 40 *Revista Española de Derecho Constitucional* 15.

and interpret a single rule, with the particularity that two different normative wills, so to speak, coincide.

Two cases, one of a rather exceptional nature, the other with a much more ordinary character, deserve brief comment here. Firstly, it is worth pointing out that the cases mentioned at the outset involving rule of law backsliding and in particular judicial independence, notably in Hungary and Poland, are also interesting from a semantic point of view in that they are frequently alluded to by an express reference to the CJEU as the 'guardian' of the national constitution.[25] Secondly, at a level of constitutional normality, the situation of the guarantee of fundamental rights should be clarified, particularly in cases where a procedural remedy is available to individuals for the guarantee of these rights in the Member State. Recall the well-known development in the constitutional case law, first in Austria and then in Germany, whereby their respective constitutional courts asserted their competence to respond to claims for the guarantee of fundamental rights as recognised in the CFR.[26] More concisely, in both cases the coincidence between the European standard and the national standard prompts the national constitutional courts to take up the mantle of guaranteeing rights formally situated in the primary law of the EU: in principle, without prejudice to their duty to ensure beforehand that their criteria are consistent with those of the CJEU.[27]

In short, from this point onwards, an *extension* of the aforementioned jurisprudential approach would be considered worthwhile: what has been valid for the CFR may be valid for all the mandates of EU law relevant to the constitution of the Member State as reproduced in the Europeanised constitution. The principle of the rule of law could be a good example.

3.2. The *Devalued* Guardian of the Self-Determined Constitution

As is to be expected, the guardian of the self-determined or original constitution is the original guardian of the constitution represented in the classical scenario by the national constitutional court. It is the paramount keeper of the primacy of the national constitution insofar as it is unaffected by the constitutionally relevant mandates emanating from EU law. This amounts to affirming the accustomed notion of 'a' guardian, in the singular, of the national constitution suffers no change concerning this second tier of the EUMSC. With a fundamental caveat nevertheless: the national constitutional court must endure the ever-growing presence of the prevalent application of EU law and consequently the relative power of the Europeanised constitution, which renders the relationship between the said first and second tier asymmetrical. In short, the national constitutional court is a single but devalued guardian.

[25] Above n 3.

[26] R Hofmann and A Heger, 'Zur neuen Grundrechte-Architektur im europäischen Mehrebenen-System (2021) 48 *EuGRZ* 1; P Cruz Villalón, 'Still on Constitutional Courts at the rescue of their Mandate' in P B Donath et al (eds), *Der Schutz des Individuums durch das Recht* (Berlin, Springer, 2023) 873–86.

[27] BVerfGE 152, 216 ('Right to be forgotten'). *cf* X Arzoz, *Transformaciones judiciales. Karlsruhe y los derechos fundamentales de la Unión Europea* (Madrid, CEPC, 2022).

3.3. The *Stressed* Guardian of the Disputed Constitution (or the Constitution of Last Resort)

If the determination of the guardian of the first two tiers of the EUMSC can be resolved in more or less rational terms, the guarantee of this third component presents something of a conundrum. In the end, it leads to the question of the guarantee of the guarantors, classically termed *quis cuestodiet custodes ipsos*, only: with the added difficulty of the presence of two competing *custodes*. The difficulty we face in this conundrum goes to the very nature of this last component of the EUMSC.

This makes the CJEU as the European guardian and the constitutional court as the national guardian mutually *neutralised* guardians, to the point of posing the question of whether they simply deserve the name of guardians. Then, if they are guardians, after all, they are obligated to uninterrupted *negotiation*, otherwise called *dialog* in friendly terms. This is the origin of images such as the *perpetuum mobile* or the 'league of the European Constitutional Courts', both proposals by Andreas Voβkuhle.[28] To conclude, the situation is about two courts looking at each other when interpreting norms of parallel, although not identical, content.

4. Conclusions

The increasingly conspicuous role of the CJEU as surrogate guardian of the constitution of the EU Member States calls for renewed attention to the characteristics both of the European constitutional aggregate and the Member State constitutions. There is a particular need to engage in a top-down analysis of the constitutions of the Member States; ie, undertaking an inquiry that, with all due caution, takes as its point of departure the singular condition of the Member States that form part of the supranational polity. The prevalent pluralistic understanding of the constitutions of the Member States should be shelved in order to concentrate attention on the common features of the members' constitutions that together comprise a unitary normative profile in its own right, that is, a strategic component of the European constitutional aggregate worthy of an acronym: the EUMSC.

The dissection of the EUMSC reveals the following three-tiered structure: (a) a *Europeanised* or *hetero-determined* constitution; (b) a *self-determined* or *original* (otherwise *residual* or *enucleated*) constitution; (c) a constitution *of last resort* (otherwise *contested* constitution).

The first tier of the EUMSC, the Europeanised or hetero-determined constitution is: (a) a *state* constitution; (b) a constitution *founded on values*; (c) a *conventional* constitution; and (d) a *torso* or *incomplete* constitution. Concerning its binding force, it reunites the principle of prevalent application of EU law and the principle of supremacy of the national constitution.

[28] A Voβkuhle, 'Der europäische Verfassungsgerichtsverbund' in A Voβkuhle, *Europa, Demokratie, Verfassungsgerichte* (Berlin, Suhrkamp, 2021) 265; A Voβkuhle, 'Pyramide oder Mobile? Menschenrechtsschutz durch die europäischen Verfassungsgerichte' in A Voβkuhle, *Europa, Demokratie, Verfassungsgerichte* (Berlin, Suhrkamp, 2021) 305–13, 313.

The second tier of the EUMSC is the self-determined or original constitution which encompasses the body of national constitutional provisions upon which EU law does not impinge or, simply put, the Europeanised constitution *by default*. As for its binding force, it conjugates the supremacy germane to the constitution vis-à-vis the rest of the national legal order with its subordinate position to the prevalent application of EU law on par with the rest of the national legal order.

The third tier of the EUMSC is the disputed constitution (or constitution of last resort) which emerges as a national reaction to the innate pressure of the Europeanised constitution. In one direction, it opens the way for a national monitoring of the quality of the EU constitutional structure; in the other, it establishes a safeguard for the essential elements of the national constitution. Its peculiarity derives from the circumstance of the parallel provisions from the EU (*reciprocal metaconstitutionality*).

Drawing on the above, the guardian of the EUMSC is to be determined in the following terms. Concerning the first tier, the *political* guarantee of the constitution (Article 7 TEU), a frequent institute in federal states, has proven impotent in the case of a supranational polity, that is, it has not been able to act as an effective guardian of the Europeanised constitution (namely the rule of law crisis). By contrast, the European and the national judiciaries are proving their capacity to act as *associated* guardians of the Europeanised constitution (namely the CFR).

As for the second tier of the EUMSC, the guardian of the self-determined or original constitution suffers no change, that is, it continues under the domain of the constitutional jurisdiction. Notwithstanding, the principle of prevalent application of EU law justifies to some degree likening it to a *devalued* guardian.

Finally, in the third tier, latent (or even open) conflict describes the situation when a national guardian intending to protect the core contents of the national constitution is on a par with a European guardian intent on preventing adulteration of the principle of primacy of EU law. Consequently, the question of the guardianship of the disputed constitution permanently oscillates between negotiation and conflict.

Bibliography

Arzoz, X, *Transformaciones judiciales. Karlsruhe y los derechos fundamentales de la Unión Europea* (Madrid, CEPC, 2022).

Bifulco, R and Paris, D, 'Der italienische Verfassungsgerichtshof' in Bogdandy, A von, Grabenwarter, CHR and Huber, PM (eds), *Handbuch Ius Publicum Europaeum, vol VI, Verfassungsgerichtsbarkeit in Europa: Institutionen* (Heidelberg, CF Müller, 2016) 271–356.

Bogdandy von, A, *Strukturwandel des öffentlichen Rechts. Entstehung und Demokratisierung der europäischen Gesellschaft* (Berlin, Suhrkamp, 2022).

Bogdandy, A von and Schill, S 'Die Achtung der nationalen Identität unter dem reformierten Unionsvertrag. Zur unionsrechtlichen Rolle nationalen Verfassungsrechts und zur Überwindung des absoluten Vorrangs' (2010) 70 *Zeitschrift für ausländisches öffentliches Recht und Völkerrecht (ZaoRV)* 701.

Claes, M and De Witte, B, 'The Roles of Constitutional Courts in the European Legal Space' in Bogdandy von, A, Huber, PM and Grabenwarter, CHR (eds), *Constitutional Adjudication. Common Themes and Challenges, The Max Planck Series in European Public Law*, vol IV (Oxford, Oxford University Press, 2023).

Collins, J, *Democracy's Guardians: a history of the German Federal Constitutional Court (1951–2001)* (Oxford, Oxford University Press, 2015).

Cruz Mantilla de los Ríos, P, *La identidad nacional de los Estados miembros en el Derecho de la Unión Europea* (Madrid, Thomson Reuters Aranzadi, 2022).

Cruz Villalón, P, 'Bemerkungen zu Begriff und Funktion der Verfassung des EU-Mitgliedstates' in Hofmann, R et al (eds), *Festschrift für Franz Merli* (Baden-Baden, Nomos, 2023) 671–83.

—— 'Constitución nacional y Constitución europea' in Cruz Villalón, P, *La constitución inédita. Estudios ante la constitucionalización de Europa* (Madrid, Trotta, 2004).

—— 'Experiencia y jurisprudencia de la coerción estatal' (2020) 40 *Revista Española de Derecho Constitucional* 15.

—— 'La constitución (del Estado miembro de la UE) como logro evolutivo' in N Luhmann, *La constitución como logro evolutivo. Introducción, traducción y epílogo de Pedro Cruz Villalón* (Madrid, Tecnos, 2024) IL-LXXV.

—— 'La Constitución del Estado miembro: Un intento de recapitulación' in Gordillo, L (ed), *Spanish Constitution and European Integration. Treinta años de Derecho Constitucional de la integración. Actas del XIV Congreso de la Asociación de Constitucionalistas de España* (Valencia, Tirant, 2018) 19–29.

—— 'La identidad constitucional de los Estados Miembros: Dos relatos europeos' (2013) 17 *Anuario de la Facultad de Derecho de la Universidad Autónoma de Madrid* 501.

—— 'The Evolution of Constitutional Adjudication in Europe' in Bogdandy von, A Huber, PM, Grabenwarter, CHR (eds), *Constitutional Adjudication. Common Themes and Challenges, The Max Planck Series in European Public Law*, vol IV (Oxford, Oxford University Press, 2023).

—— 'Still on Constitutional Courts at the rescue of their Mandate' in Donath, P et al (eds), *Der Schutz des Individuums durch das Recht* (Berlin, Springer, 2023) 907–18.

Faraguna, P, 'Constitutional Identity in the EU – A Shield or a Sword' (2017) 18 *German Law Journal* 1617.

Grimm, D, 'Die Rolle der nationalen Verfassungsgerichte in der europäischen Demokratie' now in Grimm, D, *Europa ja – aber welches? Zur Verfassung der europäischen Demokratie* (Munich, CH Beck, 2016) 199–224.

—— 'Three Meanings of Constitutional Identity and their Prospects in the European Union' in Poorter, J et al (eds), *A Constitutional Identity for the EU?* (2022) 4 *European Yearbook of Constitutional Law* 13.

Hofmann, R and Heger, A, 'Zur neuen Grundrechte-Architektur im europäischen Mehrebenen-System' (2021) 48 *EuGRZ* 1.

Izquierdo Sans, C, 'Preferencia aplicativa y diálogo judicial' (2019) 1 *InDret. Revista para el análisis del Derecho* 1.

Krisch, N, 'The Spanish constitutional crisis: Law, legitimacy and popular sovereignty in question', *Verfassungsblog. On matters constitutional*, 7 October 2017.

Martín y Pérez de Nanclares, J, 'The Cooperation of Constitutional Courts in the European Legal Space' in Bogdandy, A von, Huber, M and Grabenwarter, CHR (eds), *Constitutional Adjudication. Common Themes and Challenges, The Max Planck Series in European Public Law*, vol IV (Oxford, Oxford University Press, 2023).

Merli, F, 'Die Konstitutionalisierung der EU-Grundrechte: Das österreichische Beispiel' in Donath, P et al (eds), *Der Schutz des Individuums durch das Recht* (Berlin, Springer, 2023) 873–86.

Millet, F-X, *L'Union Européenne et l'identité constitutionnelle des États membres* (Paris, LGDJ, 2013).

Requejo Pagés, JL, 'Primacía de la Unión y soberanía nacional. Consideraciones sobre una posible solución normativa de un conflicto de principio' in Urías Martínez, J and Álvarez-Ossorio

Micheo, F, *Cultura constitucional en Europa. Encuentro hispalense en torno a la obra del profesor Pedro Cruz Villalón* (Seville, Publicaciones de la Universidad de Sevilla, 2022) 255–71.

—— 'The Decline of the European Model of European Constitutional Jurisdiction' in Bogdandy, von A, Huber, PM and Grabenwarter, CHR (eds), *Constitutional Adjudication. Common Themes and Challenges, The Max Planck Series in European Public Law*, vol IV (Oxford, Oxford University Press, 2023).

Sadurski, W, *Poland's Constitutional Breakdown* (Oxford, Oxford University Press, 2019).

Saiz Arnaiz, A, Alcobero Livina, C, (eds), *National constitutional identity and European integration* (Cambridge, Antwerp, Poland, Intersentia, 2013).

Van der Schiff, G, 'EU Member State Constitutional Identity: A Comparison of Germany and the Netherlands as Polar Opposites' (2016) 76 *Zeitschrift für ausländisches öffentliches Recht und Völkerrecht (ZaoRV)* 167.

Vincx, L, *The Guardian of the constitution. Hans Kelsen and Carl Schmitt on the Limits of Constitutional Law*. Translation, Introduction and Notes by Lars Vinx (Cambridge, Cambridge University Press, 2015).

De Visser, M, *Constitutional Courts in Europe. A Comparative Analysis* (Oxford, Hart, 2014).

Voβkuhle, A, 'Der europäische Verfassungsgerichtsverbund' in Voβkuhle, A, *Europa, Demokratie, Verfassungsgerichte* (Berlin, Suhrkamp, 2021) 265–89.

—— 'Pyramide oder Mobile? Menschenrechtsschutz durch die europäischen Verfassungsgerichte' in Voβkuhle, A, *Europa, Demokratie, Verfassungsgerichte* (Berlin, Suhrkamp, 2021) 305–13.

Zglinski, J, 'The new judicial federalism: the evolving relationship between EU and Member State Courts' (2023) 2 *European Law Open* 345.

9

The Europeanisation of the Constitutional Parameter of Review: A By-Product of the Charter of Fundamental Rights

XABIER ARZOZ

1. Introduction

The area of jurisdiction in which every court must play its role is defined and can be described in general terms as review. Judicial review is performed according to a programme set previously, step by step, by different actors; mainly the constitution-maker and the lawmaker, but also often by the body or set of bodies responsible for review. The judicial review programme assigned to a court results from the identification and combination of four basic elements: object; parameter; standard or intensity; and the effects of the review.

These four coordinates define and determine what a court can review, with the help of which parameter, to which degree of scrutiny and with which substantive and temporal effects. These coordinates not only serve to assign responsibility for review; they also allow us to contrast the review programmes of different courts (ordinary, constitutional, international and supranational) since different courts tend to perform distinct review programmes in which one or more of those elements entirely or partially vary. This also explains, at least in part, the divergent outcomes often arrived at in cases involving the same or similar facts.

Since its conception in 1920, the European model of constitutional justice has developed in two directions. On the one hand, it has evolved from the negative legislator paradigm to a more complex constitutional role which to some extent occurred through a natural process of maturation and for which the term 'review' does not properly describe its impact on the legal order. Nevertheless, for the purposes of this chapter, the notion of review will be confined to describing the function generally assigned to constitutional courts. The other development involves the increasing internationalisation of law, which has also understandably affected constitutional adjudication. Over the past few decades in European Union (EU) Member States, the main driving force transforming the European model of constitutional justice has been European integration.

The process of EU integration has been more conflictive than the evolution from the negative legislator paradigm of constitutional jurisdiction. An ample literature demonstrates the well-known *Simmenthal* doctrine of the Court of Justice of the European Union (CJEU) and the great overthrow of the concentrated European model of constitutional justice.[1] However, less attention has been devoted to the transformation of the main coordinates of constitutional adjudication in terms of the change in the object, parameter, level of scrutiny and effects of that adjudication.

Focusing on the less noticeable transformation of the review programme of constitutional courts will enable us to assess the impact of European integration on constitutional justice by means of this less travelled path. Two different ways of assessing the Europeanisation of constitutional justice are possible, depending on whether one looks at its substantive or formal aspect. The substantive approach looks at the content of the case law, at the convergence of values and principles and at the reception and intertwining of constitutional principles between orders. The formal approach, by contrast, looks at key aspects that define the review function of constitutional courts in their legal orders.

This chapter will analyse the influence of the EU Charter of Fundamental Rights (CFR) on the transformation of the review function of European constitutional courts. It has two intertwined objectives. One is assessing the capacity to discipline constitutional courts' review programmes over time. The other is examining the degree of autonomy constitutional courts display when they accommodate their review programmes to evolving EU law. Due to space limitations, the chapter will look only at one of the review coordinates, the parameter of judicial review, which is probably the most significant and at least the most peculiar element of constitutional review by constitutional courts.

The adaptation of the review programmes of constitutional courts can be distinguished from the generally recognised evolutive interpretation of constitutional texts, which mainly affects substantive case law. It is through evolutive interpretation that the meaning of the constitution develops and adapts to societal needs. EU law or European integration are both factors to be considered in the dynamic interpretation of constitutional provisions; however, dynamical interpretation of a constitutional provision that does not change over time is one thing, while another is adjusting the very review programme of the constitutional jurisdiction (generally established by constitutional and legal provisions), in that it involves incorporating new provisions of a non-constitutional character. In other words, we must distinguish, on the one hand, between the evolutive interpretation of the content of the parameter of review and, on the other, the broadening or eventually even the replacement of the parameter of review.[2]

[1] See M Bobek, 'The Impact of the European Mandate of Ordinary Courts on the Position of Constitutional Courts' in M Claes et al (eds), *Constitutional Conversations in Europe* (Cambridge, Intersentia, 2012); D Piqani, 'The Simmenthal revolution revisited: what role for constitutional courts?' in B de Witte et al (eds), *National Courts and EU Law. New Issues, Theories and Methods* (Cheltenham, Edward Elgar, 2016).

[2] On the continuous evolution of the substantive parameter of constitutional review, see A Spadaro, 'Dalla Costituzione come "atto" (puntuale nel tempo) alla Costituzione come "processo" (storico): Ovvero della continua "evoluzione" del parametro costituzionale attraverso i giudizi di costituzionalità' (1998) *Quaderni costituzionali* 343.

EU law does not in itself modify the understanding and relevance of the basic elements of constitutional review, but it can indirectly require adjustments to their configuration. The hypothesis underlying this chapter is that the emergence of a new parameter of validity (for instance, EU law, or more specifically the CFR) and a new court, responsible for its exclusive review in an already populated constitutional space, will trigger a process of adjustment for either the object or the parameter of review (or both) that constitutional courts apply regarding domestic acts and norms in cases related to EU law.[3]

The Europeanisation of the constitutional parameter of review started before the CFR came into force. In Italy, the Constitutional Court has jurisdiction to review the compatibility of regional laws 'with the constraints deriving from EU legislation and international obligations' by virtue of Article 117 of its Constitution, introduced in 2001.[4] In Belgium, it was the 2009 reform of legislation on constitutional jurisdiction that legitimated the use of international and EU fundamental rights to review national legal norms inasmuch as they are analogous to the constitutionally entrenched rights.[5]

Although the broadening of the constitutional parameter of review in those Member States took place independently of the entry into force of the CFR, Charter rights also benefited from this broadening. The adjustments looked at the convenience for the domestic legal system. Their priority was coherent application of the legal sources and preserving relevant space for concentrated constitutional jurisdiction.

By contrast, the entry into force of the CFR on 1 December 2009 and the CJEU's seminal federalising case law on the CFR's horizontal provisions made urgent a profound revision of the parameter of review being applied by constitutional jurisdictions.[6] Two judgments of the CJEU handed down on 26 February 2013 embodied that federalising case law. They mapped the situations where EU law and, consequently, the CFR must apply. According to the *Melloni* judgment, when the regulation of an issue is fully

[3] Already R Streinz, *Bundesverfassungsgerichtlicher Grundrechtsschutz und Europäisches Gemeinschaftsrecht* (Baden-Baden, Nomos, 1989) 293–304, 472.

[4] See O Pollicino, 'L'integrazione del parametro costituzionale alla luce del diritto comunitario "presa sul serio"' in G Bronzini and V Piccone (eds), *La Carta e le Corti. I diritti fondamentali nella giurisprudenza europea multilivello* (Taranto, Chimienti, 2007).

[5] See J Velaers, 'Le contrôle des lois, décrets et ordonnances au regard du titre II de la Constitution et des conventions internationales relatives aux droits de l'homme, en cas de concours de droits fondamentaux' in A Arts et al (eds), *Les rapports entre la Cour d'arbitrage, le Pouvoir judiciaire et le Conseil d'État* (Brussels, Larcier, 2006).

[6] For previous comparative works on the topic, see J Komárek, 'National constitutional courts in the European constitutional democracy' (2014) 12 *I•CON* 525; J Komárek, 'Why National Constitutional Courts Should Not Embrace EU Fundamental Rights' in S de Vries, U Bernitz and S Weatherill (eds), *The EU Charter of Fundamental Rights as a Binding Instrument – Five Years Old and Growing* (Oxford, Hart, 2015); X Arzoz, *La tutela de los derechos fundamentales de la Unión Europea por el Tribunal Constitucional* (Madrid, Instituto Nacional de Administración Pública, 2015); X Arzoz, *Transformaciones judiciales: Karlsruhe y los derechos fundamentales de la Unión Europea* (Madrid, Centro de Estudios Políticos y Constitucionales, 2022); D Paris, 'Constitutional courts as European Union courts: The current and potential use of EU law as a yardstick for constitutional review' (2017) 24 *Maastricht Journal of European and Comparative Law* 792; C Rauchegger, 'The Charter as a Standard of Constitutional Review in the Member States' in M Bobek and J Adams-Prassl (eds), *The EU Charter of Fundamental Rights in the Member States* (Oxford, Hart, 2020).

harmonised at the EU level, the situation demands the *exclusive* application of the CFR.[7] According to the other judgment, *Åkerberg Fransson*, when the regulation of an issue is not fully harmonised at the EU level, the level of protection of the CFR is still *always* applicable to that situation, but higher national standards that *improve* the protection of the right in question are admissible as long as that higher standard does not affect the autonomy, unity or effectiveness of EU law.[8]

These two judgments vigorously undermined the firm assurance of certain constitutional jurisdictions in their capacity as privileged vessels freely navigating European constitutional waters and docking only at ports of their homeland for provisions. To continue with the metaphor, the CJEU's February 2013 judgments extended its territorial sovereignty to all European constitutional waters, reigning in constitutional courts' former freedom of the seas. Constitutional courts became subject to the legal force of the CFR just like any other national court.

In this chapter, the processes of adaptation of the constitutional parameter of review in four Member States – Austria, Spain, Germany and Portugal – will be analysed (in chronological order) in the wake of the CFR before these experiences are compared and a few conclusions drawn.

2. Austria

The Austrian Constitutional Court was the first to take a kick at the ball. Until 2012, its traditional stance resembled that of most of its European homologues. Since adhesion, the Constitutional Court had acknowledged the primacy of EU law, but it did not consider EU law part of the constitutional parameter for the review of national norms and decisions. At the same time, nothing prevented the court from applying EU law

[7] Case C-399/11 *Stefano Melloni v Ministerio Fiscal* ECLI:EU:C:2013:107, [2013] ECR. See, among many, N De Boer, 'Addressing Rights Divergences under the Charter: Melloni – Case C-399/11, Stefano Melloni v. Ministerio Fiscal, Judgment of the Court (Grand Chamber) of 26 February 2013' (2013) 50 *Common Market Law Review* 1083; D Sarmiento, 'Who's afraid of the Charter? The Court of Justice, national courts and the new framework of fundamental rights protection in Europe' (2013) 50 *Common Market Law Review* 1267; A Bailleux, 'Entre droits fondamentaux et intégration européenne, la Charte des droits fondamentaux de l'Union européenne face à son destin (C.J.U.E., *Stefano Melloni* et *Åkerberg Fransson*, 26 février 2013)' (2014) 97 *Revue trimestrielle des droits de l'homme* 215; LFM Besselink, 'The Parameters of Constitutional Conflict after *Melloni*' (2014) 39 *European Law Review* 531; C Franzius, 'Grundrechtsschutz in Europa – Zwischen Selbstbehauptungen und Selbstbeschränkungen der Rechtsordnungen und ihrer Gerichte' (2015) 75 *Zeitschrift für ausländisches öffentliches Recht und Völkerrecht* 383; A Pliakos and G Anagnostaras, 'Fundamental Rights and the New Battle over Legal and Judicial Supremacy: Lessons from *Melloni*' (2015) 34 *Yearbook of European Law* 97; and C Rauchegger, 'The Interplay between the Charter and National Constitutions after *Åkerberg Fransson* y *Melloni*. Has the CJEU Embraced the Challenges of Multilevel Fundamental Rights Protection?' in S de Vries, U Bernitz and S Weatherill (eds), *The EU Charter of Fundamental Rights as a Binding Instrument. Five Years Old and Growing* (Oxford, Hart, 2018).

[8] Case C-617/10 *Åklagaren v Hans Åkerberg Fransson* ECLI:EU:C:2013:105, [2013] ECR. See, among many, Sarmiento (n 7); D Thym, 'Separation versus Fusion – or: How to Accommodate National Autonomy and the Charter? Diverging Visions of the German Constitutional Court and the European Court of Justice' (2013) 9 *European Constitutional Law Review* 391; P Wattel and B Van Bockel, 'New Wine into Old Wineskins: The Scope of the Charter of Fundamental Rights of the EU after *Åkerberg Fransson*' (2013) 38 *European Law Review* 866; Bailleux (n 7); and Rauchegger (n 7).

whenever it acted as a court of first instance in disputes over competence, patrimony and elections.[9]

In early 2012, long before the CJEU launched its federalising case law on the application of the CFR, however, the Austrian Constitutional Court handed down an impressive judgment.[10] It declared that its previous case law was no longer applicable to the CFR,[11] explaining that the CFR 'constitutes within EU law an area clearly distinguishable from the treaties'. The Court accepted that parties before it could invoke CFR rights as constitutionally entrenched rights, in light of Articles 144 and 144a of the Constitution, and that, within the scope of their application, such CFR rights enter into the constitutional parameter of review of national rules according to Articles 139 and 140 of the Constitution.

The sweeping transformation was grounded on three arguments: the EU principle of equivalence; the concentrated character of constitutional review in Austria concerning all legal rules (both laws and regulations); and the broad material identity and similar wording of CFR rights and ECHR rights, which have been constitutionally entrenched rights in Austria since the 1960s.[12] The Austrian Constitutional Court ruled that, despite the continuity by CFR rights of the fundamental rights previously recognised as general principles of law, the CFR had brought about a transformation. The force of a detailed catalogue of rights, such as those contained in the CFR, cannot be compared to the force of legal positions deduced from general principles of law. As constitutionally entrenched rights, they were deemed a parameter of review in proceedings before the Constitutional Court.[13]

[9] Indeed, two of the three preliminary references from the Constitutional Court to the CJEU before 2012 originated from those procedures. See R Müller, 'Verfassungsgerichtsbarkeit und Europäische Grundrechtscharta' (2012) 4 *Österreichische Juristen-Zeitung* 159, 159–61.

[10] Austrian Constitutional Court, judgment of 14 March 2012 (U 466/11-18), VfSlg. 19.632/2012 ECLI:AT:VFGH:2012:U466.2011. For commentary, see M Pöschl, 'Verfassungsgerichtsbarkeit nach Lissabon' (2012) 67 *Zeitschrift für öffentliches Recht* 587; G Granner, 'Grundrechtecharta und Verfassungsgerichtsbarkeit' in A Kahl, N Raschauer and S Storr (eds), *Grundsatzfragen der europäischen Grundrechtecharta* (Vienna, Verlag Österreich, 2013); R Klaushofer and R Palmstorfer, 'Austrian Constitutional Court uses the Charter of Fundamental Rights of the European Union as Standard of Review: Effects on Union Law' (2013) 19 *European Public Law* 1; E Saulnier-Cassia, 'La Cour constitutionnelle autrichienne face à la Charte des droits fondamentaux de l'Union européenne' (2013) *Revue trimestrielle de droit européen* 168; A Orator, 'The Decision of the Austrian *Verfassungsgerichtshof* on the EU Charter of Fundamental Rights: An Instrument of Leverage or Rearguard Action?' (2015) 15 *German Law Journal* 1429; S Kieber and R Klaushofer, 'The Austrian Constitutional Court Post Case-Law After the Landmark Decision on Charter of Fundamental Rights of the European Union' (2017) 23 *European Public Law* 221; G Holzinger, 'Das österreichische Verfassungsgerichtshof als Bewahrer der Grundrechte' (2018) 45 *Europäische Grundrechte Zeitschrift* 1; P Cruz Villalón, '¿Una forma de cooperación judicial no reclamada? Sobre la extensión del amparo a la Carta de Derechos Fundamentales de la UE' (2021) 25 *Anuario Iberoamericano de Justicia Constitucional* 57; and C Lechner-Hartlieb, 'The Implementation of Charter Rights in the Austrian System of Fundamental Rights Protection' in A Heger and M Malkmus (eds), *On the Relation between the EU Charter of Fundamental Rights and National Fundamental Rights* (Cham, Springer, 2024).

[11] The inspiration and some of the ideas in the judgment seem to come from a law review article entitled 'Constitutional jurisdiction and Charter of Fundamental Rights' whose subtitle deserves mention: '¿Enrichment or loss of functions?', which one of the judges on the Constitutional Court published shortly beforehand. See Müller (n 9) 165–67.

[12] Austrian Constitutional Court, judgment of 14 March 2012 (U 466/11-18), VfSlg. 19.632/2012 ECLI:AT:VFGH:2012:U466.2011, paras 26, 33 and 34.

[13] ibid para 38.

The incorporation of CFR rights into the constitutional parameter of review came with a condition and a caveat. The condition was the analogous wording and purpose of the CFR rights with rights guaranteed by the Austrian Constitution.[14] The caveat addressed the different normative structure of CFR and constitutional rights. The Constitutional Court considered that the individual guarantees contained in the CFR involve a partially different normative structure, since some of the guarantees are not identical to constitutionally entrenched rights, but rather are 'principles', as in the case of Articles 22 (cultural, religious and linguistic diversity) and 37 (environmental protection). Therefore, the Austrian Court warned that the determination of the CFR rights that constituted a parameter of review in proceedings before it should be decided on a case-by-case basis,[15] and the apparent consequence is that some CFR rights may be left out of this parameter for review.

3. Spain

The Spanish Constitutional Court was, unintentionally, one, if not the primary, driver behind the CJEU's early case law federalising the application of the CFR through the two judgments of 26 February 2013. Through three carefully worded requests for preliminary ruling (two on interpretation and one on validity), the Spanish Constitutional Court attempted to preserve the higher level of protection its case law afforded regarding the extradition to third countries of persons tried *in absentia*. In the end, the CJEU dismissed the arguments, but what is of interest for this chapter is that in the third question the Spanish Court referred to the CJEU, as an *ultima ratio* attempt to save face, it prompted the CJEU to give Article 53 of the CFR a pluralistic meaning.

The reply of the CJEU to the Spanish Constitutional Court was bitter. The CJEU rejected the pluralistic understanding of Article 53 proposed by the Spanish Court in order to safeguard its case law on the procedural guarantees to be observed in *absentia* trials.[16] While true that the content of its answer was not innovative, its implications struck a nerve at the centre of the constitutional review programme. The immediate consequence of *Melloni*, in terms of the Spanish Constitutional Court's request, was the replacement of the Spanish constitutional parameter of review by the European standard in the case at hand, which was established by the Framework Decision on the European Arrest Warrant and confirmed as valid by the CJEU. In *Melloni*, neither the terms 'replacement' nor 'displacement' are used, but, clearly, the domestic parameter of review, regardless of its content, was no longer operative, and this was due to the principle of primacy of EU law.[17] The dilemma facing the Spanish Court was how to conform with the CJEU's ruling after having repeatedly upheld the non-parametric quality of EU law.

[14] ibid para 35.
[15] ibid para 36.
[16] Case C-399/11, *Stefano Melloni v Ministerio Fiscal* ECLI:EU:C:2013:107, [2013] ECR, para 58.
[17] Ibid para 60.

The Spanish Constitutional Court, in its ruling following the *Melloni* judgment,[18] did this without discussing the CJEU's position or *Melloni*'s impact on the Spanish Court's conception of the constitutional parameter of review. Instead of a theoretical discussion, it went for a pragmatic solution. It presumed the constitutional level of protection converged with the European level of protection – to avoid the embarrassing situation of directly applying an alien parameter of review. Without admitting it, it resorted to consistent interpretation, a proven method of coordinating the interpretation of constitutional provisions with the international obligations of the state explicitly entrenched in the Constitution, albeit only regarding international human rights treaties.[19] In this case, however, consistent interpretation led to an abrupt lowering of the national constitutional standard of protection to meet the requirements of EU law. The amendment of the case law was, in addition, not limited to the pending case, but also applied for all cases going forward. Three constitutional judges, in their concurring votes, objected to the artifice of pretending to autonomously reach identical levels between the Spanish and European standards of protection.[20]

Following the saga of constitutional cases regarding the Council Framework Decision on the European Arrest Warrant came the General Regulation for the Protection of Personal Data, a regulation that brings about a deep substantive harmonisation of the exercise of a CFR fundamental right: consequentially, most of the field of application of that regulation qualifies as a *Melloni* situation.

As was inevitable, cases challenging the new right to be forgotten reached the Spanish Constitutional Court in 2016 and 2020. Both cases involved circumstances favourable to a decision calling for the direct application of the CFR. First, the structural requirements of EU law for the sole application of the CFR had been already laid down by the CJEU in *Melloni* and *Åkerberg* (2013), and their implications had been sufficiently discussed in legal scholarship. Second, the issue before the Spanish Constitutional Court dealt with an application submitted by an individual against *Google*, arguing that the Spanish Supreme Court had gone against the balancing criteria established by both the CJEU and the Spanish Constitutional Court itself, which on this issue found themselves of equal mind. Thirdly, directly applying the CFR did not seem as bold gesture as it did in 2014, especially after the German Federal Constitutional Court did exactly that in 2019; the so-called 'November (R)evolution' that will be explained later.[21]

[18] Spanish Constitutional Court, judgment 26/2014 of 13 February 2014, ECLI:ES:TC:2014:26. Unofficial English translation of the Court at STC 26-2014 EN.pdf (tribunalconstitucional.es). For an analysis see, among many, Arzoz, *Tutela* (n 6) 87–110, and JI Ugartemendia Eceizabarrena and S Ripol Carulla, *El Tribunal Constitucional en la encrucijada europea de los derechos fundamentales* (Oñati, Instituto Vasco de Administración Pública, 2017). In English, see X Arzoz, 'Avoiding the Rain or Learning to Dance in it: The Hesitations of the Spanish Constitutional Court' in A Heger and M Malkmus (eds), *On the Relation between the EU Charter of Fundamental Rights and National Fundamental Rights* (Cham, Springer, 2024).

[19] According to Art 10.2 of the Spanish constitution, 'The provisions relating to the fundamental rights and liberties recognised by the constitution shall be interpreted in conformity with the Universal Declaration of Human Rights and the international treaties and agreements thereon ratified by Spain.' For that constitutional provision, see A Saiz Arnaiz, *La apertura constitucional al Derecho internacional y europeo de los derechos humanos. El artículo 10.2 de la Constitución española* (Madrid, Consejo General del Poder Judicial, 1999); and X Arzoz, *La concretización y actualización de los derechos fundamentales* (Madrid, Centro de Estudios Políticos y Constitucionales, 2014) 159–262.

[20] Spanish Constitutional Court, judgment 26/2014 of 13 February 2014 ECLI:ES:TC:2014:26.

[21] The phrase 'November (R)evolution' comes from J Kühling, 'Das ‚Recht auf Vergessenwerden' vor dem BVerfG – November(r)evolution für die Grundrechtsarchitektur im Mehrebenensystem' (2020) 73 *Neue Juristische Wochenschrift* 275.

Notwithstanding, in its decisions in those cases, the Spanish Constitutional Court missed the opportunity to recognise the CFR as a parameter of review in so-called '*Melloni* situations' a second time.[22] The outcome in the second case is of particular interest. Because the claimant explicitly alleged that the Spanish Supreme Court had deviated from the criteria established by the CJEU in a case regarding the right to be forgotten, the Constitutional Court carefully analysed the relevant CJEU case law.[23] However, the analysis presented did not go much deeper than comparative exercise refraining from taking any normative position to the parameter of review. Following the 'introductory report', the judgment examined the infringement of the 'fundamental right to be forgotten' through the lens of the balancing criteria extracted from the CJEU's own case law, which now carried its own weight apart from EU law, and interpreted it according to the Constitutional Court's general case law on the same criteria ('public relevance of the widespread information' and 'the time factor'). The Spanish Court found that, because these criteria were not met, the challenged decisions of the national courts violated the fundamental right to informative self-determination established by Article 18.4 of the Spanish Constitution. Hence, the parameter of review being applied was undoubtedly the Spanish Constitution.

What the Spanish Court did in this case stirred some controversy, as did the direction in which it seemed to be moving. Some thought the Court was beating a path leading to the direct application of the CFR.[24] In my view, the ruling does not depart from the Spanish Court's stance in *Melloni*.[25] Its approach is to fully comply with the content of the CJEU case law without intention to extend its application beyond the constitutional parameter of review.

Two judges who dissented with judgment 89/2022 made the same point as the three judges who elaborated a concurring opinion in judgment 26/2014 (*Melloni*), namely the ambiguity of the parameter of review being applied. Nevertheless, the reasons for their dissent differed. While the dissents in 2014 advocated the direct and unequivocal application of the European standard of protection, only eight years later the dissents would have preferred judgment 89/2022 to be more intensively or unequivocally grounded on constitutional fundamental rights.

In summary, the Spanish Constitutional Court's strategy for coping with the CJEU's *Melloni* and *Åkerberg Fransson* case law is conservative from a methodological and ideological perspective, but pragmatic from a substantive perspective. It consists of affirming the formal autonomy of the constitutional parameter of review, but firmly

[22] Spanish Constitutional Court, judgments 58/2018 of 4 June 2018 ECLI:ES:TC:2018:58 and 89/2022 of 29 June 2022 ECLI:ES:TC:2022:89.

[23] Case C-131/12 *Google Spain SL and Google Inc v Agencia Española de Protección de Datos (AEPD) and Mario Costeja González* ECLI:EU:C:2014:317; Case C-136/17 *GC and Others v Commission nationale de l'informatique et des libertés (CNIL)* ECLI:EU:C:2019:773; and Case C-507/17 *Google LLC, successor in law to Google In. v Commission nationale de l'informatique et des libertés (CNIL)* ECLI:EU:C:2019:772.

[24] They argue that up to this point, the Spanish Constitutional Court was moving in the same direction as advocated by the First Chamber of the German Federal Constitutional Court in *Recht auf Vergessen II*: R Alonso García, 'El TC y el derecho al olvido: ¿Allanando un camino "a la alemana" de la CDFUE como parámetro directo de amparo?' (2022) 82 *Revista Española de Derecho Europeo* 9; P Cruz Villalón, 'De la persistencia de un viejo *dictum*: la STC 89/2022, en contexto' in D Fromage (ed), *Jacques Ziller a European scholar* (Florence, European University Institute, 2022).

[25] Spanish Constitutional Court, judgment 26/2014 of 13 February 2014 ECLI:ES:TC:2014:26.

attaching its content to the European level of protection. Within the legal technique applied to this effect lies methodological conservatism: consistent interpretation as laid down in Article 10.2 of the Constitution, a proven method for coordinating the content of constitutional provisions with international obligations for the state.

4. Germany

Whereas the CJEU's *Melloni* judgment was a bitter pill for the Spanish Constitutional Court – as *Melloni* ignored the Spanish judges' aspiration to safeguard the higher national level of protection, the *Åkerberg Fransson* judgment was like a wrench thrown into the gears of the separation model implemented by the German Constitutional Court in 1986 and practised ever since.

The traditional German separation model distinguished two objects, two parameters and two organs for review. The CJEU would review the acts and norms of the EU institutions with the help of EU law, and the German Constitutional Court would review the constitutionality of the acts and norms of the German institutions using the Constitution as its benchmark. Regarding national acts and norms adopted to execute or implement EU law, the German constitutional jurisdiction would only review the part of those acts or norms not implementing EU law or where domestic institutions have a margin of appreciation. There was a rationale in doing so; reviewing the part of those acts that were an implementation or consequence of EU law would amount to indirectly reviewing provisions or legal acts of EU law.

The separation model worked relatively well regarding the review of legal norms, which ideally speaking, can be dissociated into parts deriving from either EU or national law. By contrast, when the object of review is a judicial decision, demarcating the division between the two becomes less evident. In this case, it can be argued that the Constitutional Court could, at least, review on the basis of the right to a legal judge of Article 101.1 of the Constitution on whether the ordinary court has fulfilled its duty to refer to the CJEU and thereby respected that Court's competence to interpret EU law in a definite way. However, supervising compliance with the judicial duty to refer, though essential, does not of itself ensure full enforcement of CFR rights by national courts.

In any case, the penetration and expansion of EU law put stress on the separation model beginning in 1986 and continued to increase. The review programme of the German Constitutional Court, and consequently its jurisdiction, risked confinement to an ever smaller and less relevant space.

In principle, the CJEU judgment in *Melloni* did not directly affect the German separation model, as far as it endorsed the direct application of the CFR in certain situations. However, the implications of the CJEU's judgment in *Åkerberg Fransson* on situations not fully harmonised were far-reaching. The judgment made the separation model imminently untenable.[26] Where before they had been separate, the CJEU imposed concurring standards of protection. The CFR must be always applicable within the scope of application of EU law, with the only variance being the possibility of complementing

[26] See Thym (n 8).

the European level of protection with a higher national standard, unless it injures the unity, autonomy or effectiveness of EU law. The German Constitutional Court now had to reconcile the notion of separation with the inescapable European parameter of review. The CJEU's emerging case law implied that the content of domestic legal acts could no longer be neatly divided into different parts for the Constitutional Court and CJEU to review without stepping on the other's toes.

It took some time, around six years, for the German Federal Constitutional Court to find its footing and address the implications of the CJEU's new case law without retreating into some jurisdictional 'winter headquarters'. The bold transformation of constitutional review that the strategy called for was guided most of all by concern for effective protection of fundamental rights.

If the CJEU had distinguished two possible situations under EU law (partial and full harmonisation of the substantive regulation) through two judgments issued the same day, so did the German Federal Constitutional Court, and in fact it copied the CJEU by addressing the two situations in two judgments also handed down on the same day.[27] The adaptation comprised not a uniform but a dual approach to accommodate *Melloni* and *Åkerberg Fransson*. A bold and innovative strategy, the constitutional jurisdiction would directly and exclusively apply the EU standard in so-called '*Melloni* situations', and preferentially apply the constitutional standard in other situations ('*Åkerberg Fransson* situations'), always with the self-imposed commitment to consistency with – deference towards – the supranational over national standards. In other words, even in so-called '*Åkerberg Fransson* situations' the constitutional standard must give way to the EU standard if it implied a higher level of protection.

In sum, in fully harmonised situations, the constitutional parameter and the CFR do not merge; they maintain separate lives and separate status. It is the Constitutional Court that in certain situations is to directly and exclusively apply the EU standard as a parameter of review. At the same time, the Court recognises that it is obliged to

[27] German Federal Constitutional Court, First Senate, judgments of 6 November 2019, 1 BvR 16/13 (*Right to be forgotten I*) ECLI:DE:BVerfG:2019:rs20191106.1bvr001613 and 1 BvR 276/17 (*Right to be forgotten II*) ECLI:DE:BVerfG:2019:rs20191106.1bvr027617. For a critical assessment, see S Burchardt, 'Backlash against the Court of Justice of the EU? The Recent Jurisprudence of the German Constitutional Court on EU Fundamental Rights as a Standard of Review' (2020) 21 *German Law Journal* 1; A Edenharter, 'Die EU-Grundrechte-Charta als Prüfungsmaßstab des Bundesverfassungsrechts' (2020) 73 *Die Öffentliche Verwaltung* 349; S Geiger, 'Allemagne: césure jurisprudentielle en matière de protection des droits fondamentaux européennes' (2020) *Revue trimestrielle de droit européen* 225; JM Hoffmann, 'Unionsgrundrechte als verfassungsrechtlicher Prüfungsmaßstab' (2020) *Neue Zeitschrift für Verwaltungsrecht* 33; JA Kämmerer and M Kotzur, 'Vollendung des Grundrechtsverbunds oder Heimholung des Grundrechtsschutzes?' (2020) *Neue Zeitschrift für Verwaltungsrecht* 177; D Thym 'Friendly Takeover, or: The Power of the "First Word". The German Constitutional Court embraces the Charter of Fundamental Rights as a Standard of Domestic Judicial Review' (2020) 16 *European Constitutional Law Review* 187; C Rauchegger, 'National Constitutional Courts as Guardians of the Charter: A Comparative Appraisal of the German Federal Constitutional Court's *Right to Be Forgotten* Judgments' (2020) 22 *Cambridge Yearbook of European Legal Studies* 258; M Wendel, 'The two-faced Guardian – Or how one Half of the German Federal Constitutional Court became a European Fundamental Rights Court?' (2020) 57 *Common Market Law Review* 1383; CD Classen, 'Über das Ziel hinausgeschossen? Anmerkung zu den zwei Beschlüssen des BVerfG zum Recht auf Vergessen vom 6.11.2019, 1 BvR 16/13, 276/17' (2021) *Europarecht* 92; R Hofmann and A Heger, 'Zur neuen Grundrechte-Architektur im europäischen Mehrebenensystem' (2021) 48 *Europäische Grundrechte Zeitschrift* 1; D Preßlein, 'Grundgesetz vs. Grundrechtscharta? Zur „europäisierten Grundrechtsprüfung" des BVerfG und nach den Beschlüssen zum „Recht auf Vergessen" und „Europäischer Haftbefehl III"' (2021) *Europarecht* 247; and Arzoz, *Transformaciones* (n 6) 201–93.

refer to the CJEU when the interpretation or the extent of the EU level of protection is unclear. In situations that are not fully harmonised, the Constitutional Court endorses the preferential use of the national standard while favouring attentiveness to the CFR in remaining cases, which in current circumstances might well statistically constitute most of them.

The scope of the new strategy was as yet only applied to the constitutional review of judicial decisions. Regarding the review of legal norms, the German Constitutional Court made no change. As before, it would only review the elements of legal norms which were not an execution or implementation of EU law or did not correspond to the national margin of discretion.

5. Portugal

The Portuguese Constitutional Court has traditionally kept a prudent distance from the line of application of EC/EU law. Only in 2020, after 34 years of EU membership, did it pronounce a *Solange*-like judgment recognising the full compatibility of European integration with the Constitution and affirming, albeit nominally, the *contralimiti* doctrine.[28] It is likely that the lack of any previous pronouncement and the relative kindness of the aforementioned 2020 judgment towards EU law have to do with Article 8.4 of Portugal's Constitution, which delivers a comfortably broad landing strip to receive and apply both primary and secondary EU law 'in the terms defined by it' within the Portuguese legal order.

In 2022, the Constitutional Court reviewed Law 32/2008 of 17 July 2008 implementing Directive 2006/24 on the conservation of personal data in electronic communications.[29] We should remember that the CJEU, after several other national laws implementing the Directive were declared unconstitutional,[30] and at the request of the High Court of Ireland and the Constitutional Court of Austria, declared the Directive invalid because of its indiscriminate retention of personal data.[31] Following the CJEU judgment, around 10 Member States also declared their respective national legislation implementing the Directive unconstitutional. Furthermore, in other rulings the CJEU insisted that national legislation providing for general and indiscriminate

[28] Portuguese Constitutional Court, judgment 422/2020 of 15 July 2020 (English translation at www.tribunalconstitucional.pt/tc/en/acordaos/20200422s.html).

[29] Portuguese Constitutional Court, judgment 268/2022 of 19 April 2022. On the background and development of the case see T Violante, 'How the Data Retention Legislation Led to a National Constitutional Crisis in Portugal' (2022) *Verfassungsblog.de*, 9 June 2022; and F Pereira Coutinho, 'The Charter of Fundamental Rights of the European Union at the Portuguese Constitutional Court: The Data Retention Cases' in A Heger and M Malkmus (eds), *On the Relation between the EU Charter of Fundamental Rights and National Fundamental Rights* (Cham, Springer, 2024).

[30] The most extensive declaration of unconstitutionality was the one by the First Senate of the German Federal Constitutional Court in judgment of 2 March 2010, 1 BvR 256/08 ECLI:DE:BVerfG:2010:rs20100302.1bvr025608.

[31] Joined Cases C-293/12 and C-594/12 *Digital Rights Ireland Ltd v Minister for Communications, Marine and Natural Resources and Others and Kärntner Landesregierung and Others* ECLI:EU:C:2014:238, [2014] ECR.

retention of personal data relating to means of electronic communication needed to be suppressed.[32]

In Portugal, however, Law 32/2008 of 17 July 2008 implementing the troublesome Directive 2006/24 remained formally in force, because of uncertainty over whether the grounds considered by the CJEU to invalidate the Directive applied to it. Despite the existence of doubts over the national law's validity, the legislature did not seek to amend it and no judges referred any request for preliminary ruling to the CJEU for an explicit pronouncement. The situation came to a head when, in 2017, the Portuguese authority for the protection of personal data invoked the '*Costanzo* doctrine'[33] and did not apply Law 32/2008, for being incompatible with EU law. Simultaneously, the Portuguese Ombudsperson challenged the constitutionality of Law 32/2008 before the Constitutional Court.

The constitutional challenge against Law 32/2008 was seen as an occasion to clarify the constitutionality of a law whose validity was doubted. The relevance of the challenge to this chapter is neither the outcome nor the content of the review, but rather the parameter selected to carry out that review.

The Portuguese Constitutional Court affirmed that its exclusive abstract review of constitutionality differs substantially from the diffuse review that Portuguese ordinary courts carry out regarding constitutionality and compatibility with European norms. While the ordinary courts perform applicability review, the Constitutional Court focuses on normative validity. To explain these different forms of review, the judgment referred to the distinction between the primacy (of EU law) and the supremacy (of the Constitution) on which the Spanish Constitutional Court in 2004 based the compatibility of the principle of primacy of EU law with the supremacy of the Constitution.[34] The Portuguese Constitutional Court held that reviewing validity and applicability were not incompatible, just different.

After asserting the distinctiveness of the abstract review procedure, the Court proclaimed that the Portuguese Constitution was the only parameter to be applied in this procedure for the invalidity of a national norm. Nevertheless, it also left room for the interpretative openness of the constitutional parameter. Unlike the Spanish context, however, it found the legal grounds for said openness not within the national constitution, but within EU law; it was the principle of consistent interpretation *established by EU law* that was the basis for this interpretative openness. Consequently, in abstract review the constitutional parameter of review incorporates the EU level of protection as laid down by EU secondary law and the abundant case law of the CJEU.

The judgment of the Portuguese Constitutional Court prompted a dissenting opinion joined by six out of the 13 judges on the Court objecting to the legal reasoning, though not to the solution being reached, for reasons connected to EU law. The dissent

[32] Among others, Joined Cases C-203/15 and C-698/15 *Tele2 Sverige AB v Post- och telestyrelsen and Secretary of State for the Home Department v Tom Watson and Others* ECLI:EU:C:2016:970, [2016] ECR, paras 112 and 125.

[33] Case 103/88 *Fratelli Costanzo SpA v Comune di Milano* ECLI:EU:C:1989:256, [1988] ECR 1839.

[34] Spanish Constitutional Court, declaration 1/2004 of 13 December 2004 ECLI:ES:TC:2004:1D (unofficial English translation of the court at www.tribunalconstitucional.es/ResolucionesTraducidas/STC%20 26-2014%20EN.pdf). The distinction of primacy and supremacy goes back to German case law and the distinction between *Anwendungs-* and *Geltungsvorrang*.

questioned the use made of consistent interpretation, claiming that the purpose of the principle of consistent interpretation, as laid down in EU law, is to compensate for the lack of direct effect of certain EU legal provisions through the unfolding of *effet utile*. The dissenting judges criticised the Court for using this principle to condition the outcome of the review of validity. In their opinion, the Court should have assumed the EU standard for reviewing the proportionality of the challenged legislation as established by the CJEU.

In summary, the judges of the Portuguese Constitutional Court were even more divided about the proper conduct of the abstract review of a legal norm passed to implement EU law than the Spanish judges in *Melloni*. The discord of almost half of the composition of the court (six judges out of 13) is reminiscent of the opposition in 2014 of three dissenting judges (out of a total of 12) to the *Melloni* judgment by the Spanish Constitutional Court. Both groups of dissenting judges criticised the artifice of erecting a supposedly autonomous constitutional parameter of review, to the aim of complying with the requirements of EU law. At one point, the Portuguese dissenters even went beyond what some of their Spanish colleagues advocated. Since, in the Portuguese case, the review was of a norm, they not only criticised the lack of assumption of the European *standard*, but also the *result* of the review of proportionality conducted by the CJEU, which was 'functionally equivalent' and performed with 'materially equivalent parameters'.

6. Conclusions

The legal force of the CFR and the CJEU's federalising case law on the CFR's horizontal clauses strongly added impetus to the progress of Europeanisation of the constitutional parameter of review. The EU standard of protection of fundamental rights attained a new position within the scope of the application of EU law. It was no longer merely a source of inspiration nor a minimal standard. In specific circumstances (so-called '*Melloni* situations'), it became the exclusive standard for the whole EU, complete and definitive, displacing the standard of any Member States, even those of a higher level of protection or constitutional rank. In 'non-*Melloni* situations', which for the time being are the majority, the CFR represents the minimum level of protection that Member States are generally allowed to raise voluntarily, but never lower.

In this chapter we have looked at the different techniques and strategies that several European constitutional courts have used with a similar purpose: to expand the constitutional parameter of review, either directly or indirectly, in order to align it with the CFR.

Some constitutional jurisdictions have taken those adjustments quite far, while others have been more hesitant or favoured less drastic solutions. The factors that lead to or discipline this adjustment vary enormously and include the reasoning deployed (use of constitutional legal grounds or of reasons derived from EU law or a combination of both), the semantics of solutions (incorporation, application, consistent interpretation or two of them in combination) and their extent and scope of application (abstract review of norms, review of individual judicial decisions or both).

Notwithstanding, two basic modalities of adjustment of the constitutional parameter can be identified: one being its replacement by the EU parameter and the other being hybridisation, bringing the constitutional parameter in line with the European standard. Some of these adjustments are open to further specifications and will obviously evolve over time, but already show a profound transformation of the main coordinate of the constitutional review programme: the parameter of review.

Comparatively, the boldest and most sophisticated adjustment was carried out by Germany. It combined the Constitutional Court's self-empowerment to directly apply the CFR rights in the less numerous '*Melloni* situations' and the application of the constitutional parameter consistently interpreted in line with the CFR in remaining situations. Furthermore, the new adjustment was limited to the review of individual judicial decisions, in as much as it maintained the old adjustment, the separation approach adopted in 1986 for the review of legal norms connected with EU law.

The broadening of the constitutional parameter of review in Austria was also boldly done. Explicitly reacting to the entry into force of the CFR, an aspiration to keep the review of legal norms concentrated on fundamental rights also played a role. The fact that the European Convention of Human Rights and several of its Protocols were already of constitutional rank in Austria provided an element of continuity, facilitating the adjustment. As with the Belgian legal reform of 2009, the incorporation of CFR rights to the constitutional parameter of review was conditioned on total or partial correspondence with the constitutionally entrenched rights.

By contrast, the Spanish adjustment was the least bold or sophisticated. Indeed, it did not properly constitute an adjustment, but rather a confirmation in the new scenario of case law already practised much earlier, starting with the adhesion to the European Communities in 1986. The Spanish Constitutional Court effectively tested and confirmed its existing approach to EU fundamental rights (and the EU more generally). Therefore, the reaction to the federalisation of the CFR was to maintain the status quo prior to the CFR's coming into force. It was also less sophisticated, for it applied the same approach to the review of both legal norms and judicial decisions.

The hybridisation of the constitutional parameter of review is a strategy of adjustment that has been attractive for several constitutional jurisdictions, whether as the only form of adjustment (as in Spain and Portugal) or as the form of adjustment for most cases in combination with the direct application of the European level of protection (the German case).

Constitutional courts likely encourage the hybridisation of the constitutional parameter of review as an adjustment strategy for a combination of reasons. First, a hybridisation strategy is less disruptive to the court's conception of its mandate to fully preserve the supremacy of the constitution, supremacy which it understands as the obligation to keep both the object and the parameter of constitutional review unamended. Second, it allows the courts to comply with the EU level of protection, or at least not deviate from it. Third, this strategy allows them to calibrate the extent to which EU law enters the national constitutional order and maintains the illusion of preserving sovereignty in areas deeply determined by EU law where the CJEU has already pronounced itself. The price of preserving this illusion is the permanent instrumentalisation of the constitutional parameter of review to avoid deviating from the EU level of protection.

Hybridisation as a solution is not always compatible with the federalising understanding of the CFR derived from *Melloni*, in which the CJEU imposed the exclusive application of the CFR. According to this judgment,

> where an EU legal act calls for national implementing measures, national authorities and courts remain free to apply *national standards of protection of fundamental rights*, provided that the level of protection provided for by the CFR, as interpreted by the Court, and the primacy, unity and effectiveness of EU law are not thereby compromised.[35]

Therefore, in the opposite situation, when an EU legal act does not call for national implementing measures, because there is full harmonisation of the regulation at the EU level, the mentioned premise fails and national authorities and courts are barred from applying 'national standards of protection', whatever their content, even if after hybridisation of those standards, the level of protection provided by the CFR is not compromised.

Some constitutional courts (Spain, Portugal) are internally divided over the compatibility of consistent interpretation of the constitutional parameter of review with the principle of primacy of EU law and the unequivocal content of the *Melloni* judgment. This may suggest that the hurdles for a bolder (and perhaps more correct) strategy of adjustment are not formal or material, but mainly ideological.

The process of adaptation of constitutional review may be driven by the evolution of EU law, but it is managed by each constitutional court against the backdrop of its legal culture. In each of the cases studied, adaptation has been steered exclusively by the constitutional court. Each constitutional court decides the timing and avenues for accommodation and gives its own reasons for it. In other words, the constitutional courts' contribution to the refinement of the constitutional review programme is crucial; the lawmaker can only deliver a basic framework that must be fine-tuned during its implementation in relation to other courts acting in the same areas (ordinary courts, the European Court of Human Rights and the CJEU).

The broad procedural autonomy enjoyed by most constitutional courts lets them adapt the constitutional review programme to the evolving factual and normative context of the constitutional state, which in the European setting is a cooperative state integrated in a supranational union. After all, the emergence at the supranational level of a new parameter of validity and a new review organ for using it as a benchmark was what generated the need to readjust the object and the parameter of constitutional review at the national level regarding acts and norms connected to EU law.

The EU-driven expansion of the national parameter of constitutional review will continue to erode the predominantly introverted understanding of national constitutional justice, which may set off a self-asserted relocation of the constitutional courts of EU Member States within the European constitutional space.

[35] Case C-399/11 *Stefano Melloni v Ministerio Fiscal* ECLI:EU:C:2013:107, [2013] ECR, para 60 (added emphasis).

Bibliography

Alonso García, R, 'El TC y el derecho al olvido: ¿Allanando un camino "a la alemana" de la CDFUE como parámetro directo de amparo?' (2022) 82 *Revista Española de Derecho Europeo* 9.

Arzoz, X, 'Avoiding the Rain or Learning to Dance in it: The Hesitations of the Spanish Constitutional Court' in A Heger and M Malkmus (eds), *On the Relation between the EU Charter of Fundamental Rights and National Fundamental Rights* (Cham, Springer, 2024).

—— *La concretización y actualización de los derechos fundamentales* (Madrid, Centro de Estudios Políticos y Constitucionales, 2014).

—— *La tutela de los derechos fundamentales de la Unión Europea por el Tribunal Constitucional* (Madrid, Instituto Nacional de Administración Pública, 2015).

—— *Transformaciones judiciales: Karlsruhe y los derechos fundamentales de la Unión Europea* (Madrid, Centro de Estudios Políticos y Constitucionales, 2022).

Bailleux, A, 'Entre droits fondamentaux et intégration européenne, la Charte des droits fondamentaux de l'Union européenne face à son destin (C.J.U.E., *Stefano Melloni* et *Åkerberg Fransson*, 26 février 2013)' (2014) 97 *Revue trimestrielle des droits de l'homme* 215.

Besselink, LFM, 'The Parameters of Constitutional Conflict after *Melloni*' (2014) 39 *European Law Review* 531.

Bobek, M, 'The Impact of the European Mandate of Ordinary Courts on the Position of Constitutional Courts' in M Claes et al (eds), *Constitutional Conversations in Europe* (Cambridge, Intersentia, 2012).

Burchardt, S, 'Backlash against the Court of Justice of the EU? The Recent Jurisprudence of the German Constitutional Court on EU Fundamental Rights as a Standard of Review' (2020) 21 *German Law Journal* 1.

Classen, CD, 'Über das Ziel hinausgeschossen? Anmerkung zu den zwei Beschlüssen des BVerfG zum Recht auf Vergessen vom 6.11.2019, 1 BvR 16/13, 276/17' (2021) *Europarecht* 92.

Cruz Villalón, P, 'De la persistencia de un viejo *dictum*: la STC 89/2022, en contexto' in D Fromage (ed), *Jacques Ziller a European scholar* (Florence, European University Institute, 2022).

—— '¿Una forma de cooperación judicial no reclamada? Sobre la extensión del amparo a la Carta de Derechos Fundamentales de la UE' (2021) 25 *Anuario Iberoamericano de Justicia Constitucional* 57.

De Boer, N, 'Addressing Rights Divergences under the Charter: Melloni – Case C-399/11, Stefano Melloni v. Ministerio Fiscal, Judgment of the Court (Grand Chamber) of 26 February 2013' (2013) 50 *Common Market Law Review* 1083.

Edenharter, A, 'Die EU-Grundrechte-Charta als Prüfungsmaßstab des Bundesverfassungsrechts' (2020) 73 *Die Öffentliche Verwaltung* 349.

Franzius, C, 'Grundrechtsschutz in Europa – Zwischen Selbstbehauptungen und Selbstbeschränkungen der Rechtsordnungen und ihrer Gerichte' (2015) 75 *Zeitschrift für ausländisches öffentliches Recht und Völkerrecht* 383.

Geiger, S, 'Allemagne: césure jurisprudentielle en matière de protection des droits fondamentaux européennes' (2020) *Revue trimestrielle de droit européen* 225.

Granner, G, 'Grundrechtecharta und Verfassungsgerichtsbarkeit' in A Kahl, N Raschauer and S Storr (eds), *Grundsatzfragen der europäischen Grundrechtecharta* (Vienna, Verlag Österreich, 2013).

Hofmann, R and Heger, A, 'Zur neuen Grundrechte-Architektur im europäischen Mehrebenensystem' (2021) 48 *Europäische Grundrechte Zeitschrift* 1.

Hoffmann, JM, 'Unionsgrundrechte als verfassungsrechtlicher Prüfungsmaßstab' (2020) *Neue Zeitschrift für Verwaltungsrecht* 33.

Holzinger, G, 'Das österreichische Verfassungsgerichtshof als Bewahrer der Grundrechte' (2018) 45 *Europäische Grundrechte Zeitschrift* 1.

Kämmerer, JA and Kotzur, M, 'Vollendung des Grundrechtsverbunds oder Heimholung des Grundrechtsschutzes?' (2020) *Neue Zeitschrift für Verwaltungsrecht* 177.

Kieber, S, and Klaushofer, R, 'The Austrian Constitutional Court Post Case-Law After the Landmark Decision on Charter of Fundamental Rights of the European Union' (2017) 23 *European Public Law* 221.

Klaushofer, R and Palmstorfer, R, 'Austrian Constitutional Court uses the Charter of Fundamental Rights of the European Union as Standard of Review: Effects on Union Law' (2013) 19 *European Public Law* 1.

Komárek, J, 'National constitutional courts in the European constitutional democracy' (2014) 12 *I•CON* 525.

—— 'Why National Constitutional Courts Should Not Embrace EU Fundamental Rights' in S de Vries, U Bernitz and S Weatherill (eds), *The EU Charter of Fundamental Rights as a Binding Instrument – Five Years Old and Growing* (Oxford, Hart, 2015).

Kühling, J, 'Das ‚Recht auf Vergessenwerden' vor dem BVerfG – November(r)evolution für die Grundrechtsarchitektur im Mehrebenensystem' (2020) 73 *Neue Juristische Wochenschrift* 275.

Lechner-Hartlieb, C, 'The Implementation of Charter Rights in the Austrian System of Fundamental Rights Protection' in A Heger and M Malkmus (eds), *On the Relation between the EU Charter of Fundamental Rights and National Fundamental Rights* (Cham, Springer, 2024).

Müller, R, 'Verfassungsgerichtsbarkeit und Europäische Grundrechtscharta' (2012) 4 *Österreichische Juristen-Zeitung* 159.

Orator, A, 'The Decision of the Austrian *Verfassungsgerichtshof* on the EU Charter of Fundamental Rights: An Instrument of Leverage or Rearguard Action?' (2015) 15 *German Law Journal* 1429.

Paris, D, 'Constitutional courts as European Union courts: The current and potential use of EU law as a yardstick for constitutional review' (2017) 24 *Maastricht Journal of European and Comparative Law* 792.

Pereira Coutinho, F, 'The Charter of Fundamental Rights of the European Union at the Portuguese Constitutional Court: The Data Retention Cases' in A Heger and M Malkmus (eds), *On the Relation between the EU Charter of Fundamental Rights and National Fundamental Rights* (Cham, Springer, 2024).

Piqani, D, 'The Simmenthal revolution revisited: what role for constitutional courts?' in B de Witte et al (eds), *National Courts and EU Law. New Issues, Theories and Methods* (Cheltenham, Edward Elgar, 2016).

Pliakos, A, and Anagnostaras, G, 'Fundamental Rights and the New Battle over Legal and Judicial Supremacy: Lessons from *Melloni*' (2015) 34 *Yearbook of European Law* 97.

Pollicino, O, 'L'integrazione del parametro costituzionale alla luce del diritto comunitario "presa sul serio"' in G Bronzini and V Piccone (eds), *La Carta e le Corti. I diritti fondamentali nella giurisprudenza europea multilivello* (Taranto, Chimienti, 2007).

Pöschl, M, 'Verfassungsgerichtsbarkeit nach Lissabon' (2012) 67 *Zeitschrift für öffentliches Recht* 587.

Preßlein, D, 'Grundgesetz vs. Grundrechtscharta? Zur „europäisierten Grundrechtsprüfung" des BVerfG und nach den Beschlüssen zum „Recht auf Vergessen" und „Europäischer Haftbefehl III"' (2021) *Europarecht* 247.

Rauchegger, C, 'National Constitutional Courts as Guardians of the Charter: A Comparative Appraisal of the German Federal Constitutional Court's *Right to Be Forgotten* Judgments' (2020) 22 *Cambridge Yearbook of European Legal Studies* 258.

—— 'The Charter as a Standard of Constitutional Review in the Member States' in M Bobek and J Adams-Prassl (eds), *The EU Charter of Fundamental Rights in the Member States* (Oxford, Hart, 2020).
—— 'The Interplay between the Charter and National Constitutions after *Åkerberg Fransson* y *Melloni*. Has the CJEU Embraced the Challenges of Multilevel Fundamental Rights Protection?' in S de Vries, U Bernitz and S Weatherill (eds), *The EU Charter of Fundamental Rights as a Binding Instrument. Five Years Old and Growing* (Oxford, Hart, 2018).
Saiz Arnaiz, A, *La apertura constitucional al Derecho internacional y europeo de los derechos humanos. El artículo 10.2 de la Constitución española* (Madrid, Consejo General del Poder Judicial, 1999).
Sarmiento, D, 'Who's afraid of the Charter? The Court of Justice, national courts and the new framework of fundamental rights protection in Europe' (2013) 50 *Common Market Law Review* 1267.
Saulnier-Cassia, E, 'La Cour constitutionnelle autrichienne face à la Charte des droits fondamentaux de l'Union européenne' (2013) *Revue trimestrielle de droit européen* 168.
Spadaro, A, 'Dalla Costituzione come "atto" (puntuale nel tempo) alla Costituzione come "processo" (storico): Ovvero della continua "evoluzione" del parametro costituzionale attraverso i giudizi di costituzionalità' (1998) *Quaderni costituzionali* 343.
Streinz, R, *Bundesverfassungsgerichtlicher Grundrechtsschutz und Europäisches Gemeinschaftsrecht* (Baden-Baden, Nomos, 1989).
Thym, D, 'Friendly Takeover, or: The Power of the "First Word". The German Constitutional Court embraces the Charter of Fundamental Rights as a Standard of Domestic Judicial Review' (2020) 16 *European Constitutional Law Review* 187.
—— 'Separation versus Fusion – or: How to Accommodate National Autonomy and the Charter? Diverging Visions of the German Constitutional Court and the European Court of Justice' (2013) 9 *European Constitutional Law Review* 391.
Ugartemendia Eceizabarrena, JI and Ripol Carulla, S, *El Tribunal Constitucional en la encrucijada europea de los derechos fundamentales* (Oñati, Instituto Vasco de Administración Pública, 2017).
Velaers, J, 'Le contrôle des lois, décrets et ordonnances au regard du titre II de la Constitution et des conventions internationales relatives aux droits de l'homme, en cas de concours de droits fondamentaux' in A Arts et al (eds), *Les rapports entre la Cour d'arbitrage, le Pouvoir judiciaire et le Conseil d'État* (Brussels, Larcier, 2006).
Violante, T, 'How the Data Retention Legislation Led to a National Constitutional Crisis in Portugal' (2022) *verfassungsblog.de*, 9 June 2022.
Wattel, P and Van Bockel, B, 'New Wine into Old Wineskins: The Scope of the Charter of Fundamental Rights of the EU after *Åkerberg Fransson*' (2013) 38 *European Law Review* 866.
Wendel, M, 'The two-faced Guardian – Or how one Half of the German Federal Constitutional Court became a European Fundamental Rights Court?' (2020) 57 *Common Market Law Review* 1383.

10

European Criminal Law and Constitutional Courts. Constructing a Fundamental-Rights Narrative Through Militant Cooperation

MARIBEL GONZÁLEZ PASCUAL

1. European Criminal Law; an Increasing Challenge for European Courts

European criminal law refers to a set of standards adopted in various forums together with the case law of the European Court of Human Rights (ECtHR) and the Court of Justice of the European Union (CJEU), making the notion of European criminal law comparable to a patchwork of regimes.[1] Neither can we speak of a European criminal justice system in a proper sense. There is no EU police force, no criminal courts, prisons or trials. European criminal law is applied in the context of national criminal justice systems, which are a product of divergent historic experiences.[2]

Nonetheless, that some European criminal law is emerging has become an undeniable reality. The EU has established norms for prosecution and investigation of crime, pre-trial measures (recognition of arrest warrants, evidence warrants, freezing orders and decisions on bails), procedural criminal law (particularly on the rights of both victims and accused), offences, and penalties and enforcement of penalties. Furthermore, this legislation is increasingly applicable to domestic cases, a case in point being the directives on procedural rights. At the same time come calls for the CJEU to address the precise content of the emerging European criminal law by elaborating autonomous concepts that will significantly influence national law, 'changing both perceptions and practice in national criminal justice systems'.[3] The establishment of a

[1] U Sieber, 'Die Zukunft des Europäischen Strafrechts' (2009) *121 Zeitschrift für die gesamte Strafrechtswissenschaft* 1, 1–2.

[2] S Coutts *Citizenship, Crime and Community in the European Union* (Oxford, Hart Publishing, 2019) 190.

[3] V Mitsilegas, 'Legislating for human rights after Lisbon' in M Fletcher et al (eds), *The European Union as an Area of Freedom, Security and Justice* (Oxford, Routledge, 2017) 210.

European Public Prosecutor is a particularly remarkable development, one that drives home the point that 'Member States are no longer in the driving seat of criminal policy'.[4]

According to a traditional view, however, criminal law forms part of the core of national sovereignty,[5] according to which each society may strike the balance between freedom and security according to their beliefs. Ultimately, deciding what actions constitute an offence or the severity of the offence depends on the idiosyncrasies of each community, and thus 'criminal law is a code that reflects the national society's set of values'.[6] Strict adherence to the principle of legality, both materially and formally, furthermore, is required to justify the state's power to act punitively in a democratic system. In a material sense, this requirement provides the system legal certainty. In a formal sense, it ensures the participation of citizens in setting criminal laws by requiring their regulation by statute. Finally, criminal law is particularly sensitive to fundamental rights concerns. Traditionally, the limits on the state's coercive powers have been moulded by strict negotiation in national forums, and also often involve symbolic links to the affective foundation of national identity.[7]

This is the scenario in which constitutional courts must increasingly manage the impact of the emerging EU criminal law in their jurisdictions. The growing concern of constitutional courts with the role of the EU in criminal law has gone through three distinguishable phases. First, constitutional courts took a purely internal approach to the emergence of EU criminal law as the parameters and the procedures followed remained strictly national. Later came a phase in which constitutional courts engaged in dialogue with the CJEU; however, their preliminary rulings were generally riddled with mistrust. Now in a third phase, constitutional courts protect fundamental rights by accepting EU law as the 'only game in town'. This changing and increasing role of fundamental rights in European criminal law can be seen in the decisions of the CJEU. The CJEU is slowly changing the axis of its argumentation from the effectiveness of EU law to respect for fundamental rights in a composite rights system. Hence, the 'fundamental rights narrative' has become the crossroads where the case law of both the CJEU and the constitutional courts intersects in criminal matters.

Fundamental rights currently lie at the core of European criminal law. This development has gone hand in hand with the entry into force of the Charter of Fundamental Rights of the European Union (CFR), and the impressive number of preliminary rulings requested by national courts concerning the protection of fundamental rights in the area of freedom, security and justice.[8] Still, constitutional courts have also played an important role, as some of the CJEU's hallmark cases in criminal matters, directly or indirectly, found their impulse in constitutional court decisions.[9]

[4] J Öberg, *The normative foundations for EU criminal justice* (Oxford, Hart Publishing, 2004) 114.

[5] Case 554/14 *Ognyanov* EU:C:2016:319 pt 121I (AG Bot).

[6] Couts (n 2) 115.

[7] N Walker, 'In search of the Area of Freedom, Security and Justice: A constitutional Odyssey' in Walker N (ed), *Europe's Area of Freedom, Security and Justice* (Oxford, Oxford University Press, Oxford, 2006) 18.

[8] S Iglesias and M González-Pascual, 'Fundamental Rights at the Core of the EU AFSJ' in S Iglesias and M González-Pascual (ed), Fundamental *Rights in the EU Area of Freedom, Security and Justice* (Cambridge, Cambridge University Press, 2021) 1.

[9] Case C-303/05 *Advocaten voor de Wereld* EU:C:2007:261; Case C-306/09 *IB* EU:C:2010:626; Case C-399/11 *Melloni* EU:C:2013:107; Case C-168/13 PPU *Jeremy F* EU:C:2013:358; Case 293/12 *Digital*

In this framework, the chapter examines the main hallmark cases on European criminal law in which the constitutional courts played a key role. First, it analyses the cases regarding the European Arrest Warrant Framework Decision[10] (EAW FD). Then the chapter looks into the main controversies regarding European substantive criminal law by focusing on the principle of legality. Finally, it highlights how constitutional courts have gradually come to a shared 'rights narrative' among European courts in criminal matters.

The key role played by the ECtHR itself, however, will not be analysed, in order to respect the length limits established by the editors. Even though I will not go into it, the ECtHR has developed an extensive and influential case law on criminal law that has important implications for the States parties to the Convention. Furthermore, the impact of ECtHR case law on the EU is increasing. This growing relevance of the ECHR in EU law, and particularly in EU criminal law, is partially instigated by the national courts when they frame their reference to the CJEU by relying on the ECtHR case law or even suggesting the CJEU follow the ECtHR in the case at hand.[11] Finally, the ECtHR has sent strong messages to the CJEU which resulted in a leap forward in fundamental rights protection.[12]

2. Constitutional Courts and the European Arrest Warrant: From Deep Mistrust to Militant Cooperation

What triggered the decisions of the constitutional courts as regards the influence of EU law on criminal law was the EAW FD. As is well known, the EAW differs from extradition primarily in that it is a mechanism used by judges that simplifies and streamlines the process of arrest and surrender and eliminates the double incrimination requirement for 32 offences. Moreover, the EAW must be applied automatically by national judges based on the presumption that the criminal systems of all EU Member States have sufficient procedural guarantees and fundamental rights protection.

When the EAW was first applied in the EU, there was little harmonisation in either substantive or procedural criminal law. This would change, however, because the EAW system concerns classic constitutional rights and safeguards applied in the process of depriving an individual of his or her personal liberty. National constitutions typically contain extensive and elaborate provisions, often including special chapters, to ensure *nulla poena sine lege*, the presumption of innocence, fair trial, access to judicial protection

Rights Ireland EU:C:2014:238; Case C-404/15 *Aranyosi and Caldararu* EU:C:2016:198; Case C-216/18 PPU *LM* EU:C:2018:586; Case C-42/17 *MAS and MB* EU:C:2017:936 (*Taricco II*); Case 128/18 *Dorobantu* EU:C:2019:334 Case 699/21 *EDL* EU:C:2023:295; Case 700/21 *OG* EU:C:2023:444.

[10] 2002/584/JHA: Council Framework Decision of 13 June 2002 on the European arrest warrant and the surrender procedures between Member States. OJ L 190.

[11] S Imamovic, *The architecture of fundamental rights in the EU* (Oxford, Hart Publishing, 2022) 11–12.

[12] The seminal judgment *Aranyosi and Caldararu* was fostered indirectly by the German Constitutional Court, but the basis for the ruling of the CJEU was set by the ECtHR in *MSS v Belgium* and Greece App no 30696/0921.

and competent defence.[13] Unsurprisingly, cases involving the EAW FD and the protection of fundamental rights have come before the CJEU on numerous occasions.

Initially, constitutional courts' main concern was the surrender of their own nationals, since nationality was no longer grounds for refusing a request for cooperation under the EAW. This development represented a considerable challenge for European legal systems, especially those in which the ban on extradition of nationals had constitutional rank. The so-called 'nationality exception' reflected an idea of the relationship between the state and its citizens that was grounded in both history and philosophy and accompanied mistrust in the legal systems of other states.[14] In fact, even though recourse to the 'nationality exception' had been decreasing in post-World War II Europe, the EAW represented a watershed moment in the history of the extradition of nationals that provoked great controversy.[15]

The Polish and the German Constitutional Courts declared their national laws implementing the EAW FD unconstitutional, whereas the Supreme Court of Cyprus considered the surrender of nationals incompatible with its national constitution. The Czech Constitutional Court, for its part, considered the law implementing the Framework Decision constitutional. These Courts only addressed the national law transposing the EAW FD, which led them to different conclusions.[16] None of these Courts, it is worth noting, requested a preliminary ruling.

Constitutional courts took a different approach, however, in cases related only to fundamental rights' protection.[17] The seminal cases *Advocaten vor den Wereld*, *Jeremy F* and *Melloni* brought crucial questions for the protection of fundamental rights within the EU to the attention of the CJEU, including the interpretation of Article 53 CFR, the requirements of double criminality in transnational cases and the compatibility with the EAW of additional national safeguards.

Unfortunately, the case law rendered by the CJEU disappointed national courts and scholars. *Melloni* in particular provoked deep unrest.[18] As is well known, the CJEU

[13] A Albi, 'The European Arrest Warrant, Constitutional Rights and the Changing Legal Thinking: Values Once Recognized Lost in Transition to the EU Level' in M Fletcher, et al (ed), *The European Union as an Area of Freedom, Security and Justice* (Oxford, Routledge, 2017) 138.

[14] Case C-66/08 *Kozłowski* EU:C:2008:253, pt 85 (AG Bot).

[15] Z Deen- Racsmán and Judge Blekxtoon, 'The Decline of the Regulation of (Non) Surrender of Nationals and Dual Criminality under the European Arrest Warrant' (2015) 13 *European Journal of Crime, Criminal Law and Criminal Justice* 317, 340.

[16] On these cases, see S Iglesias, 'La Jurisprudencia Constitucional Comparada sobre la Orden Europea de Detención y Entrega, y la Naturaleza Jurídica de los Actos del Tercer Pilar' (2010) 36 *Revista de Derecho Comunitario Europeo* 169.

[17] The judgments of the constitutional courts regarding the ban on surrendering nationals advanced nationality as the essence of EU citizenship. 'Citizenship of the Union is an accidental and dependent relationship [.] It is therefore an additional element, a structure built up on top of citizenship of the Member States.' Judgment of the Polish Constitutional Court, 27 April 2005, para 4.3.

[18] See L Besselink, 'The Parameters of Constitutional Conflict After Melloni' (2014) 39 *European Law Journal* 531. The judgment rendered in *Advocaten vor de Wereld* (n 9) was also quite disappointing. The Belgian Constitutional Court referred to the key question of the fundamental rights compatibility of the lack of verification of double criminality requirements for the offences listed in the EAW FD. However, the CJEU simply held that the EAW FD is compatible with the principle of legality of criminal offences and penalties if their definitions 'are those which follow from the law of the issuing State' (para 52). On this case see D Sarmiento, 'European Union: The European Arrest Warrant and the quest for constitutional coherence' (2008) 6 *International Journal of Constitutional Law* 171.

emphasised in *Melloni* that, when the EU has harmonised the standard of protection of a given right, then national laws, including national constitutions, must not undermine the uniformity of the standard since doing so would compromise the efficacy of EU law. Therefore, domestic courts were no longer to rely on their own standards of fundamental rights protection if it entailed failing to apply EU law. Briefly put, Article 53 CFR forbids the disapplication of 'EU legal rules which are in fully compliance with the Charter' even if applying the EU rules 'infringes the fundamental rights guaranteed by that State's constitution'.[19]

The CJEU thus affirmed the primacy and autonomy of EU law in relation to the national law without giving due regard to the fundamental rights at stake. This reading of Article 53 CFR, along with the Opinion 2/13,[20] impaired the credibility of the EAW and renewed fears among constitutional courts that fundamental rights protection in criminal matters could be weakened.[21]

Still, the Spanish Constitutional Court, which took for granted its own understanding that the right not to be convicted in absentia must prevail without further consideration, should also be pointed out.[22] The Spanish Constitutional Court construed the right to a fair trial in case of extradition, however, using a sometimes contradictory and inconsistent argument. In fact, the Spanish Constitutional Court's request of retrial was deeply criticised in all the cases because it considered neither the rights of the victims nor the need for public security. Furthermore, the argument was derived from an interpretation of Article 6 ECHR that the ECtHR did not endorse.[23] Furthermore, the Spanish Constitutional Court neither questioned nor reviewed its own case law. It simply tried to impose the national interpretation of the fundamental right at stake. Undoubtedly, the question referred by the Spanish Constitutional Court was extremely important for the protection of rights in Europe, but the Spanish court failed to frame it in accordance with the European context in which the answer would be formulated.

In a nutshell, it would seem neither the Spanish Constitutional Court nor the CJEU pondered the impact of their decisions on an integrated, cooperative European criminal legal system. The CJEU seemed unaware of the ultimate consequences of its decisions in a particularly sensitive field for fundamental rights. For its part, the Spanish Constitutional Court disregarded the difference between the EAW and extradition law and shied from collaborating in the elaboration of a common standard of fundamental rights to be shared by the CJEU and national courts.[24]

Such was the situation when the German Constitutional Court contested *Melloni* and introduced the requirement of identity review for measures implementing the EAW.[25]

[19] *Melloni* (n 9) para 58.

[20] Opinion 2/13 EU:C:2014:2454.

[21] V Mitsilegas, 'Mutual Recognition and Fundamental Rights in EU Criminal Justice' in S Iglesias and M González-Pascual (eds), *Fundamental Rights* (Cambridge, Cambridge University Press, 2021) 261.

[22] Order of the Spanish Constitutional Court, 86/2011, 6 June of 2011.

[23] M González-Pascual, 'The first preliminary reference of the Spanish Constitutional Court' in M Claes et al (eds), *Constitutional Conversations in Europe* (Amberes, Intersentia, 2012) 170.

[24] A critical stance on the rulings of both Courts can be found in A Torres, 'Melloni in Three Acts: From Dialogue to Monologue' (2014) 10 *European Constitutional Law Review* 308–33.

[25] German Constitutional Court BverfG, Order of 15 December 2015- EAW II, 2 BvR 2735/14.

Even though the German Constitutional Court concluded that there was no conflict between EU law and the German constitutional law in the case at hand, it regrettably neither requested a preliminary ruling nor waited for the CJEU decision in *Aranyosi* which was already pending.[26] Still, the German Constitutional Court indirectly caused a shift in the case law regarding the cooperation between national authorities responsible for issuing and executing EAWs. In the joined cases *Aranyosi and Caldararu* the CJEU not only took up the question of whether the execution of an EAW could be refused on the grounds of concern for potential fundamental rights violations, but also adopted an approach similar to that of the German Constitutional Court.[27] *Aranyosi and Caldararu* represents a huge step by the CJEU in the direction of the position taken by the German Constitutional Court (and the ECtHR) because it drastically reduced the distance between them created by *Melloni*.[28] Hence, even though the German Federal Constitutional Court did not raise a preliminary ruling, it pushed the CJEU towards a comprehensive understanding of the EU fundamental rights.[29]

This impulse to reach a European understanding of the safeguards and guarantees that must govern a cooperative European criminal law was further fleshed out by both the Irish High Court and the Italian Constitutional Court when they brought before the CJEU the *LM* and *OG* cases.

At the origin of *LM* originated was a negative appraisal of the rule of law in Poland made by the Irish High Court. The specific issue addressed in the preliminary reference was whether a Member State may refuse the execution of an EAW because of a systematically deficient rule of law in the requesting Member State. The extreme relevance of the case for the EU led some to consider *LM* as a 'potential constitutional moment for the European Rule of Law'.[30]

Following *Araynosi and Caldararu*, the Irish High Court gave the CJEU the chance to answer the questions whether Ireland could refuse surrendering a Polish citizen to Poland following a EAW because of systemic breaches of the rule of law in Poland and whether the Irish court must also carry out a thorough assessment of the individual's chances of obtaining a fair trial in his home country. Furthermore, the Irish High Court provided the CJEU with a unique opportunity to address specific criticism involving the rule of law crisis in Poland.

The CJEU made clear that defending European values is a task national courts share with the CJEU. Furthermore, since the CJEU relied on the rule of law by linking it to the right to a fair trial, it gave individuals standing to challenge violations of a European

[26] T Reinbacher and M Wendel (2016), 'The Bundesverfassungsgericht's EAW II Decision' (2016) 23 *Maastricht Journal of European and Comparative Law* 702, 712–13.

[27] Mitsilegas (n 21) 264.

[28] M Hong, 'Human Dignity, Identity Review of the European Arrest Warrant and the Court of Justice as Listener in the Dialogue of Courts' (2016) 12 *European Constitutional Law Review* 549, 562.

[29] The German Constitutional Court continued instigating for higher fundamental rights protection in EAW cases by forcing the ordinary courts to raise preliminary rulings, of which the order of German Constitutional Court of 19 December 2017 was particularly relevant (BverfG, Order of 19 December 2017- EAW III, 2 BvR 427/17). This reference, requested by the German Constitutional Court, led to the CJEU judgment in *Dorobantu*. About this case, X Arzoz, 'Euroorden, condiciones de reclusión y derechos fundamentales' (2018) 113 *Revista Española de Derecho Europeo* 113.

[30] A von Bogdandy, 'A potential constitutional moment for the European Rule of Law: The importance of Red Lines' in A von Bogdandy et al, *Defending Checks and Balances in EU Member States* (Berlin, Springer, 2021) 387.

value.[31] *LM* thus created new tools to ensure judicial independence across the EU. Even though endorsing criteria for the non-execution of an EAW hardly solves the rule of law crisis,[32] the rule of law has become a legally enforceable value within the EU through the LM judgment.

Also worth mentioning is the interpretation followed by the Irish High Court in its reference. The Irish High Court asserted that 'Poland shows a significant disregard for what is recognised in the TEU as an important common value of the EU and its Member States … Poland appears no longer to accept that there are common European values'.[33] The Irish High Court therefore questioned whether the *Aranyosi and Caldararu* test was the correct test to apply, having found that Poland had breached the common value of rule of law as established by Article 2 TEU. Furthermore, the Irish High Court's doubts over the respect for the rule of law in Poland were backed up by reports from European bodies, such as the Venice Commission and the EU Commission. The Irish High Court thus framed its questions in the European context by prioritising the EU's concern for Poland's respect of a European common value enshrined in the Treaties.

The Italian Constitutional Court also followed this interpretation when raising a reference questioning differential treatment of third-country nationals (TCNs) in EAW cases.[34] Differentiated treatment has been the subject of recurrent controversy in the EU. Several Member States have tried to prevent the surrender of their own nationals by looking for loopholes in the EAW FD, for which purpose Article 4(6) of the EAW FD is particularly useful.[35]

Several domestic laws transposing this provision adopted it not only for automatic protection of their own citizens, but also to limit its scope or even to disregard it when the person to be surrendered was foreign. These national provisions gave rise to four preliminary rulings before the CJEU: the well-known *Kozlowsky, Wolzenburg, IB* and *Lopes da Silva* judgments.[36]

In them, the CJEU applied the non-discrimination principle and crafted an autonomous interpretation of the terms 'staying' and 'resident' to be applied homogeneously throughout the EU. In sum, the CJEU allowed Member States to protect their own nationals but not to disregard the rights of other Member States' citizens. The CJEU chose not to take up the right to family life, which was suggested by the General Advocates, opting for a particularly cautious approach instead.

[31] ibid 395.

[32] A Frąckowiak and Adamska, A, 'Drawing Red Lines with No (Significant) Bites' in A von Bogdandy et al, *Defending Checks and Balances in EU Member States* (Berlin, Springer, 2021) 453.

[33] Judgment of the High Court, *Celmer* [2018] IEHC 154, 12 March 2017, para 129.

[34] The Italian Constitutional Court also raised a preliminary ruling on the refusal of an EAW when the surrender may expose the person in question to the risk of serious harm to his or her health. This reference increased the reach of fundamental rights since, in the case EDL the CJEU followed the case law in Aranyosi and Caldararu, as suggested by the Italian Constitutional Court. Order of the Italian Constitutional Court of 23 of September of 2021, No 2016/2021.

[35] Article 4(6) EAW FD: 'The executing judicial authority may refuse to execute the European arrest warrant: … where the requested person is staying in, or is a national or a resident of the executing Member State and that State undertakes to execute the sentence or detention order.'

[36] Case C-66/08 *Kozłowski* EU:C:2008:437; Case C-123/08 *Wolzenburg* EU:C:2009:616; IB; Case C-42/11 *Da Silva* EU:C:2012:517.

This case law, however, left TCNs unprotected. In fact, the Italian legislation implementing the EAW FD only allowed for the denial of surrender of Italian citizens or those of another Member State who had been legally and effectively living in Italian for at least five years. The surrender of TCNs was endorsed in unconditional terms. In this context, the Court of Appeal of Bologna asked the Italian Constitutional Court to declare the national law on EAW unconstitutional. In the Court of Appeal's view such provision was incompatible with both the right to family life and rehabilitation as the purpose of criminal sentencing.

The Italian Constitutional Court, however, deemed the question one to be solved at the EU level. In its reference to the CJEU, the Italian Constitutional Court extensively addressed not only the CJEU case law on Article 4(6) EAW FD, but also cases in which the CJEU had mentioned the rehabilitation of the person convicted.[37] The Italian Constitutional Court also cited the EU legislation protecting TCNs and underscoring the relevance of rehabilitating offenders. Finally, the Italian Constitutional Court emphasised the ECtHR case law in cases concerning both the reintegration of offenders and the expulsion of aliens from a Member State. In its words, the case law 'establishes the minimum level of protection that must be guaranteed in connection with the corresponding right according to Article 7 EU Charter under Article 52 (3) EU Charter'.[38]

In this framework, the Italian court asked the CJEU whether Article 4(6) EAW FD precludes legislation that bars the executing judicial authorities from refusing to surrender TCNs, irrespective of the links maintained by those individuals with the territory. Hence, the Italian Constitutional Court grounded its doubts on EU law (including the ECtHR case law) and implicitly backed the approach that it considered more adequate, namely the link to the right to family life and the rehabilitation of the offenders.

The CJEU, however, did not fully follow the approach of the Italian Constitutional Court. It mainly relied on the principle of non-discrimination. According to the CJEU, any national law refusing the TCNs 'absolutely and automatically, the benefit of the ground for optional non-execution of a EAW … even where those TCNs are staying or resident in the territory of the Member State and without account being taken of the degree of integration of those TCNs within the society of that Member State'[39] fails to comply with Article 20 CFR, because the differentiated treatment is not objectively justified.

The CJEU considered the right to family life, but only as criteria to be applied by national judges to assess whether refusing or executing an EAW issued against a TCN is appropriate. Therefore, the scope of the right to family life is left to the discretion of the national judicial authorities, whereas respect for the non-discrimination principle is imposed on national legislators. The CJEU allows nationality (and EU citizenship) as a relevant criterion in EAW cases, but it reinterprets nationality 'in light of social links and connections rather than through some pre-social, ethnocultural notion of

[37] Among others, Case C-149/09 *Tsakouridis* ECLI:EU:C:2010:708 and Case 316/16B *Vomero* EU:C:2018:256.
[38] Order of the Italian Constitutional Court of 21 of October of 2021; No 217/2021, para 8.5.
[39] *OG* (n 9) para 51.

belonging, or some idealized link between the sovereign and its subjects'.[40] Whereas the scarce role still played by the rehabilitation objective in the European criminal law might be disappointing,[41] *OG* balances the protection of the rights involved in the case with the discretion that the EU usually leaves to the Member States in criminal matters. Since public security policy is largely set at the national level, even in transnational cases, and the supranational protection of fundamental rights is far from fully developed, the rehabilitation of offenders at the EU level tends to be forgotten.[42]

Be that as it may, the reference made by the Italian Constitutional Court opened new avenues for the protection of rights in EAW cases. In fact, in a case concerning the surrender of a mother whose young children lived with her, the CJEU accepted the judicial authorities' decision to deny her surrender on the exceptional basis of the children's right to family life, the best interest of the minor, and certain systemic or generalised deficiencies in the issuing Member State.[43]

This judgment, brought before the CJEU by the Italian Supreme Court, aligns perfectly with the reasoning of the Italian Constitutional Court in *OG* insofar as the right to family life offers a solid basis to condition (or even deny) the execution of an EAW. The CJEU accepts this reasoning only when children are involved, thus limiting the potential of Article 7 CFR.[44] Nonetheless, the reference submitted by the Italian Constitutional (and Supreme) Courts pushed the CJEU towards a proactive defence of fundamental rights.

Constitutional courts eventually found a battlefield on which their requirements hold fast, that of fundamental rights. The references made by the constitutional courts that are fully aware of EU law and sensible to its requirements have expanded the scope of the fundamental rights and shaped the CJEU case law. Instead of insisting on the link between diminishing sovereignty and criminal law, constitutional courts increasingly play at the EU level following the EU rules, and the shift from mistrust to militant cooperation has borne fruit.[45]

[40] Coutts (n 2) 81.

[41] L Mancano, 'Punishment and Rights in the European Union Citizenship: persons or criminals?' (2018) 24 *European Law Journal* 206, 208.

[42] M González-Pascual, 'La creciente irrelevancia de la reinserción social en la UE' (2020) *118 Revista Española de Derecho Constitucional* 167, 188.

[43] Case C-261/22, *GN* ECLI:EU:C:2023:1017.

[44] Even though the reluctance of the CJEU to link the right to family life with the rehabilitation of offenders is disappointing, the most controversial cases have been the ones affecting infants, *F-L (FC) v Polish Judicial Authority* [2012] UKSC 25 being a case in point. The UK Supreme Court applied the ECtHR case law regarding the compatibility of foreigners who have committed a crime with Art 8 ECHR. Still, this case law is not easily applicable to the EAW cases since one of the criteria is the severity of a crime, which in the EAW cases means that of a crime committed in another state. The UK Supreme Court eluded this intricate question by weighing the interests of the children, which carried only when the criminal offence was not considered serious. On this case, M González-Pascual, 'Mutual Recognition of judicial decisions and the right to family life' in M González-Pascual and A Torres (eds), *The right to family life in the European Union* (Oxford, Routledge, 2017) 70–72. The reference submitted by the Italian Constitutional Court, however, led to a more adequate solution for both the interest of the children and the principle of mutual trust.

[45] Cooperation among the CJEU and the constitutional courts has also been fruitful for the protection of personal data in criminal matters. The constitutional courts of Germany, Romania and Czech Republic declared the law implementing the so-called 'Data Retention Directive' unconstitutional. Eventually, however, the Supreme Court of Ireland and the Austrian Constitutional Court raised a preliminary ruling which led to a leading case in fundamental rights protection within the EU. The CJEU judgment was a turning point in the fundamental rights protection, not only because it annulled the Data Retention Directive, but also for

Consequently, we see the standard of rights protection in the EU rising in criminal matters thanks to constitutional courts. This is clearly the case in horizontal cooperation, since the CJEU no longer denies courts the possibility of suspending mutual recognition instruments, the seminal cases on this matter mostly being brought by constitutional courts. Still, suspension is more feasible in theory than in practice in criminal matters, given the significant amount of information about the actual situation of the criminal system in another Member State that must be available for a domestic court to competently order a suspension. This situation logically follows from the aims of judicial cooperation in criminal matters. Balancing security and liberty has long posed a conundrum for constitutional systems. In the EU, the balance is even more difficult to strike because of the concurrence of different levels and actors whose competencies vary widely.[46]

Nonetheless, the pressure of national courts (not only constitutional courts), the legal strength of the CFR, the increasing number of Directives on the rights of both the accused and the victims in criminal cases that are also applied in purely domestic cases, and the case law of the CJEU on managing diversity, stressing the coherence of EU law and ensuring its effective application all signal a paradigm shift from a system focused primarily on law enforcement rules to a system in which the fundamental rights are brought to the fore, protected and enforced in EU law.[47]

3. Substantive European Criminal Law and Constitutional Courts: The Legality Principle at the Crossroad

In its judgment on the Lisbon Treaty the German Constitutional Court made a statement that attracted much attention regarding the hypothetical future for a proper European criminal law. In its view, criminal law

> depends on cultural processes of previous understandings that are historically grown and also determined by language, and on the alternatives which emerge in the process of deliberation which moves the respective public opinion … The penalization of social behaviour can, however, only partially be normatively derived from values and moral premises that are shared Europewide.[48]

Still, from 1989 on, the CJEU has repeatedly supported the use of criminal law to ensure the effectiveness of EU law, which remains to date the primary justification for modifications to EU regulatory criminal policy.[49] However, the legitimacy of the EU's criminal

the approach followed by the CJEU. Still, only the Constitutional Court of Austria and the Supreme Court of Ireland raised a preliminary ruling. On this case M González-Pascual, 'El TJUE como garante de los derechos en la UE tras Digital Rights Ireland' (2014) 49 *Revista de Derecho Comunitario Europeo* 943.

[46] M González-Pascual, '*A European Standard of Human Rights Protection*' in S Iglesias and M González-Pascual (eds), *Fundamental Rights* (Cambridge, Cambridge University Press, 2021) 56.

[47] Mitsilegas (n 2) 214.

[48] BverfG 30 June 2009, 2 BvE 2/08, *Lisbon*, para 1-421, 253.

[49] Case 68/88 *Commission v Greece* EU:C:1989:281. Effectiveness subsequently appeared as a justification for EU competence in criminal law in the seminal rulings *Environmental Crimes* (Case 176/03 *Commission v Council* EU:C:2005:542) and *Ship-Source Pollution* (Case 440/05 *Commission v Council* EU:C:2007:393).

jurisdiction in absence of any clear mandate in the Treaties still faces challenges. Be that as it may, since the entry into force of the Lisbon Treaty, EU criminal law is increasingly mediated by a robust rights-based approach. Hence, the CJEU case law on criminal law is imbued with these two apparently contradictory paradigms: security-effectiveness of EU law enforcement alongside a strong catalogue of rights. It is in this framework that the principle of legality has become the battlefield between the CJEU and the Italian Constitutional Court in the so-called *Taricco* saga.

The judicial *Taricco* saga has its origins in the Italian statute of limitations for prosecution of VAT offences and the need for prolongation to ensure the efficient prosecution of several serious cases of fraud at the European level. The controversy was whether Article 325 TFEU obliged national authorities to extend current limitation periods. The CJEU held that, when 'interruption of the limitation period has the effect that, in a considerable number of cases, the commission of serious fraud will escape criminal punishment … the measures laid down by national law to combat fraud and any other illegal activity affecting the financial interests of the European Union could not be regarded as being effective and dissuasive, which would be incompatible' with EU law.[50] Moreover, the CJEU dismissed the potential violation of the principle of legality with a limited understanding of the scope of Article 49 CFR,[51] following the ECHR case law on that point even though the national legal traditions did not easily support such a narrow application of the principle of legality.[52] Nonetheless, after *Taricco* led to the reopening of thousands of criminal charges in Italy, the Italian Constitutional Court raised a preliminary ruling challenging the assessment of the CJEU.

The Italian Constitutional Court starts its referral by noting that the ruling of the CJEU lacked the essential foreseeability and certainty required of criminal law. The ambiguity of the judgment, therefore, was incompatible with the principle of legality enshrined in the Italian Constitution. Secondly, the Italian Constitutional Court asks whether the CJEU has implicitly accepted that its interpretation in *Taricco* 'is only applicable, if it is compatible with the constitutional identity of the Member State, and that it falls to the competent authorities of that State to carry out such assessment'.[53] Were that interpretation correct, the ruling of the CJEU would be constitutional. Thirdly, the Italian Constitutional Court emphasises that its interpretation does not compromise the uniform application of EU law. In its view, whether the limitation of offences is considered substantive or procedural criminal law depends on national law, and the distinction is not uniform among the national constitutional traditions. In the cases in which the limitation period for the prosecution of offences is considered substantive criminal law, as in the Italian system, the question refers to the principle of legality. Furthermore, in these cases the protection provided by the national constitutional system is higher than that granted by the Charter, the applicable provision being Article 53 CFR.

[50] Case C-105/14 *Taricco and Others* EU:C:2015:555 (*Taricco I*) para 47.
[51] *Taricco I* (ibid) para 56.
[52] C Peristeridou, 'The Principle of Legality in the Area of Freedom, Security and Justice' in S Iglesias and M González-Pascual (eds), Fundamental *Rights* (Cambridge, Cambridge University Press, 2021) 347.
[53] Order of the Italian constitutional Court of 26 November of 2016, 24/2017 para 7.

Finally, even if the limitation of offences was considered procedural in nature by the CJEU, the ruling in *Taricco* failed to indicate in sufficient detail the path that the national courts must follow to achieve the required effectiveness of EU law. Consequently, the judiciary could potentially disregard any 'normative element whatsoever pertaining to liability for punishment or to the trial, where it was considered to be an obstacle to the punishment of the offence'.[54] This conclusion could hardly be compatible either with the exercise of judicial powers in a system governed by the rule law or with the principle of legality enshrined in Article 49 CFR.

Therefore, the Italian Constitutional Court clearly demonstrates frontal opposition to the interpretation of the principle of legality made by the CJEU. Its disapproval goes hand in hand with an alternative interpretation of the interaction of national and EU law, its main proposal being the non-application of *Taricco* in Italy grounded on national constitutional identity. Alternatively, the Italian Constitutional Court advances a thicker interpretation of Article 49 CFR. In any case, the Italian Constitutional Court warns that disregarding its interpretation (or failing to find a proper solution for the contradiction between national constitutional law and EU law) will lead it to consider the ruling of the CJEU in *Taricco* unconstitutional. However, this 'unconventional' use of the preliminary ruling, one that clearly resembles an ultimatum, is also a call for dialogue.[55]

The CJEU took the opportunity to reverse implicitly yet clearly its ruling in *Taricco*. In *Taricco II*, the CJEU observes that the protection of the EU financial interests by the enactment of criminal penalties is a shared competence between the EU and the Member States. Furthermore, the time limitation for the prosecution of criminal offences concerning the VAT had not been harmonised at the time of the main proceedings, meaning Italy was free to establish those rules. This implies that national authorities could apply the national standards of fundamental rights' protection, provided that doing so would not compromise the primacy, unity and effectiveness of EU law. This argumentation is in line with the well-known *Fransson* case[56] in which the CJEU allowed some leeway for national authorities in sectors of the national legislation whose link to EU law was weak. Therefore, the requirements of foreseeability, precision and non-retroactivity of offences and penalties also apply, in the Italian legal system, to the limitation periods for criminal offences, even when it prevents 'the application of effective and deterrent criminal penalties in a significant number of cases of serious fraud affecting the financial interests of the Union'.[57]

In *Taricco II*, the CJEU finds middle ground by focusing on the plurality of constitutional traditions regarding the principle of legality. The CJEU implicitly seeks support in Article 6(3) TEU, thereby avoiding the application of Article 4(2) that the Italian Constitutional Court brought up in its reference.[58] The narration of rights, as a common

[54] ibid para 9.

[55] G Scaccia, 'The Lesson Learned from the Taricco Saga: Judicial Nationalism and the Constitutional Review of E.U. Law' (2020) *35 American University International Law Review* 821, 859–60.

[56] Case C-617/10 *Åkerberg Fransson* EU:C:2013:105.

[57] *Taricco II* para 62.

[58] M Bassini and O Pollicino, 'Defusing the Taricco Bomb through fostering Constitutional Tolerance' Verfassungsblog, 5 December 2017, verfassungsblog.de/defusing-the-taricco-bomb-through-fostering-constitutional-tolerance-all-roads-lead-to-rome.

task of both national courts and the CJEU is preferred to constitutional identity by the CJEU. The rights-based narrative gains even more terrain when the effectiveness of EU law might be jeopardised, which falls in line with the CJEU case law handed down in *Aranyosi and Caldararu.*

It goes without saying that this conflict is rooted in the shortcomings of EU criminal law. Effectiveness of EU law as the underlying reason for imprisonment without further reflection unavoidably leads to constitutional dilemmas. The case brings to the fore 'the connection between direct applicability of EU law, consequences in terms of individual liability, and different understandings of legality'.[59] When it comes to criminal law, the balance between effectiveness and fundamental rights should be struck with great care. The controversy could have easily been avoided if CJEU had paid due regard to fundamental rights in *Taricco I.* Nonetheless, the ruling in *Taricco II* was the starting point for a partial solution in a subsequent conflict with the Romanian Constitutional Court.

The Romanian Constitutional Court confronted the CJEU in the framework of the rule of law crisis and Romanian judicial reform. The intricacies of the Romanian cases regarding the rule of law go well beyond the scope of this chapter,[60] since most of the cases do not specifically concern criminal law, but in *Lin*[61] the CJEU dealt with the compatibility of the principle of legality in the Romanian constitutional system and the effectiveness of EU law. In 2018, the Romanian Constitutional Court declared the provision permitting exceptions to the country's statute of limitation for criminal offences unconstitutional in the event of 'any procedural act'. However, four years later, the Romanian legislature only amended the law to stipulate that only procedural acts communicated to the suspect or accused may suspend the time limitation for prosecution. In 2022, the Romanian Constitutional Court stated that, between the date of publication of its judgment in 2018 and the entry into force of the new legislative measure, there was no ground for interrupting the limitation period for criminal liability.

In addition, the Romanian Supreme Court stated that, under Romanian law, the rules relating to the interruption of the limitation period for criminal liability fall within the scope of substantive criminal law and that, consequently, they are subject to the principle of non-retroactivity of criminal law. Consequently, a final conviction may, in principle, be subject to extraordinary appeal based on the effects of the judgment of the Constitutional Court as a more lenient criminal law (*lex mitior*). In this framework, the Court of Appeal in Braşov asks to the CJEU how it should apply the judgment of the Romanian Constitutional (and Supreme) Courts, since applying it entailed the 'risk that thousands of defendants would not face criminal liability'[62] including in cases affecting EU financial interests.

The CJEU quotes its ruling in *Taricco II*, recalling that the protection of EU financial interests is a shared competence, emphasising the duty of the Member States to

[59] L Mancano, *The European Union and Deprivation of Liberty* (Oxford, Hart Publishing, 2019) 67.
[60] On this matter, see P Cruz Mantilla de los Ríos, 'La saga rumana del Estado de Derecho' (2024) 128 *Revista Vasca de Administración Pública* 177.
[61] Case C-107/23 *PPU Lin* EU:C:2023:606.
[62] Case C-107/23 *PPU Lin* EU:C:2023:532, pt 90 (AG Campos Sánchez-Bordona).

guarantee the effectiveness of EU law and the plurality of standards within the EU in this matter. Moreover, the 'Romanian Constitutional Court applied a national standard of protection of fundamental rights which supplements the protection against arbitrariness in criminal matters offered by EU law'.[63] Therefore, even though the application of the ruling of the Romanian Constitutional Court could affect a significant number of cases involving the financial interests of the EU, the national courts are not compelled by EU law to disapply it. Thus, the CJEU follows the argument of *Taricco II* and allows the application of the national standard against the financial interests of the EU. Furthermore, the CJEU praises the judgment of the Romanian Constitutional Court on this specific subject, thus defusing the confrontation between the two courts.

Yet the CJEU also comes to another conclusion concerning the judgment of the Romanian Supreme Court. According to the CJEU, the national lex *mitior* standard compromises the unity, primacy and effectiveness of EU law. For that reason, the Romanian courts

> are required to disapply a national standard of protection relating to the principle of the retroactive application of the more lenient criminal law which makes it possible, including in the context of appeals brought against final judgments, to call into question the interruption of the limitation period for criminal liability in such cases by procedural acts which took place before such a finding of invalidity.[64]

Regrettably, the CJEU does not explain why the national standard on the *lex mitior* principle is not applicable in this case. Apparently fundamental rights do not play any role with regard to the *lex mitior* principle in the Romanian legal system, as the effectiveness of EU law apparently displaces them. The Advocate General extensively addressed, however, the *lex mitior* principle. After explaining that there is neither agreement on its applicability to final judgments in the process of enforcement among the Member States nor any conclusive ECtHR case law on the matter, the Advocate General held that Article 49 CFR should provide a high level of protection of the *lex mitior* principle. The CJEU, for its part, shies away from these findings, relying instead only on effectiveness to disregard the judgment of the Romanian Supreme Court. The CJEU, however, could have easily followed a different interpretation of the *lex mitior* principle,[65] given the deep differences among national legal traditions regarding this principle. Even qualifying the *lex mitior* principle as an aspect of the legality principle is disputed.[66] Yet no

[63] ibid para 115.

[64] ibid para 125.

[65] It could have followed the interpretation proposed by the Advocate General regarding also the *lex mitior* principle; 'the focus of effective protection of fundamental rights ought to be: the individual and the impact a rule has on his position, not the taxonomic labels attached to it by the respective national law." This guideline implies that whether "a person subject to criminal proceedings or his representation could have taken certain procedural decisions or modified their course of action in a manner relevant to the further development of those proceedings' must be taken into consideration as a consequence of the more lenient rules promulgated in criminal law. Case C-574/15 *Scialdone* EU:C:2017:553, pt 152 (AG Bobek).

[66] Peristeridou (n 53) 339.

reflection at all on the fundamental rights at stake is offered in relation to the scope of the *lex mitior* principle in the judgment of the CJEU.

This case shows that the potential of *Fransson* cannot be overestimated. A fully fledged catalogue of rights of constitutional rank, such as the CFR, demands a balanced approach vis-à-vis fundamental rights protection at the EU level.[67] Furthermore, this ruling reinforces the criticism of EU criminal policy for excessively relying on a security and effectiveness-based rationale, one that eventually leads to a repressive EU criminal policy which trumps justice and freedom.[68] The CJEU is trying to overcome this criticism by replacing the security narrative with a fundamental rights rationale, seeking legitimation for the coercive power of the EU.[69]

The principle of legality is at the crossroads of national and EU law because the EU cannot create criminal liability for individuals. The process by which an offence acquires the quality of legality takes place at the national level. 'It is the national legislation that binds the individual, and it is that legislation that must conform to the principle of legality.'[70] Nonetheless, the national legislation must comply with the duties arising from the membership to the EU, including the effectiveness of EU law. This duty implies deep consideration for fundamental rights, while regard for effectiveness might require the adoption of criminal measures.

Obviously, the risk that Member States fail to pay due regard to the EU interests, remains, but that risk should be mitigated without disregarding the fundamental rights at stake. The balance between the risk of impunity and the fundamental rights must be carefully carved out with due reflection for the level provided by the CFR (that is not a minimum), the level guaranteed by the ECHR and the level guaranteed by the national legal framework.

The CJEU offered such a reflection on *Taricco II*, albeit only after the harsh reference submitted by the Italian Constitutional Court, but it only partially gave due regard to the principle of legality in *Lin*. Nonetheless, if the CJEU wants to avoid causing the constitutional courts unease, let alone the latent threat to national constitutional identity, it must develop a convincing, consistent fundamental rights framework. This task is particularly pertinent in criminal law, given the sensitivity of criminal law to fundamental rights. Consequently, constitutional courts will be on permanent watch. The steps taken towards improved protection of fundamental rights through the CJEU's openness to judicial cooperation must also be followed with regard to substantive criminal law. It is doubtful that a substantive EU criminal law can be grounded solely on the protection of fundamental rights, but such protection is a *condition sine qua non* of any criminal law in a community governed by the rule of law.

[67] G Martinico and G Repetto, 'Fundamental Rights and Constitutional Duels in Europe: An Italian Perspective on Case 269/2017 of the Italian Constitutional Court and Its Aftermath' (2019) 15 *European Constitutional Law Review* 731, 749–50.

[68] Öberg (n 4) 136.

[69] M Fichera, 'Criminal Law beyond the State: The European Model' (2013) 19 *European Law Journal* 174, 184.

[70] Coutts (n 2) 189.

4. Concluding Remarks

Constitutional courts are increasingly taking part in the building of a European criminal law based on fundamental rights. The cases concerning the EAW are particularly relevant. Constitutional courts have challenged the initial understanding of mutual trust as a hurdle to apply any fundamental rights' argumentation. The references that were submitted by or arose from several constitutional courts have resulted in the possibility of suspending, in specific circumstances, the execution of EAWs and added rights that justify such this suspension. Furthermore, some of the references made by the constitutional courts have given the CJEU the chance to deepen key values of the EU and have enhanced the EU fundamental rights by aligning the CFR with the ECHR. The initial reluctance to engage in a dialogue with the CJEU is slowly fading, and the preliminary rulings raised by constitutional courts are increasingly well-thought out. The references made by the Italian Constitutional Court are particularly relevant in this regard.

In the context of extraordinary growth in European criminal law, several constitutional courts eventually decided that fundamental rights are properly protected by convincing Luxembourg of the need for and the path to protecting those rights. Mistrust transformed into militant cooperation. The CJEU is fully aware of this development and the standard of protection of fundamental rights of its case law is slowly increasing, often applying the standard and the argumentation proposed by constitutional courts. Obviously, the secondary EU law on fundamental rights in criminal proceedings is another very helpful tool for fundamental rights protection, since it fleshes out the CFR and reinforces the legitimacy of the CJEU towards national legislatures. Still, that national courts, and particularly constitutional courts, now seem to be on permanent watch is opening new and promising avenues for fundamental rights protection.

This shared narrative of rights, however, grows weaker when it comes to substantive criminal law. The inherent shortcomings of European criminal law, the well-settled case law on effectiveness and, probably, the conflictive relationship between the national and the EU level in specific cases all increase the complexity of protecting fundamental rights and coming to a shared understanding of the key principle of legality. Lastly, it is worth noting that not all constitutional courts have engaged in dialogue with the CJEU. Once the Irish Supreme Court and the Italian Constitutional Court have proved that dialogue represents a very successful means to protect fundamental rights, it is to be expected that other constitutional courts will eventually follow the same path.

Bibliography

Albi, A, 'The European Arrest Warrant, constitutional rights and the changing legal thinking', in Fletcher, M et al (eds), *The European Union as an Area of Freedom, Security and Justice* (Oxford, Routledge, 2017).

Arzoz, X, 'Euroorden, condiciones de reclusión y derechos fundamentales' (2018) 113 *Revista Española de Derecho Europeo* 145.

Besselink, L, 'The Parameters of Constitutional Conflict After Melloni' (2014) 39 *European Law Review* 531.
Coutts, S, *Citizenship, Crime and Community in the European Union* (Oxford, Hart Publishing, 2019).
Cruz Mantilla de los Ríos, P, 'La saga rumana del Estado de Derecho' (2024) 128 *Revista Vasca de Administración Pública* 177.
Deen-Racsmány, Z and Judge Blekxtoon, R, 'The Decline of the Regulation of (Non) Surrender of Nationals and Dual Criminality under the European Arrest Warrant' (2005) 13 *European Journal of Crime, Criminal Law and Criminal Justice* 317.
Fichera, M, 'Criminal Law beyond the State: The European Model' (2013) 19 *European Law Journal* 174.
Frąckowiak-Adamska, A, 'Drawing Red Lines with No (Significant) Bites' in von Bogdandy, A et al (eds), *Defending Checks and Balances in EU Member States* (Berlin, Springer, 2021).
González-Pascual, M, 'The first preliminary reference of the Spanish Constitutional Court' in Claes, M et al (eds), *Constitutional Conversations in Europe* (Amberes, Intersentia, 2012).
González-Pascual, M, '*A European Standard of Human Rights Protection?*' in Iglesias Sánchez, S and González-Pascual, M (eds), Fundamental *Rights in the EU Area of Freedom, Security and Justice* (Cambridge, Cambridge University Press, 2021).
—— 'El TJUE como garante de los derechos en la UE tras la sentencia Digital Rights Ireland' (2014) 49 *Revista de Derecho Comunitario Europeo* 943.
—— 'La creciente irrelevancia de la reinserción social en la UE' (2020) 118 *Revista Española de Derecho Constitucional* 167.
González-Pascual, M, 'Mutual Recognition of judicial decisions and the right to family life' in González Pascual, M and Torres Pérez, A (eds), *The right to family life in the European Union* (Oxford, Routledge, 2017).
Hong, M, 'Human Dignity, Identity Review of the European Arrest Warrant and the Court of Justice as Listener in the Dialogue of Courts: Solange-III and Aranyosi' (2016) 12 *European Constitutional Law Review* 549.
Iglesias Sánchez, S 'La Jurisprudencia Constitucional Comparada sobre la Orden Europea de Detención y Entrega, y la Naturaleza Jurídica de los Actos del Tercer Pilar' (2010) 35 *Revista de Derecho Comunitario Europeo* 169.
Iglesias Sánchez, S and González-Pascual, M, 'Fundamental Rights at the Core of the EU AFSJ' in Iglesias Sánchez, S and González-Pascual, M (eds), *Fundamental Rights in the EU Area of Freedom, Security and Justice* (Cambridge, Cambridge University Press, 2021).
Mancano, L, 'Punishment and Rights in the European Union Citizenship: persons or criminals?' (2018) 24 *European Law Journal* 206.
—— *The European Union and Deprivation of Liberty* (Oxford, Hart Publishing, 2019).
Martinico, G and Repetto, G, 'Fundamental Rights and Constitutional Duels in Europe: An Italian Perspective on Case 269/2017 of the Italian Constitutional Court and Its Aftermath' (2019) 15 *European Constitutional Law Review* 73.
Mitsilegas, V, 'Legislating for human rights after Lisbon', in Fletcher, M et al (ed), *The European Union as an Area of Freedom, Security and Justice* (Oxford, Routledge, 2017).
—— 'Mutual Recognition and Fundamental Rights in EU Criminal Justice' in Iglesias Sánchez, S and González-Pascual, M (ed), *Fundamental Rights in the EU Area of Freedom, Security and Justice* (Cambridge, Cambridge University Press, 2021).
Öberg, J, *The normative foundations for EU criminal justice* (Oxford, Hart Publishing, 2024).
Peristeridou, Ch, 'The Principle of Legality in the Area of Freedom, Security and Justice' in Iglesias Sánchez, S and González-Pascual, M (eds), *Fundamental Rights in the EU Area of Freedom, Security and Justice* (Cambridge, Cambridge University Press, 2021).

Reinbacher, T and Wendel, M, 'The Bundesverfassungsgericht's European Arrest Warrant II Decision' (2016) 23 *Maastricht Journal of European and Constitutional Law* 702.

Sarmiento, D, 'European Union: The European Arrest Warrant and the quest for constitutional coherence' (2008) 6 *International Journal of Constitutional Law* 171.

Scaccia, G, 'The Lesson Learned from the Taricco Saga: Judicial Nationalism and the Constitutional Review of E.U. Law' (2020) 35 *American University International Law Review* 821.

Sieber, U, 'Die Zukunft des Europäischen Strafrechts' (2009) 121 *Zeitschrift für die gesamte Strafrechtswissenschaft* 1.

Torres Pérez, A, 'Melloni in Three Acts: From Dialogue to Monologue' (2014) 10 *European Constitutional Law Review* 308.

von Bogdandy, A, 'A potential constitutional moment for the European Rule of Law: The importance of Red Lines' in von Bogdandy A et al, *Defending Checks and Balances in EU Member States* (Berlin, Springer, 2021).

Walker, N (ed), *Europe's Area of Freedom, Security and Justice* (Oxford, Oxford University Press, 2006).

11

The Controversial Question of Constitutional Protection Regarding the Primacy of Union Law

CRISTINA IZQUIERDO SANS

1. Introduction

For more than three decades, the Spanish Constitutional Court (SCC) hardly dealt with the principle of the primacy of European Union (EU) law (EUL) – and made use of it only on rare occasions. Through several decisions, however, EUL primacy has been established as a key principle regulating the relationship between EUL and national legal systems. Declaration 1/2004 of 13 December 2004 is a prime example, which was issued in response to a request by the Spanish Government regarding a possible contradiction between the Spanish Constitution and the principle of EUL primacy. The SCC found no contradiction between the principle of EUL primacy and Article 9(1) of the Spanish Constitution (SC), as the supposed regulation set forth in Article 95(1) SC is not applicable, adding:

> In the unlikely case where, in the ulterior dynamics of the legislation of the European Union, said law is considered irreconcilable with the Spanish Constitution, without the hypothetical excesses of the European legislation with regard to the European Constitution itself being remedied by the ordinary channels set forth therein, in a final instance, the conservation of the sovereignty of the Spanish people and the given supremacy of the Constitution could lead this Court to approach the problems which, in such a case, would arise … through the corresponding constitutional procedures.[1]

That same year, the SCC upheld the first appeal for constitutional protection (appeal for *amparo)* for failure to file a preliminary ruling which, due to the circumstances surrounding the case, implied a violation of due process.

[1] This pronouncement is based on the idea that there cannot be a hierarchy between different legal systems, but rather that they are constructed in terms of applicability. See JL Requejo, 'El futuro de un vértice jurisdiccional cada vez más complejo' (2018) 22 *Anuario de la Facultad de Derecho de la UAM* 109.

This is the shocking – and not expected – SCC judgment 58/2004 in which the Court affirmed:

> It must be taken into account that Spain has been a member State of the European Communities since 1 January 1986, in accordance with the provisions of Art. 93 SC and, therefore, subject to the rules of the Community legal system that have direct effect for citizens and have primacy over domestic provisions, as has been declared by the CJEU of the European Communities (Judgments of 5 February 1963, Van Gend and Loos case, and 15 July 1964, Costa v. E.N.E.L. case) and has been recognised by this Court (SCC judgment no 28/1991 and 64/1991, among others) (SCC judgment no130/1995 of 11 September 1995, paragraph 4).[2]

Once again, the SCC corroborates its respect for the principle of primacy of EU law. In 2012 a change occurred, and the SCC progressively began to exercise the function of defender of EU law by facilitating the correct application of the principle of primacy by ordinary judges. In other words, the SCC went from declaring respect for the principle of primacy to ensuring compliance with it with the exceptional landmark case of SCC judgment no 145/2012. For the first time the SCC uses the principle of primacy as *leitmotiv* of the decision:

> [T]the contested judicial decisions, by granting ex nunc effects to the CJEU ruling in the aforementioned judgment of 17 July 2008 – arguing that the judgment comes subsequent to the sanctioning decision that was appealed and has not conditioned the validity of any provision of Spanish law – disregard the principle of EUL primacy(which obliges the national judges and courts to apply the prevailing rule), as well as the enforceability of judgments of the CJEU handed down in infringement proceedings (which oblige the courts of the Member States to ensure that they are put into effect) and the ex tunc effects of those judgments (which project the effectiveness of their rulings to the time of entry into force of the domestic rule held to be contrary to the EUL, and not to the date on which those judgments were handed down (paragraph 6).

As everybody knows, this case is unique because there was a judgment of the Court of Justice of the European Union (CJEU) issued in a procedure for non-compliance against Spain and the judicial body refused to annul a sanction that had the national rule that the CJEU declared contrary to the EU law as its only basis, denying the *ex tunc* effectiveness of CJEU judgments. The SCC starts by recalling its traditional position in relation to the EU law: the EU law conflict is not a constitutional issue and acquires constitutional relevance when the judicial decision – which was supposed to solve that conflict – results in a violation of Article 24 SC. The SCC considered Article 24(1) SC in its aspect of unreasonable and arbitrary selection of the rule:

> [I]t can be stated that the Contentious-Administrative Chamber of the High Court of Justice of Madrid has made an unreasonable and arbitrary selection of the rule applicable to the proceedings by not taking into account that the CJEU has declared in its Judgment

[2] SCC judgment no 28/1991 of 14 February 1991, paras 4 and 5. See C Izquierdo Sans, 'Cuestión prejudicial y artículo 24 de la Constitución española' (2011) 23 *Revista General de Derecho europeo* 1; C Izquierdo Sans, 'Amparo constitucional y cuestión prejudicial ¿un nuevo giro del tribunal constitucional? Comentario a la STC 212/2014, de 18 de diciembre' (2015) 55 *Revista Española de Derecho Europeo* 107.

of 17 July 2008, with ex tunc effects, that the obligations incumbent on Spain by virtue of Articles 43 and 56 of the Treaty establishing the European Community (currently Articles 49 and 63 of the Treaty on the functioning of the European Union) – provisions that have direct effect and take precedence over Spanish domestic law – have been breached by issuing the eleventh additional provision, paragraph 1, function 14 of Law 34/1998 of 7 October 1998 on the hydrocarbons sector (as amended by Royal Decree-Law 4/2006 of 24 February 2006).

Since that decision, now a little more than a decade old, the SCC's constitutional case law has abounded which, despite the criticism directed towards it, is more congruent and reasonable than is usually appreciated, irrespective to the possibility that our constitutional judges have shown self-restraint or exceeded their role. The following should be definitely mentioned with great emphasis: throughout the case law that we are going to analyse, although it is true that the SCC has peacefully recognised the primacy of EU law over domestic law – in the scope of the powers whose exercise Spain has conferred to the European institutions – the SCC has also declared without hesitation that EU law does not fully integrate the canon of constitutionality and that the primacy of EU law cannot be invoked as an argument justifying the unconstitutionality of a rule:

> [N]either the phenomenon of European integration, nor Article 93 SC through which it is instrumented nor the principle of primacy of EUL that governs the relations between both legal systems have endowed the rules of EUL, whether original or derived, 'with constitutional rank and force' (SCC judgment no 75/2017, paragraph 2).

However, without prejudice to this clear and correct position, the SCC made two clarifications: a) that EU law has an intense hermeneutic value, based on Article 10(2) SC, which involves not only the founding treaties and their successive amendments, but also their derived law, as well as the interpretation of such rules by the CJEU (SCC judgment no 91/2019, paragraph 7); and b) that the SCC must ensure respect for the principle of primacy of EU law when an authentic interpretation by the CJEU is available, since

> in these cases the disregard and pretermission of that EU law rule, as interpreted by the CJEU, may involve 'unreasonable and arbitrary selection of a rule applicable to the process', which may give rise to a violation of the right to effective judicial protection [SCC judgments no 145/2012, paragraphs 5 and 6; no 232/2015, paragraph 4 (b); no 31/2019, paragraph 7].

This chapter analyses this case law and highlights its value, without prejudice to its dark zones. Despite the occasional controversy, it is clear that the SCC has a relevant role to play in the implementation of EU law in Spain. This chapter examines the complexity of the role that the SCC has played as a defender of the principle of primacy, although, surely, the most interesting aspect of this work is, more than the role assumed, the concern over the role the SCC can and/or should play in the future. Depending on the eye of the beholder, we might spy on some Europeanist voluntarism in the SCC or, from another perspective, a function more akin to the necessity of constitutional control of the application of EU law by ordinary jurisdictions. As always, virtue lies in balance.

2. Purely External Control of Judicial Protection (Article 24(1) SC)

Following SCC judgment no145/2012, the two next judgments handed down by the SCC in relation to EU law begin by assuming *solely external control*, because national law has not been displaced. The SCC affirms that, when the law is applied,[3] it will limit the control over the judicial decision denying the preliminary ruling to the usual external control that it exercises over any other judicial decision. I refer to SCC judgments no 27/2013 and no 212/2014, in which the Court limits itself to a mere formal analysis.

SCC judgment no 27/2013 of 11 February[4] addressed a case in which the plaintiff for *amparo* was denied aid in application of regional rules that, according to the plaintiff, were contrary to EU law. The plaintiff requested the filing of a preliminary question to the CJEU both to the High Court of Extremadura and the Spanish Supreme Court. Both courts, without referring a question to the CJEU for a preliminary ruling, found the autonomous community rule in accordance with the EU law applicable to the case and dismissed the appeal. In their opinion, the preliminary ruling was unnecessary 'since it was clearly evident how the autonomous community provision should be interpreted'.

When an appeal for *amparo* is filed, the SCC first specifies the contours of the canon of constitutionality it will use in its judicial decision, whose reasoning must be based on law and contain the elements and grounds for judgment that make it possible to know the legal criteria on which the decision was based. The SCC immediately points out that the right to effective judicial protection of Article 24(1) SC 'does not include an alleged right to judicial correctness in the selection, interpretation and application of legal provisions, unless it affects the content of several constitutional rights other than the right to effective judicial protection'. That the mere disagreement of the parties with a judicial decision, even if based on a plausible interpretation of the law applied, does not make the corresponding judicial reasoning arbitrary or manifestly unreasonable, nor does it oblige the SCC to decide which among the possible interpretations should

[3] Until SCC judgment no 145/2012, the SCC had only upheld one appeal for *amparo* for incorrect application of EU law in SCC judgment no 58/2004. This was a case of non-application of national law and application of the EU law by the judicial body, but without a preliminary ruling, in a case in which the SCC understood that the principles of *acte clair* and *acte éclairé* were not fulfilled and, consequently, it was mandatory for the judicial body to have filed a preliminary ruling. On that occasion, as I have already examined in some of my other studies, the SCC understood that the guarantees of due process had been violated and the system of sources had been altered, and therefore the judicial resolution infringed Art 24(2) SC. In 2012, when the SCC became a defender of the principle of primacy of EUL, it noticed that it was faced with cases in which the national law has been applied and it respected the work of the judicial body more, as opposed to the time when, in principle, it only intended to carry out external control of protection. See C Izquierdo Sans, 'Cuestión prejudicial y artículo 24 de la Constitución española' (2011) 23 *Revista General de Derecho europeo* 1; C Izquierdo Sans, 'Amparo constitucional y cuestión prejudicial ¿un nuevo giro del tribunal constitucional? Comentario a la STC 212/2014, de 18 de diciembre' (2015) 55 *Revista Española de Derecho Europeo* 107.

[4] For comments on this judgment, see M Carlón Ruiz 'El TC como garante del derecho comunitario. Reflexiones al hilo de la STC 27/2013, de 11 de febrero' (2013) 47 *Revista Española de Derecho Europeo* 99.

prevail. The application of this canon to the factual situation leads to the dismissal of this *amparo* complaint, since

> to determine whether the Spanish Supreme Court correctly interpreted EU law in inferring the compatibility or not of the crop rotation requirement is a question on which this Court, which is not a third-level court, as we have repeatedly stated, cannot in fact rule, unless the judicial reasoning is unreasonable, arbitrary or in patent error, circumstances that are not present in this case since the contested judgment is also based on a reasonable interpretation'

SCC judgment no 212/2014, of 18 December 2014, which also dismisses the appeal for *amparo*, again, clarifies the canon of constitutionality that is to be applied and must be surpassed by the challenged judicial decision: the judicial decision must be reasoned, and the mere disagreement of the parties with a judicial decision, even if based on another possible interpretation of the law applied, however plausible it may be, does not make the corresponding judicial reasoning arbitrary or manifestly unreasonable, nor does it oblige this Court to choose among the possible interpretations which one should prevail. The SCC affirms that, once this canon has been surpassed, no violation of the rights guaranteed by Article 24(1) SC has occurred if the judicial body has no doubts about the interpretation to be given to a EU rule, or about its application in relation to the facts of the dispute, and therefore decides not to seek consultation.[5] In short, the refusal to submit a request for a preliminary ruling does not imply, per se, a violation of effective judicial protection. The SCC makes it clear that, from the perspective of Article 24(1) SC, the canon of review established in relation to the raising of preliminary questions before the CJEU does not differ from that established in general for judicial decisions that are the result of the interpretation and application of the law to the specific case, and the only consideration that it must make is whether the judicial decision is based on law and is the result of a rational exegesis of the ordinary law.[6]

The SCC then applies the above canon to the specific case and declares that the judicial body issuing the contested judgment explains its decision and its observance of the CJEU case law. For the SCC, the reasons offered by the judicial body reach the threshold established by the constitutional case law, since the appellate body adequately externalises the legal criteria on which the decision adopted was based and its arguments do not incur in arbitrariness, nor do they suffer from lack of reasonableness. Furthermore, the conclusions reached by the appellate court must be disregarded and it is irrelevant whether they are shared or not,[7] because it is only necessary to

[5] The SCC adds that the same applies to the decision not to raise a question of unconstitutionality ex Art 163 SC. This shows that the SCC has in mind a parallelism in the treatment that it itself grants to the decisions of the judicial bodies regarding the non-filing of a question of unconstitutionality or a preliminary ruling. The reasoning would go in the following direction: If the SCC is the highest guarantor of the Spanish Constitution and does not question the decision of the judge on whether or not to file a question of unconstitutionality, out of respect for the function of the body under Art 117 SC, it is even less legitimate for it to question the decision of a judicial body on whether or not to file a preliminary question.

[6] SCC judgment no 212/2014, of 18 December 2014, para 3.

[7] The mere disagreement of the parties with a judicial decision, even if based on another possible interpretation of the law applied, however plausible it may be, does not make the corresponding judicial reasoning arbitrary or manifestly unreasonable, nor does it oblige this Court to choose among the possible

judge whether the arguments are arbitrary or unreasonable, since the judicial bodies are the only ones competent, ex Article 117(3) SC, to rule on matters of strict ordinary legality.

In paragraph 5, the SCC quickly dismisses the complaints related to the violation of the guarantees of due process and the right to a judge predetermined by law. Regarding the first guarantee, it is clear from this judgment that the SCC opts for the application of its case law on the question of unconstitutionality to the preliminary ruling: the non-application of a law as unconstitutional without resorting to the question of unconstitutionality gives rise to a decision that is not based in law, a breach of the principle of *iura novit curia* and a violation of the guarantees of due process. The analogical application of the aforementioned case law to the preliminary question of validity is not difficult, since, just as it states that the constituent has removed from the ordinary judge the possibility of not applying a law in the event of a possible judgment of incompatibility with the Constitution,[8] it can be argued that EUL has taken from the national judge – as the EU judge that he or she is – the power to make a negative judgment of the validity of EU law, the CJEU being the only competent court to declare the invalidity of the act in question.[9] As regards the preliminary question of interpretation, the SCC has been able to transfer this case law in cases in which the judicial body opts for the non-application of the law, since for the SCC the same injuries occur when a rule is not applied without a ground to support that non-application, being indifferent whether the cause is the failure to file the question of unconstitutionality or preliminary ruling, so that it draws the same legal consequences. On the contrary, ordinary judicial bodies are empowered to make positive judgments of constitutionality and validity, so that such decisions are not, in principle, susceptible to constitutional protection, except for the external analysis of tutelage that can be made of any judicial decision.

With regard to the violation of the right to a judge predetermined by law, the SCC takes this opportunity to draw attention to the fact that the content of this right in the case law of our SCC does not fit into the debate on the violation of Article 24 SC for the failure to file a preliminary ruling, since that case law is limited to granting the right that the judicial body has been created by a legal rule and is vested with jurisdiction prior to the event motivating the judicial action or process, which is not under discussion in the aforementioned debate. In this regard, it had already been stated that the CJEU is, without a doubt, the organ predetermined by law to decide on the interpretation of the EU's legal system.

interpretations which one should prevail (SCC judgments no 59/2003, of 24 March 2003, para 3; no 221/2003, of 15 December 2003, para 4; no 140/2005, of 6 June 2005, para 5; and no 221/2005, of 12 September 2005, para 5). The SCC assumes that its control of judicial decisions through the *amparo* appeal is not about the correctness of the judge, since the right to effective judicial protection has been constructed in our constitutional case law according to a model of deference or respect for the judge that is unavoidable. This deferential distance which, by legal imperative, is maintained by the SCC, is not obligatory for the ordinary courts, where the distinction between questions of legality and constitutionality loses all meaning. In this regard, see J Jiménez Campo, *Derechos Fundamentales, Concepto y garantías* (Madrid, Trotta, 1999) 91 and J Mercader Uguina, 'Tutela judicial efectiva, control de razonabilidad de las decisiones judiciales y canon reforzado de motivación en la doctrina del TC' (2008) 73 *Revista del Ministerio de Trabajo y Asuntos Sociales* 127.

[8] SCC judgment no 17/1981, of 1 June 1981, para 1.

[9] SCC judgment no 58/2004, of 19 April 2004, para 11.

The case law was described as unfortunate in the dissenting opinion of the then vice-president of the Court, Judge Adela Asua. For the vice-president, opting to apply the general canon of interpretation of ordinary legality produces a regrettable step backwards with respect to the case law resulting from SCC judgment no 58/2004, which took a new position on the constitutional relevance of the failure to raise a preliminary question. Personally, I agree with the SCC that the case law of SCC judgment no 58/2004 was not applicable to the matter it had to resolve. However, I also share Judge Adela Asua's concern, as it is somewhat dizzying that the SCC only commits itself to the correct application of EU law when the case involves non-application of national law. Fortunately, our fears proved to be unfounded sooner rather than later.

3. The Right to Obtain a Reasoned and Legally Founded Decision from Judges and Courts

Indeed, those disappointed by SCC judgments no 27/2013 and no 212/2014 were immediately comforted. In application of the same canon of reasoning, the SCC reaches the opposite conclusion and upholds the *amparo* in the SCC judgment no 232/2015, of 5 November 2015. In the case it was argued that the CJEU had interpreted Directive 1999/70 on fixed-term work and had declared that a national rule such as the Spanish one, which discriminated between interim teachers and civil servant teachers in the granting of six-year periods of continuing education in secondary education, would be contrary to EU law. Despite the CJEU judgment, the court applies the discriminatory national rule and ignores the CJEU ruling. For the SCC, the regulatory selection is unreasonable and arbitrary, violates the principle of primacy of EU law and causes a violation of effective judicial protection (Article 24(1) SC) because, as far as the Chamber failed to reason on a substantial allegation of the appealed party, namely the CJEU on the rule applicable to the case, the reasoning is clearly defective.

The SCC states that the judicial body

> resolved with an 'unreasonable and arbitrary selection of a rule applied to the process' (SCC judgment no 145/2012, para. 6), insofar as it disregarded by its own, autonomous and exclusive decision, the interpretation of clause 4(1) of Directive 1999/70/SC imposed and indicated by the competent body to do so with binding character (SCC judgment n°145/2012, para. 5) thereby violating the principle of primacy of EU law.

What characterises this case is the presence of a CJEU precedent in an identical case making it easy to affirm that the authentic interpretation of the EU law was pretermitted by the judicial body, since transferring the answer given by the CJEU to an identical case was not complicated. Sharing this pronouncement of the SCC, what is difficult is transferring the answer given by the CJEU in a judgment to a case that is not identical. This requires an additional effort on the part of the judicial body to examine the pronouncement of the CJEU, interpret its scope and declare that it was truly applicable, which implies significant risk, first by the ordinary jurisdiction and, even more, by the SCC, if it decides to check the decision adopted by the judicial body. See, for example, SCC judgment no 37/2019, of 19 April 2009, in relation to the social bonus. The Spanish Supreme Court did not apply the Spanish law because it considered it contrary to the EU law, but did not ask for a preliminary ruling, in application of the principle of the *acte éclairé*.[10] For the SCC, there was no *acte éclairé* because the cases did not present the required degree of similarity and the same rule of the EU law was not even interpreted, so that the system of sources had been pretermitted, with disregard for the guarantees of due process and, consequently, the SCC upheld the appeal for *amparo* filed and annulled the judgment of the Spanish Supreme Court challenged.

However, two pieces of information are worth mentioning: (i) the Spanish Supreme Court had made a negative judgment on the compatibility of the national law with the EU law, and therefore did not apply the national rule, raising the alarms of the SCC; and (ii) a judge filed a dissenting vote in the decision of the Spanish Supreme Court because of his disagreement with the consideration of *acte éclairé* by the majority.

Let us return, however, to SCC judgment no232/2015 and the application of a canon of reinforced reasoning, linked to a decision based in law, which will serve the SCC to consolidate a constitutional case law aimed at safeguarding the primacy of EU law. Indeed, with SCC judgment no 148/2016, the constitutional case law on consumer protection in the light of the CJEU case law begins and the SCC decides to uphold the *amparo* appeal. However, this judgment involves extremely uncommon facts and the right of access to jurisdiction, which also implies a more incisive canon than the general canon of protection. The upholding of *lis pendens* alleged by the other party, with respect to a collective process against a bank claiming the nullity of the floor clause when the appellant was not a party to the collective process, prevented it from availing itself of this process, when the CJEU had interpreted Directive 93/13 in the opposite direction. This is the only case of all the cases in which the SCC, out of respect for the principle of primacy of EU law, upholds the *amparo* appeal for violation of the right of access to jurisdiction.

However, the Court relies on the same grounds as the decisions that we will see later on:

> [I]t is up to this Court to ensure that the principle of primacy of EU law is respected when, as is the case here and we have already seen, there is an authentic interpretation made by the CJEU itself. In these cases the disregard and pretermission of that EU law rule, as interpreted by the CJEU, may involve an 'unreasonable and arbitrary selection of a rule applicable to the process.

This may give rise to a violation of the right to effective judicial protection (SCC judgments no 145/2012, of 2 July 2012, paragraphs 5 and 6; and no 232/2015, paragraph 5(c)).

The family of SCC pronouncements aimed at safeguarding the primacy of EU law in the field of unfair terms consolidates this constitutional case law linking the role of the SCC as defender of the principle of primacy of EU law to the right to a decision based on law. Thus, the unreasonable and arbitrary selection of the rule applicable to the process is taken up again in SCC judgment no 75/2017, a foreclosure case in which

[10] The Spanish Supreme Court dedicated all of para 8 of the challenged judicial decision to explain why it was an *acte éclairé*: these were identical rules, with the same provision, in different industries – gas and electricity – although approved on the same day by the Council of the Union and with the same purpose, to establish common rules for the internal market in the gas and electricity industries.

the judicial body had denied the appellants the status of consumers[11] contrary to the CJEU case law. The SCC considers that a violation of effective judicial protection has occurred 'insofar as it disregarded by its own, autonomous and exclusive decision', the interpretation of Article 2 (b) of Directive 93/13/EEC imposed and indicated by the competent body to do so has binding character and, consequently, the aforementioned principle of primacy was infringed in an 'unreasonable and arbitrary selection of a rule applied to the process' thus violating the appellant's right to effective judicial protection (Article 24(1) SC).

The paradigm of this change is found in SCC judgment no 31/2019. The case involved a mortgage foreclosure in which the national judge did not assess the existence of abusive clauses *ex officio*, and the SCC reached the conclusion that the court had not complied with the CJEU case law by failing to analyse the abusiveness of the early termination clause and failing to raise a question for preliminary ruling. The differential fact of this case is that, in order to reach this conclusion, the SCC interprets the CJEU case law alleged by the appellant, in order to determine whether or not that case law was applicable to the cases, *BBVA* (C-8/14) and *Banco primus* (C-421/14), and obliged the judicial body to make this analysis. For the SCC, the refusal of the judicial body to analyse the abusiveness of the clauses violated the principle of primacy, incurred an unreasonable and arbitrary interpretation of a rule applied to the process and violated the appellant's right to effective judicial protection. In addition to applying a reinforced canon of reasoning, it should be noted that the SCC abandoned the unreasonable selection of the rule applied to the process in favour of the unreasonable interpretation.

As González Alonso aptly observes,[12] the scope of the duty to give reasons is not identical for all judicial decisions regardless of the matter to which they refer. The SCC has linked the right to the reasoning of judicial decisions with the right to obtain a decision based on law and, according to this last side of Article 24(1) SC, the judicial body can only give reasons based on law to justify the *decisum*, so that, if the judicial decision is devoid of this type of reasoning, the requirement of reasoning will only be apparent, not real, thus violating the fundamental right (SCC judgment no 23/1987).[13] The author states that

> [T]he inclusion of this aspect in the right to effective judicial protection is related to one of the most important issues affecting the constitutional jurisdiction, such as the limits of

[11] The appellants, although natural persons, do not have the status of consumers, since they secured by mortgage a loan arranged for the benefit of a commercial company and, consequently, the control of unfairness of contractual clauses imposed by Council Directive 93/13/EEC of 5 April 1993 on unfair terms in consumer contracts (Directive 93/13/EEC) is not applicable to them, nor in the Law on general contracting conditions, which clearly indicates that the concept of unfairness is circumscribed to contracts concluded with consumers.

[12] A González Alonso, 'La tutela jurisdiccional de los derechos del artículo 24.1 de la Constitución Española, Tesis doctoral inédita' Universidad Autónoma de Madrid, Facultad de Derecho. Departamento de Derecho Público y Filosofía Jurídica, March 2012 224 ff, repositorio.uam.es/bitstream/handle/10486/9207/48355_gonzalez_alonso_alicia.pdf?sequence=1&isAllowed=y.

[13] The SCC has stated that it would 'incur in excessive formalism if it were to admit as reasoned decisions those which, at first sight and without the need for further intellectual and argumentative effort, it is proven that they start from non-existent or patently erroneous premises or follow an argumentative development that incurs logical breakdowns of such magnitude that the conclusions reached cannot be considered based on any of the reasons given' (PoL 4), criteria subsequently reiterated (for example, SCC judgment no 96/2006 of 27 March 2006, para 6; SCC judgment no 105/2009, of 4 May 2009, para 2).

> the latter's knowledge and resolution of appeals for amparo. Although the overreaching of the SCC in matters of ordinary legality can also occur through the interpretation of other provisions that recognise fundamental rights – especially Articles 14, 25 and 28 – the risk is especially evident in this aspect of the right to effective judicial protection, insofar as the High Court can enter any area of ordinary legality. The control of this aspect of the law should never be that of the greater reasonableness or correctness in the interpretation of ordinary legality, or in the selection of the rule applicable to the case. This is why it is so important to define the contours of what is to be understood by unreasonableness and arbitrariness, which, as will be explained below, is an aspect to which the SCC has not paid particular attention, perhaps because of the difficulty involved in defining these concepts a priori.

This aspect of the right to a reasoned decision is what the SCC has used to analyse whether the right recognised in Article 24(1) SC is violated when the decision in relation to the EU law lacks sufficient motivation or, if it is offered, is arbitrary, unreasonable or not based on law. In application of the 31/2019 the SCC has issued more than 20 judgments. All are based on the right to obtain a decision based on law, a right that is not fulfilled with the mere issuance of a declaration of will in one sense or another, but must be the result of a rational exegesis of the legal system and not the result of arbitrary judgment. The case law of the SCC has been progressing hand in hand with the pronouncements of the CJEU.[14] The CJEU has not only brought about legal reform so it can oppose enforcement of a clause due to its abusive nature,[15] but has also carried out interpretations of Directive 93/13 that collide with national procedural rules, in particular with the rules on time-barring and *res judicata*. This has led some judges to demonstrate reluctance towards accepting the interpretation of the CJEU, as accepting it would mean contravening the rules contained in the Spanish Code of Civil Procedure and is in this context where the SCC has played the defender of the primacy of EU law. This defensive role was obviously not going to be easy: It requires additional effort of the SCC to examine the CJEU pronouncements, interpret their scope and find the interpretation of the CJEU contrary to the interpretation of the ordinary jurisdiction. The risk of the SCC erring in the interpretation pursued by the CJEU judgment that it intends to apply is clear.[16] Which is why, in my view, prudence is called for.

Without prejudice to the undeniable prominence of consumer protection in the SCC's role of defending the principle of primacy of EU law, the truth is that very similar reasoning is found in areas other than unfair terms in mortgage foreclosure proceedings. SCC judgment no 13/2017, which upholds an appeal for *amparo* for violation of the right to legal counsel (Article 17(3) SC), is, in this sense, striking. The judicial body denied the lawyer access to the police file, being a right enforceable by the appellants

[14] CJEU judgment of 17 May 2022, Case C-600/19, *Ibercaja Banco and others*.

[15] The legal reform occurs with Law 1/2013 of 14 May 2013 on measures to strengthen the protection of mortgage debtors, debt restructuring and social renting and was the consequence of the CJEU judgment of 14 March 2013, Case C-415/11, *Aziz*.

[16] In relation to SCC judgment no 31/2019, see MJ García Valdecasas Dorrego, 'La sentencia de 28 de febrero de 2019 del TC: preclusión procesal, cosa juzgada y derecho de propiedad en la declaración de abusividad de una cláusula contractual' in (2020) 37 *Derecho privado y Constitución* 343, 380. On a general note, regarding the case law of the SCC on abusive clauses, see C Martínez Escribano, 'El control judicial de oficio de las cláusulas abusivas en los procedimientos de ejecución hipotecaria. La STC 141/2022, de 14 de noviembre (2023) 4 *Anuario de derecho civil* 1703, 1766.

in custody in accordance with the provisions of Article 7 of Directive 2012/13/EU of the European Parliament and of the Council of 22 May 2012, not yet transposed into Spanish law, although the deadline for transposition had already passed. The SCC stated that,

> in accordance with the CJEU case law, since Spain has not complied with this obligation in substantial terms and always in relation to the useful effect of the Directive in a vertical sense (enforceability of the individual against the State, which is the hypothesis that concerns us here), individuals are entitled to invoke against the State and before the national courts those provisions of the Directive that, from the point of view of their content, are unconditional and sufficiently precise.

Personally, I find of particular interest SCC judgment no 152/2021, which upheld the appeal for *amparo* filed by the father of three children for violation of the right to effective judicial protection by disregarding and pretermitting an anti-discrimination rule of the EU. The appellant claimed that his retirement pension should be increased by the 'maternity supplement' regulated in Spain, which only provided for a pension supplement in favour of women. The appellant complained in the judicial proceedings that the regulation discriminated on the grounds of sex contrary to Article 14 SC and the case law of the SCC on male discrimination in pension matters, and contrary to Directive 79/7/EEC and the CJEU case law interpreting it, requesting the direct application of that EU legislation and, if appropriate, the raising of a preliminary ruling or a question of unconstitutionality. The courts ruled out the infringement of the fundamental right and the contravention of the Directive, arguing that the provision in question was a provision relating to the 'protection of women' and that raising a question was not necessary. The judicial body did not evaluate the CJEU case law invoked by the appellant, which led the SCC to affirm that an 'unreasonable and arbitrary selection of the rule applied to the process' had been incurred, since the interpretation of the EU rule imposed by the competent body to do so with binding character was disregarded, thus violating the 'principle of primacy of European Union Law'.[17]

Finally, SCC Plenary judgment no 47/2023, of 10 May 2023 is worth mentioning, a judgment that deals with the thorny issue of expulsion as a sanction that may be imposed on a private individual whose presence in the territory is illegal. In this judgment, the SCC reviews the domestic regulatory framework enabling the possible applicable sanctions; the main provisions of Directive 2008/115/SC and the case law that has been gradually established by the CJEU in response to several questions referred for a preliminary ruling by the Spanish courts. These questions refer to the compatibility between this directive and its transposition in 2009 to the provisions of the Organic Law on the rights and freedoms of foreigners in Spain. The appeal for *amparo* was filed against both the decision of the Government Delegation in Madrid that imposed the sanction of expulsion from national territory and the consequent prohibition of returning to

[17] The provision was subsequently amended as a result of the CJEU judgment of 12 December 2019, which was handed down in the preliminary ruling C-450/18, *WA v Instituto Nacional de la Seguridad Social (INSS)*. The judgment declared the incompatibility of the provision with respect to Council Directive 79/7/EEC of 19 December 1978 on the progressive implementation of the principle of equality between men and women in matters of social security.

Spain for a period of three years and the subsequent judicial decisions that confirmed the original administrative decision. A violation of the fundamental right to effective judicial protection (Article 24(1) SC) was found in all these decisions, since they all lack sufficient grounds for the imposition of the expulsion measure.

In effect, the judicial decisions declared the expulsion appropriate based on the direct application of the provisions of Article 6(1) of Directive 2008/115/SC, but in invoking those grounds, the judicial bodies failed to apply the consequences provided for in Spanish law for situations of irregular stay, since, in Spanish law, the sanction of expulsion is not called for in cases when foreigners are merely in a situation of irregular stay unless aggravating or negative circumstances are found. The SCC found that this interpretation of the Spanish courts, which marginalised the most favourable national legislation and gave direct inverse effect to the return Directive, was erroneous and contrary to the case law of the CJEU on the effectiveness of such rules in domestic legal systems. The SCC declares that:

> 'as stated in the CJEU judgment of 8 October 2020, "it must be observed that, in accordance with the Court's settled case law, a directive cannot, of itself, impose obligations on an individual, since a provision of a directive may not be relied upon as such by a Member State against such an individual"' (paragraph 35).

The operative section of the judgment finds a violation of the right to the legality of penalties of Article 25(1) SC which has given rise to successive decisions on its application.

4. Primacy and Constitutional Review

The SCC is to ensure the supremacy of the Constitution when reviewing the constitutionality of laws, both through the constitutional challenge and the question of unconstitutionality. A priori, it might seem that this function is alien to EU law, since the SCC reviews the constitutionality of national law, without interference from EU law. In reality, however, this is far from the case.

Our first focus should be on the issue known as double defect or, in other words, the coincidence in the same process of a rule that possibly infringes both the SC and EU law. The friction involves the constitutional norms relating to fundamental rights. Faced with an unexpected relationship between the preliminary question and the question of unconstitutionality, the SCC has also assumed the role of guarantor of EU law in its judgment no 168/2016 of 4 October 2016, when it declared in paragraph 4 that, in response to an allegation of double defect, the national judicial body should bring a preliminary question before requesting a finding on constitutionality. This case law has been reiterated on several occasions:

> [W]hen a preliminary ruling is still pending on a legal rule, it is not possible to raise at the same time a question of unconstitutionality until the CJEU has issued its decision. The potential incompatibility of the domestic rule with the EU Law results in the inapplicability of the former. Therefore, the question of unconstitutionality would lack of one of its admissibility requirements in that the questioned rule with the force of law is 'applicable to the case' [Articles 163 SC and 35(1) OLCC] … from the Spanish point of view, a judicial body that has doubts about the constitutionality of a legal provision cannot raise a question of

unconstitutionality before this Constitutional Court if at the same time considers that very legal provision contrary to the EU law, because it would be obliged by this latter not to apply it. Whilst it has doubts about the compatibility of the domestic legal provision with the European Union Law, then it must first raise a preliminary ruling before the Court of Justice of the European Union and once this Court has decided on its compatibility, may lodge a question of unconstitutionality'.[18]

The question came from the debate in France over the so-called priority question of unconstitutionality,[19] which sought to resolve dilemmas that might occasionally arise for judicial bodies assessing the conformity of a law with both the Constitution and EU law when the priority of the question of unconstitutionality was established. The CJEU was called upon to rule on whether the French option was correct in *Melki and Abdeli*.[20] In SCC judgment no 168/2016, the SCC took a position that has been peacefully applied up to this point.[21] Perhaps the incisive intervention of the EU in matters relating to the protection of the rule of law may turn such a respectful position, in order to preserve, by our SCC, the constitutionality review of national law.

Last, but not least, I highlight a lesser-known issue: the strengthened hermeneutic role of EU law in the review of laws that the SCC is to conduct. Take SCC judgment no 156/2021, a constitutional challenge in which the SCC declares the unconstitutionality of Article 4(2)[22] of Royal Decree-Law 1/2017 of 20 January 2017 on urgent measures for the protection of consumers regarding floor clauses. For the SCC, the regulation established in the provision, put in relation to the content of the CJEU judgment *Gutiérrez Naranjo*, was unreasonable from the perspective of Article 24 SC. By making it difficult to impose costs on financial institutions, the Royal Decree-Law had disincentivised consumers from claiming their rights. The SCC states that, although EU law cannot be treated as a canon of constitutionality for domestic rules, it can serve to confirm the unreasonableness of the consequences entailed by the contested provision in relation with the objectives of the CJEU judgment *Gutiérrez Naranjo v. Cajasur Banco*, SAU, of 21 December 2016. Based on the dissuasive effect caused to consumers, the SCC declares the unconstitutionality of the regulation for violating the right to effective judicial protection enshrined in Article 24(1) SC.

For its part, SCC judgment no 91/2019 of 3 July 2019, represents an internal question of unconstitutionality in conjunction with Article 5(2) of Royal Decree-Law 11/2013

[18] SCC judgment no 205/2016, of 13 December 2016, para 5.

[19] LM Díez-Picazo, 'Las transformaciones de la Constitución francesa de 1958' (2008) 34 *Cuadernos de Derecho Público* 21.

[20] CJEU judgment of 22 June 2010, C-118/10. See D Sarmiento Ramírez-Escudero, 'Cuestión prejudicial y control previo de constitucionalidad. Comentario a la sentencia Melky TJUE' (2010) 37 *Revista española de Derecho europeo* 97.

[21] Following SCC judgment no 168/2016 of 4 October 2016, this case law has been applied on 12 occasions: SCC judgment no 185/2016 of 15 November 2016; judgment nos 202, 203, 204 and 205/2016 of 13 December 2016; no 90/2020 of 9 September 2020; nos 115 and 116/2020 of 22 September 2020; no 125/2020 of 21 October 2020; no 173/2020 of 15 December 2020 and nos 5 and 6/2021 of 27 January 2020. In all cases it has entailed the inadmissibility of the question of unconstitutionality by application of the case law of SCC judgment no 168/2016.

[22] Article 4(2) of Royal Decree Law 1/2017 was very restrictive of awarding costs to financial institutions, which meant that the consumer would have to bear his or her own costs, thus causing a deterrent effect when claiming their rights.

of 2 August 2013 for the protection of part-time workers together with urgent measures meant to preserve the economic and social order. In this judgment, the SCC states that both direct discrimination and indirect discrimination in the prohibition of discrimination of Article 14 SC are included since SCC judgment no 145/1991 of 1 July 1991. Indirect discrimination is considered constitutional case law whose origin lies in the concept developed by the case law of the CJEU in reference to measures that, despite their neutral formulation, harm a much higher percentage of women than men. Based on this premise, the SCC declared the partial nullity of the legal provision because it incurred, by regulating the amount of the retirement pension accorded to part-time workers, in indirect discrimination.

SCC judgment no 134/2018 is also worth mentioning. This was a constitutional challenge against Law 9/2017 of 3 August 2017 on the regulation of bullfighting and animal protection in the Balearic Islands alleging a violation of the principle of market unity and free movement, insofar as it mandated that the trip from the livestock farm to the bullring be the indispensable minimum and that the livestock farm supplying the bulls be the closest in distance to the bullring where the bullfighting spectacle was held. The state invoked its powers in the area of market unity and free movement and the SCC upheld the constitutionality of the rule. Although the invocation of the primacy of EU law cannot be accepted on its own as an argument justifying the constitutionality of a rule, in this case the sufficiently open nature of the prescriptions of the contested provision and the consideration of animal welfare within the overriding reasons of general interest defined by EU law allow for the affirmation that the contested rule is justified by the Community rules on animal protection.

Thirdly, the specific impact of EU law on the internal distribution of competences is noteworthy. Constitutional challenge no 130/2013 of 4 June 2013 is striking in this sense. The Government of Aragon filed the challenge against multiple articles of Law 38/2003 of 17 November 2003 on general assistance, alleging the challenged legislation exceeds the state's constitutionally conferred powers to provide assistance. For the purposes that interest us, Article 6(2) stipulated that 'the procedures for the granting and control of assistance regulated in this Law shall be supplementary to the rules of direct application of assistance financed by European Union funds'. A priori, asserting that the internal distribution of powers is not altered by EU law contradicts the case law. The *SCC* dismissed the challenge to this provision, reasoning that

> in the absence of the subsequent legislative or regulatory activity of the Autonomous Communities, this supplementary State legislation may be necessary to ensure compliance with European secondary legislation … and … because, otherwise, a preposterous conclusion could be reached that, given the regulatory passivity of all or some Autonomous Communities, the farmers and stockbreeders of these regions could not receive the aid that corresponds to them according to the applicable EU regulations.

5. Conclusions

The SCC quickly understood that the obligation of the Member States to guarantee the effectiveness of the rights that EU law confers to persons on trial implied a requirement of effective judicial protection and that, based on this premise, different aspects of Article 24 SC, in general terms, have justified the intervention of the constitutional judge in the application of EU law by the ordinary judge. In that sense, I believe that the SCC has been a forerunner of the pronouncements that we subsequently find in the CJEU case law, for example, the CJEU judgment of 17 May 2022 (C-600/19 *Ibercaja*), which maintained 'that the obligation on the Member States to ensure the effectiveness of the rights that individuals derive from EU law implies a requirement for effective judicial protection, reaffirmed in Article 47 of the Charter of Fundamental Rights of the European Union' (see, to that effect, judgment of 10 June 2021 C-776/19 to C-782/19 *BNP Paribas Personal Finance* EU:C:2021:470, paragraph 29 and the case law cited).

The SCC has applied a general canon of protection and purely external review solely guarding against arbitrariness, unreasonableness or patent error in cases in which no preliminary ruling has been made because the judge or court found no conflict, had no doubt about the interpretation to be given to a European rule and, proceeding to an interpretation of national law in accordance with EU law, applied the former without pretermission of the latter. The canon of review to be applied in these cases does not differ from the established general norm for judicial decisions that are the result of the interpretation and application of the law to the specific case, leaving the only question to be considered whether the judicial decision follows a rational exegesis of the ordinary law and, even if the reasoning assumes another possible interpretation of the ordinary law, does not incur in arbitrariness, unreasonableness or patent error. The restrictive scope of review chosen by the SCC in cases where the judicial body has taken a decision on the compatibility of the national rule with European law, by applying the national law without a preliminary ruling, should, in my opinion, be judged positively.

The SCC has also applied, in its role as defender of the principle of primacy of EU law, a canon of reinforced reasoning linked to the right to a decision based on law. In my opinion, the SCC must be meticulous, precise and careful in the application of this canon of control when monitoring the application of EU law by national courts. This is because, on the one hand, the SCC must respect the role of ordinary judges as judges of the Union, but also and above all, because of the danger of SCC reviewing the interpretation that the ordinary judges have made of the CJEU case law. While some ordinary judges ask the SCC for a preliminary ruling when they have doubts about CJEU case law or its interpretation by the ordinary courts, they often forget the main premise: the conflict between EU law and national law is a conflict without constitutional relevance and therefore, unless it affects a fundamental right, the conflict is to be resolved in the ordinary jurisdiction. The SCC should only play the role of judge of the EU when there is a direct conflict between the EU law and the Constitution, as was the case in *Melloni*. This leaves cases when the constitutionality of a national law demands review because it develops the EU law, most commonly when transposing a Directive. This is the case of SCC judgment no 1/2018. In such cases, preliminary rulings by the SCC might be called for.

For the rest, I believe that we ought to welcome the clarity with which the SCC, in its exercise of constitutionality control, recognises in its case law the hermeneutic value based on Article 10(2) SC even though EU law does not integrate the canon of constitutionality. This recognition leads it to situate the European case law on preliminary questions together with the applicable constitutional case law so that both serve as interpretative criteria for the constitutionality control of our laws.

Bibliography

Carlón Ruiz, M, 'El Tribunal Constitucional como garante del Derecho comunitario: Reflexiones al hilo de la STC 27/2013, de 11 de febrero' (2013) 47 *Revista Española De Derecho Europeo* 47.

García Valdecasas Dorrego, MJ, 'La sentencia de 28 de febrero de 2019 del Tribunal Constitucional: preclusión procesal, cosa juzgada y derecho de propiedad en la declaración de abusividad de una cláusula contractual' (2020) 37 *Derecho privado y Constitución* 343.

González Alonso, A, 'La tutela jurisdiccional de los derechos del artículo 24.1 de la Constitución Española, Tesis doctoral inédita' Universidad Autónoma de Madrid, Facultad de Derecho. Departamento de Derecho Público y Filosofía Jurídica, March 2012, repositorio.uam.es/bitstream/handle/10486/9207/48355_gonzalez_alonso_alicia.pdf?sequence=1&isAllowed=y.

Huelin Martínez de Velasco, J, 'La Sentencia del Tribunal Constitucional 26/2014 (Melloni)' (2014) *Revista de Jurisprudencia* 1

—— 'La tormentosa relación del Tribunal Constitucional con el derecho de la Unión Europea. Comentario a la STC 37/2019' Lefrebvre, 6 February 2020, elderecho.com/la-tormentosa-relacion-del-tribunal-constitucional-con-el-derecho-de-la-union-europea-comentario-a-la-stco-37-2019.

Izquierdo Sans, C, 'Amparo constitucional y cuestión prejudicial ¿un nuevo giro del tribunal constitucional? Comentario a la STC 212/2014, de 18 de diciembre' (2015) 55 *Revista Española de Derecho Europeo*, 107.

—— 'Cuestión prejudicial y artículo 24 de la Constitución española' (2011) 23 *Revista General de Derecho europeo*, 1.

Jiménez Campo, J, *Derechos Fundamentales, Concepto y garantías* (Madrid, Trotta,1999).

Martínez Escribano, C, 'El control judicial de oficio de las cláusulas abusivas en los procedimientos de ejecución hipotecaria. La STC 141/2022, de 14 de noviembre' (2023) 4 *Anuario de derecho civil* 1703.

Mercader Uguina, J, 'Tutela judicial efectiva, control de razonabilidad de las decisiones judiciales y canon reforzado de motivación en la doctrina del Tribunal Constitucional' (2008) 73 *Revista del Ministerio de Trabajo y Asuntos Sociales* 127.

Requejo, JL, 'El futuro de un vértice jurisdiccional cada vez más complejo' (2018) 22*Anuario de la Facultad de Derecho de la UAM* 109.

Sarmiento Ramírez-Escudero, D, 'Cuestión prejudicial y control previo de constitucionalidad. Comentario a la sentencia Melky TJUE' (2011) 37 *Revista española de Derecho europeo* 97.

INDEX

www.ingramcontent.com/pod-product-compliance
Ingram Content Group UK Ltd.
Pitfield, Milton Keynes, MK11 3LW, UK
UKHW020815290926
15470UKWH00003B/1178

9 781509 975709